Classical Music in Weimar Germany

Classical Music in Weimar Germany

Culture and Politics before the Third Reich

Brendan Fay

BLOOMSBURY ACADEMIC
LONDON • NEW YORK • OXFORD • NEW DELHI • SYDNEY

BLOOMSBURY ACADEMIC
Bloomsbury Publishing Plc
50 Bedford Square, London, WC1B 3DP, UK
1385 Broadway, New York, NY 10018, USA
29 Earlsfort Terrace, Dublin 2, Ireland

BLOOMSBURY, BLOOMSBURY ACADEMIC and the Diana logo
are trademarks of Bloomsbury Publishing Plc

First published in Great Britain 2020
Paperback edition first published 2021

Copyright © Brendan Fay, 2020

Brendan Fay has asserted his right under the Copyright,
Designs and Patents Act, 1988, to be identified as Author of this work.

For legal purposes the Acknowledgements on p. vii constitute
an extension of this copyright page.

Cover design: Chris Bromley
Cover image: Wilhelm Furtwängler conducting an orchestra, 1931.
(© Alfred Eisenstaedt/Getty Images)

All rights reserved. No part of this publication may be reproduced or
transmitted in any form or by any means, electronic or mechanical,
including photocopying, recording, or any information storage or retrieval
system, without prior permission in writing from the publishers.

Bloomsbury Publishing Plc does not have any control over, or responsibility for,
any third-party websites referred to or in this book. All internet addresses given
in this book were correct at the time of going to press. The author and publisher
regret any inconvenience caused if addresses have changed or sites have
ceased to exist, but can accept no responsibility for any such changes.

A catalogue record for this book is available from the British Library.

A catalog record for this book is available from the Library of Congress.

ISBN: HB: 978-1-3501-1480-7
PB: 978-1-3502-2624-1
ePDF: 978-1-3501-1481-4
eBook: 978-1-3501-1482-1

Typeset by Integra Software Services Pvt. Ltd.

To find out more about our authors and books visit
www.bloomsbury.com and sign up for our newsletters.

Contents

Illustrations	vi
Acknowledgments	vii
Introduction: German Music and the Nazi Past	1
1 (Re)Composing the Nation: Music, War, and the German Inflation, 1918–1924	17
2 Radios and Records: Image and Reality in Weimar Technology	55
3 Internationalism, Nationalism, and the Case of Hans Joachim Moser	89
4 Wagner under Weimar	121
5 Judging Performance, Performing Judgments: Race and Performance in Weimar Germany	147
Epilogue: Rethinking Tradition	171
Select Bibliography	184
Index	198

Illustrations

1	Stump of the "Goethe Oak" in Buchenwald, 2007	4
2	German War Bond Advertisement. *Neue Musik Zeitung*, 1919	27
3	*Neue Musik Zeitung* Production costs July 1914 and present, 1923	28
4	"The Glass House Public and Picture 8611," *Simplicissimus*, 1920	31
5	"Eight against One," *Simplicissimus*, 1921	33
6	"The Book. The Books," *Simplicissimus*, 1926	35
7	"Cultural Exchange," *Simplicissimus*, 1921	37
8	"Tannhäuser on the Radio," *Simplicissimus*, 1924	59
9	"Finale Furioso," Wilhelm Busch, 1860s	65
10	"Two Corners of the World," *Simplicissimus*, 1924	68
11	"Radio Endangers Poor Souls," *Simplicissimus*, 1924	69
12	Poster for the 1938 *Entartete Musik* Exhibition	107
13	"Bayreuth," *Simplicissimus*, 1924	128
14	"Jews against Wagner," *Entartete Musik Exhibition Catalog*, 1938	137
15	"Destroy This Mad Brute," US Government poster, ca. 1917	173
16	Raemaekers's War Cartoons, *Century Magazine*, 1916	174

Tables

1	"Concert Statistics: Mannheim and Berlin Philharmonic, 1922–1925"	43
2	Future Bayreuth	133

Acknowledgments

It is a real pleasure to finally be able to thank all of the individuals and institutions who made the writing of this book possible. Much of the research on which this project is based was made possible by a grant from the Office of the Vice President for International Affairs at Indiana University. I count the year I spent in Berlin, Germany, in 2010–2011 with my family among the most rewarding and stimulating of my life. Thanks also to the Department of History, the School of Library and Information Science, and the Institute for European Studies at Indiana University for providing crucial academic and financial support during my time as a graduate student. I would also like to thank my colleagues at the School of Library and Information Management at Emporia State University who offered encouragement and advice at every step.

I would like to thank the many archivists and librarians in Germany and the United States whose assistance and expertise impacted this book in ways large and small. A special thanks as well to my research assistant, Emily Alexander, who copyedited large parts of the manuscript and greatly assisted with properly formatting the source citations. The interlibrary loan staff at Emporia State University has been particularly helpful in tracking down obscure items. My interdisciplinary interests in history and musicology were fostered dating back to my undergraduate years at the University of Texas, and I would particularly like to thank David Crew, Brian Levack, and Kevin E. Mooney without whose encouragement I likely would not have taken up these interests in the first place. A number of colleagues' comments and criticisms greatly helped improve this book, especially Celia Applegate, Erin Corber, Patrick Gilner, Carl Ipsen, Stephanie Koscak, Christopher A. Molnar, Bryan Parkhurst, Pamela Potter, Mark Roseman, Julia Roos, Robert A. Schneider, Rebecca Spang, Laura Stokes, Kira Thurman, Michael Widdersheim, Jonathan O. Wipplinger, and Jonathan Yeager. Chapters of this book were presented at many academic conferences over the past several years, and I extend a special thanks to the commenters whose insights helped strengthen the book's arguments. I could not have asked for better editors in Tom Stottor at I. B. Tauris and Laura Reeves at Bloomsbury Academic, whose sure hands helped guide the manuscript through all stages of the publication process. Lastly, a special thanks goes to the two anonymous reviewers for their incisive comments on the manuscript. Needless to say, any remaining shortcomings or errors are mine alone.

This book would never have seen the light of day without the love and support of my family and friends. Jennifer Fay and Enrique Davila—who I just as easily could have thanked in any of the above sections—have read my work and offered sage advice over the years. Although my parents, Paula Page and Thomas Fay, would not appear to have bestowed any of their considerable musical talents on me, they awakened in me a love of music for which I will always be grateful. I also want to thank other family members, including my sister, Kathleen Fossan, Chris Fossan, grandparents, Robert and Glynn Page, Joan Squires, Alexander Gemignani, Carolann Page, and father-in-law Eggehard Rother for their unstinting support over the years. I have been exceedingly fortunate to have not one but many best friends, and would particularly like to thank Matt Begley, Danny Droubi, Ivan Neel, Rick Lockton, and Ezana Tesfaye for their friendship over the years. Finally, my wife Sonja and our children, Madeleine and Maxim, have borne the brunt of the travel, relocation, and time away from home that the writing of this book required. I hope my dedicating it to them serves as some small token of appreciation for all that they have sacrificed and endured.

A lightly revised version of Chapter 5 appeared as "Judging Performance, Performing Judgments: Race and Performance in Weimar Germany" in *Current Musicology*, 96 (Fall 2013), 71–96. In addition, a lightly revised version of Chapter 1 titled "Conservative Music Criticism, the Inflation and Concert Life in Weimar Germany, 1919–1924" appeared in *Cultural History*, 6 (2) (2017): 141–163. My thanks to both journals for permission to reprint.

Introduction: German Music and the Nazi Past

"Ist das Bach?" one German asks his fellow SS officer, as notes from the composer's *Partita in A Minor* punctuate the sound of gunshots during the clearing of the Kraków Ghetto in one of the more memorable scenes in Steven Spielberg's film *Schindler's List*. It was not the first time such a cultural trope has been used to depict Nazi perpetrators on screen, nor would it be the last. In Alfred Hitchcock's 1944 classic *Lifeboat*, a captured German U-boat officer seduces his captors with Schubert Lieder before murdering one of their number. Frank Pierson's film *Conspiracy* likewise sees Adolf Eichmann and Reinhard Heydrich unwind over cognac and Schubert's *String Quintet in C Major* after having casually discussed the mass murder of Europe's Jews at the notorious Wannsee Conference. As the foregoing illustrates, the relationship between "good" and "bad" Germany has found wide-ranging expression in popular culture, from contemporary film and literature to historical nonfiction.[1] Indeed, a peculiarly German sense of cultural superiority has long been seen as one of the singular driving forces behind the the Great War, which opened the century. Following the almost unimaginable destruction of the Second World War and the horrors of the Holocaust, the relationship between Germany's capacity for culture and war begged the question: how could the land of Bach, Beethoven, and Goethe have also produced Hitler and the Holocaust?

By the middle of the twentieth century, Germany had found itself transformed from the country of *Dichtern und Denkern* (poets and thinkers) to that of *Richtern und Henkern* (judges and hangmen) as the postwar period saw many scholars searching for a German *Sonderweg* (special path) that might explain the German descent into dictatorship and mass murder. Political historians found a likely culprit in Germany's "revolution from above" under Bismarck while cultural historians identified a German preference for culture over politics.[2] Germans, according to this interpretation, consciously retreated from the outer world of crass, divisive party politics to the inner, elevated one of *Kultur* and *Bildung* with disastrous consequences for civil society and, later, Germany's first experiment with democracy under the Weimar Republic (1918–1932).[3]

This was not always so. Prior to the era of the world wars, nineteenth-century observers often spoke glowingly of a German *Sonderweg* characterized by literary, philosophical, and, above all, musical dynamism and creation. Efforts geared toward uncovering a peculiar German aptitude for musical creation and Germans in general as a "peoples of music" seized upon the very fragmentation long held responsible for the development of those structures—political backwardness and a sclerotic associational life, to name only two—which made it particularly susceptible to Nazism.[4] Germany's fractured political development, which had served as cultural virtue in the eighteenth and nineteenth centuries, quickly became vice in the twentieth as the defense of *Kultur* served as a battle cry for Germans during the First World War and a rallying point amid the shattering defeat that followed in its wake. According to many scholars, Germany's cultural conservatives, wracked by the dislocations of economic instability, political violence, and an array of cultural modernisms so characteristic of the interwar period, perceived *Kultur* under threat and cast their lot with reactionary political movements of the German right. And they found them, whether in the form of the German National People's Party (DNVP) that sought to turn back the clock and return Germany to its former greatness under the imperial monarchy or the nascent National Socialists, who shared their sense of cultural conservatism and commitment toward tradition. As we will see below, an array of studies from historians, musicologists, and other scholars have shown an association between the culturally traditional and politically reactionary from Weimar to the Third Reich, whether based on a shared anti-Semitism, extreme nationalism, or hostility toward modernist art.[5] For many, the answer to the question posed earlier was clear: the German turn toward Nazism occurred not despite Beethoven and Bach but because of them.

The end of the last century saw the appearance of pathbreaking scholarship that demonstrated the complicity of German culture and its defenders with the rise of Nazism. Historians such as Georg Bollenbeck and Michael Meyer heavily documented the entrenched nationalism and anti-Semitism within conservative circles and the backlash to modernist innovations so characteristic of Weimar.[6] Some writers perceived a generational divide among Weimar cultural figures who found themselves on either side of the battle lines that hardened over the course of the Republic. According to one influential view, interwar Germany bore witness to the victory of Weimar's postwar modernist "sons" over their prewar traditionalist "fathers," the latter of whom proved receptive to and supported the

Nazi crusade against musical modernism toward the last years of the Republic in a number of guises.[7] It is not just the historians who pressed forward this line of argument. Eckhard John excavated the origins and development of the term "musical Bolshevism" over the course of Weimar in the musical press, demonstrating the international purchase the concept enjoyed well before the Nazis appeared on the scene and the important role it served in tapping into wider anxieties toward modernism and Communism.[8] Like other disciplines that came of age in the second half of the nineteenth century, musicology faced a reckoning with a disciplinary past that deeply privileged German music and composers at the expense of other traditions.[9] Pamela Potter's pioneering *Most German of the Arts: Musicology and Society between Weimar and the Third Reich* shed light into these dark corners while also highlighting important points of continuity in musical life between Weimar and the Nazi state.[10]

From the various contributions within the influential conservative music periodicals *Zeitschrift für Musik*, *Neue Musik-Zeitung*, and *Allgemeine Musik-Zeitung* to the writings of influential musicologists, journalists, and composers such as Alfred Heuss, Hans Hinkel, and Hans Pfitzner, to name only three, we can indeed often trace a correspondence between cultural conservatives on one hand and increasingly hostile views toward Jews, foreigners, atonalists, and the Republic itself on the other. For this reason, the convergences between Weimar and Third Reich within the pages of the conservative musical press have often been seen in rather straightforward terms whereby conservative-minded individuals and institutions have functioned as a kind of cultural anteroom in which reactionary fears, if not proto-Nazi ideas themselves, first germinated and later flourished. To be sure, Weimar Germany was not the only place where such cultural appropriation took place, nor musical conservatives the only ones who usurped culture for their own political and social ends. Fascinating studies of eighteenth- and nineteenth-century German masters have revealed the lengths to which various groupings went in their efforts to align past composers with their own ideological programs. The previous century, for example, had seen conservatives advertise Beethoven's völkisch-nationalist credentials, while socialists emphasized Handel's revolutionary and anti-aristocratic tendencies.[11] Not to be outdone, Nazi cultural authorities later went to great lengths to highlight Mozart's biological fitness.[12] The relationship between German *Kultur* and Nazism can be found outside the musical sphere as well, perhaps most notoriously in the *Goethe Eiche* (Goethe's Oak) seen below in image 1. Unwilling to clear a large oak tree under which the German poet was rumored to have written parts of his classic *Faust*, Nazi authorities preserved the tree in their plans for the concentration camp at Buchenwald. In many ways, the oak embodies the two dominant responses to German culture's role in the life of the nation in the era of the world wars: while some prisoners were struck by the chilling and discordant juxtaposition of the Germany of Goethe and the murderous new Germany under Nazism, others saw the tree as a fitting symbol of the darkly symbiotic relationship between German culture and German barbarism.[13]

This book approaches its subject with two overarching goals in mind. First, it seeks to reexamine the relationship between culture and politics in twentieth-century Germany by challenging the association between traditional culture and politics as revealed through conservative music criticism, the personal papers of select critics and musicologists, and the memoir literature of leading performers of the period. Second, it aims to bring the disciplines of history and musicology into greater conversation with each other. Orthodox historical scholarship, on the one hand, once highlighted the continuities between Weimar and Nazi Germany and the various ways in which social, political, economic, and cultural life in the troubled Republic prepared the ground for National Socialism.[14] Where political and social historians saw

Image 1 Stump of the "Goethe Oak" in Buchenwald, 2007. Source: Diogo, Duarte, Wikimedia Commons. Image retrieved from https://commons.wikimedia.org/wiki/File:Buchenwald_Goethe_Eiche_2007.JPG.

continuity, cultural historians and musicologists, on the other hand, emphasized rupture by depicting the cultural efflorescence and vibrant experimentation of the interwar period as having fallen silent after 1933.[15] This disciplinary divide has stemmed at least in part from differing scholarly priorities and points of view. As the musicologist Pamela Potter recently argued, while historians have tended to ignore the arts and traditional objects of culture (i.e., art, theater, dance, and music) in their scholarship, many musicologists have relied on dated understandings of totalitarianism and imbued Hitler and the Nazi leadership with far more power and control over the arts than they ever really enjoyed.[16] Recent scholarship suggests this divide is closing as scholars rethink the nature of both Weimar culture and cultural policy under the Nazi dictatorship. In his book on the fate of German theater between Weimar and Nazi Germany, for example, Gerwin Strobl vividly depicts an erratic, indecisive Nazi state riven by overlapping jurisdictions and competing agencies that was all too often amenable to compromise within the cultural sphere.[17] Within music more specifically, Nicholas Attfield's recent work has reappraised strands of conservative thought within Weimar music circles, suggesting that parallels between Nazi ideology and the ideas of Alfred Heuss, Hans Pfitzner, and other members of the conservative musical establishment had more to do with appropriation and exploitation than genuine affinity.[18] This book builds on this previous work by reexamining conservative musical culture and offers a nuanced view of many of the competing perspectives and cultural priorities of its supporters.

Just who were these cultural conservatives who wrote for conservative music journals and what did they value? They ranged from university-trained musicologists and scholars to professional music critics and amateur musicians but were bound together first and foremost by a profound admiration for the German classical tradition from the Baroque masters to the late Romantics and shared, as Brian Cherney has written, "a belief in the continuation of the traditional musical language, above all, the tonal system and the nineteenth-century concept of melody [and] a reverence for the achievements of the past period."[19] Traditionalists held the classical tradition from Bach to Wagner not only as a cornerstone of national identity but also as the driving force behind German cultural hegemony. It is worth recalling the unrivaled position German music held at the beginning of the twentieth century, one that dominated the concert stages of the world and brought to life by German musicians and conductors who breathed life into a music they viewed as truly universal.[20] As the inheritors of this patrimony, Weimar traditionalists sought to preserve this legacy and looked to *Kultur* as instrumental in helping Germans recover from a lost war and the economic misery and political violence of the interwar period. Second, next to their shared admiration for the German classics cultural conservatives were bound together by a disposition toward modern music that ranged from suspicious to hostile. Some traditionalists, while stopping short of endorsing modernist composers, argued that their music deserved to have a hearing and left it up to future generations to decide if it deserved a place in the repertory.[21] For others, however, the iconoclastic music of Schoenberg, Weill, Berg, and other modernists upended timeless conceptions of harmony, melody, rhythm, and other features of musical language and was looked on by many as sacrilegious and scandalous—even as a violation of natural law itself. A 1922 review of a Düsseldorf festival devoted to modern music by Martin Friedland offers a typical example: "musical colors ran one into the other, everything rendered mollusk-like and spineless. One wonders: just as we cannot naturally sing in quarter tones … neither can we play music (in this fashion)."[22]

Beyond these shared commitments, however, this book will show that they differed markedly in their attitudes toward the major social, political, and cultural questions of the day. Yet within the drama of German history between Weimar and the rise of Nazism, Weimar's cultural conservatives have frequently been cast in a villainous role while champions of musical modernism have often been depicted in heroic and ennobling terms. In his magisterial survey *The Rest Is Noise: Listening to the Twentieth Century*, the critic Alex Ross summed up the situation in the following terms: "The automatic equation of radical style with liberal politics and of conservative style with reactionary politics is a historical myth that does little justice to an agonizingly ambiguous historical reality."[23] Indeed, the historian who casts his net in pursuit of a particular kind of game invariably ensnares other kinds of prey in his trawl, a tendency illustrated by the binaries which often separate "tradition" from "modernism":[24]

I argue that the association of the culturally traditional with the politically and socially reactionary has a tendency to obscure more than it reveals, for reasons that are fourfold. First, defenders of conservative culture both during and after

Tradition	Modernism
Conservative	Progressive
Reactionary	Revolutionary
Backward looking	Forward looking
National	International
Nationalist	Cosmopolitan
Prescriptive	Experimental
Linear	Abstract

Weimar did not emit solely from Germany's political right. For the victims of Nazi oppression, Jewish and non-Jewish alike, faced with unimaginable suffering and brutality in camps like Auschwitz and Dachau, traditional culture was often one of the few things that sustained them. For example, music occupies a central place in the diary of the Jewish writer Victor Klemperer whose wife Eva—a talented concert pianist and organist—frequently played sonatas by Mozart and Beethoven so as to allow the couple to forget the sense of dread and foreboding of everyday life under Nazism, if only temporarily.[25] A Czech survivor imprisoned in Sachsenhausen recalled feeling himself on the edge of despair before the music of Dvořák broke his desperation and steeled his resolve not to abandon hope.[26] While much has been made of a "renaissance of Jewish culture" during Weimar, within the musicological establishment the conservative agendas of Jewish musicologists and critics such as Alfred Einstein and Robert Hernried—both later pressed into forced emigration—all too often betray their authors' nationalist and anti-modernist leanings.[27]

Second, traditional art did not merely function as a site of crisis and division, exacerbating cultural resentments among defenders seeking to preserve it from the onslaught of popular, foreign, and modernist influence. Rather, it also served in a beneficent role as the medium best suited for recovery from a war that had shattered Germany and intruded on the lives of all of its citizens in one way or another. Nadine Rossol has demonstrated the ways in which the Republic frequently sought to adapt traditional music and symbols to shore up support for the Weimar state during national holidays, state funerals, and other forms of public ritual.[28] And as Jay Winter has shown, traditionalist language often likewise proved the preferred medium among communities and families seeking to honor, mourn and commemorate their war dead.[29] Kathe Köllwitz's traditionalist language, while conveying a subdued, unspoken anger toward the sufferings of war, functioned more as an instrument of recovery than reaction. Meanwhile, the modernist paintings of an Otto Dix and George Grosz—whose postwar canvases so strikingly register the widespread sense of anger, protest, and resentment—have long been recognized as embodying the same kind of profound sense of dislocation and unease as that found in reactionary circles during the interwar period.

In fact, one need to look no further than Emil Nolde, as Peter Gay perceptively saw, to see that "Expressionism was compatible with all sorts of politics"; which brings us to a third shortcoming of the aesthetic-political association mentioned above.[30] That is, if the frequent association of the culturally conservative with the politically reactionary is often problematic, the reverse is true as well. For while many traditionalists have often been implicated on the side of the perpetrators because of their cultural affinities, not a few modernists continue to be regarded as victims despite their own personal political sympathies. Many modernist composers—even those who later fell victim to the cultural policies of Nazism—retained a conservative- nationalist outlook even in exile abroad. The case of Anton Webern is instructive. A disciple of Arnold Schoenberg and member of the so-called Second Viennese School, Webern found his music was expressly forbidden in Nazi Germany. His financial struggles grew ever greater over the course of the regime before his life was tragically cut short immediately after the war by an American GI who mistook him for a resister. Still, following Hitler's invasion of Western Europe and the conquest of Denmark and Norway, Webern wrote in his diary,

> This is Germany today! But the *National Socialist* one, to be sure! Not just any one! This is exactly the *new* state, for which the seed was already laid twenty years ago. Yes, *a new state* it is, one that has never existed before!! *It is something new*!! Created by this unique man!!! *Each day becomes more exciting.* I see such a good future.[31]

Webern's better-known colleague Arnold Schoenberg, whose serialist compositions the Nazis derided as the very essence of cultural Bolshevism, was also no friend of the Weimar Republic and remained a committed monarchist and staunch German nationalist in exile in California.[32] He envisioned his twelve-tone compositional approach as capable of securing German leadership in musical matters for at least the next hundred years and as "a living example of an art able most effectively to oppose Latin and Slav hopes of hegemony and derived through and through from the traditions of German music."[33] The violinist Gustav Havemann, who joined the avant-garde *Novembergruppe* and maintained public friendships with a number of modernist Jewish composers over the course of Weimar, privately held views that would have shocked the consciences of these same friends. A deeply committed National Socialist who joined the Nazi Party in 1932, he would go on to assume a leading role within the Nazi cultural organization Action League for German Culture.[34]

Finally, those figures whom scholars dub traditionalist or conservative based upon their aesthetic inclinations and preferences can hardly be described in monolithic terms with a common set of artistic values, social fears, or cultural priorities. In the literature, Weimar's cultural conservatives are often depicted as a stubborn and inflexible group with fixed and unchanging views on what and how—even *why*—music was to be played. In reality, things appear far different. They hailed from all parts of Germany, and while a certain number worshipped at the altar of instrumental music, others extolled vocal and operatic music. Some proselytized against the corrupting influences of the radio, record player and other modern media, while others imbued those same technologies with a rejuvenating and edifying potential. Put simply, the church of tradition may have worshipped the same creator, but it was made up of many different denominations.

This book does not—it could not—call into question the real continuities between cultural traditionalists during Weimar and the Third Reich. It does suggest, however, that such associations cannot be made without serious qualifications. Grafting xenophobia, cultural exclusivity, patrimony, and other sentiments widespread in conservative political culture onto conservative musical circles does violence to a historical reality that was more complex and nuanced. Some cultural conservatives, for example, sought to put the canon, which remained for many the most formidable weapon in Germany's illustrious cultural arsenal, to good use in healing the bitter divisions which had opened up in German society over the course of the First World War or in reestablishing international ties, which had been disrupted by the war. German music criticism, irrespective of critics' own attitudes, remained a model for critical traditions in other contexts—in places as far flung as the United States where American writers adapted German models in cultivating their own native artists and emerging critical schools.[35] Perhaps because the Nazi Party's official line vis-à-vis culture, as spelled out by formal Nazi Party organizations, Nazi publications, and leading functionaries' own well-known artistic views, tended toward the traditional, there has been a temptation to freight conservative taste under Weimar with predictive meaning.[36] Yet many critics' and musicologists' general attitudes toward race, modern technology, and foreign influence could and often did diverge in striking ways from those commonly associated with the Third Reich.

By restoring conservative musical culture to the center of the analysis, this book differs from scholars' traditional focus on the iconoclasm and cultural experimentation of Weimar Germany. Early cinema, expressionist art, and literary modernism—these are the themes that have typically attracted the attention of Weimar historians, if not as a way to register the shattering effect the First World War exerted on the European cultural landscape, then as a window onto the perpetual crises of the interwar period.[37] This book returns our focus to traditional idioms, which, for many in the postwar period, proved best suited to facilitate the widespread mourning and loss that followed in the wake of a conflict that marked the collapse of the imperial state and claimed the lives of nearly 2.5 million Germans. New "modernisms" such as the radio and mass advertising undoubtedly emerged during Weimar, but traditional content continued to exert a powerful influence over German society, above all in musical life. There has, in fact, been a growing recognition that traditionalism was far more characteristic of Weimar Germany as a whole, one that Dadaism, Bauhaus, early cinema, Expressionism, and other modernist movements concentrated in large cities like Berlin have tended to overshadow.[38] As one scholar put it, "Berlin was not Weimar. Rather, Weimar was Weimar."[39] Yet recent scholarship has often stopped short of fully explicating what this insight amounts to and its larger ramifications for Germany between the world wars. This book challenges a linear approach to the period 1918–1945 in which Weimar is so often reduced to the intellectual antechamber to Nazism. Since the 1980s, historians have increasingly eschewed a "doom and gloom" teleology that viewed Weimar as mere prelude to the Third Reich in favor of approaches emphasizing much of the Republic's promise and dynamism.[40] Alongside this, a tidal wave of new research has emerged challenging our conventional understanding of fascism, and particularly the Third Reich, as thoroughly anti-modernist.[41]

By reexamining an earlier historiography that sometimes risked seeing fascist regimes in overly simplistic terms, such revaluations have contributed immensely to our understanding of European fascism. In the case of high culture, however, the advocates of Nazi anti-modernism largely got it right the first time around. That is certainly neither to claim that all fascists were cultural traditionalists nor to ignore those select cases in which party functionaries sacrificed ideology for seemingly greater short-term gains. Nor is it to suggest that such cultural anti-modernism underlay fascist regimes across Europe as a glance at the impact of futurist intellectuals on Mussolini's Italy illustrates. Yet in Hitler's Germany, neither the lack of uniform opinion among party elites nor occasional lapses in the regime's cultural offerings should distract from the overarching conservatism of the Nazi cultural agenda, one that can be found from the start in both Hitler's public pronouncements and in the Nazi Party's earliest writings.[42] Robert Paxton was surely right when he wrote that "Mussolini and his avant-garde artist friends worried less than the Nazis about cultural modernism."[43] Hence it is not, in my view, the orthodox historiography surrounding Nazi cultural anti-modernism that needs revisiting but rather the perceived cultural streams that fed into it over the course of Weimar. New studies have caused us to reassess the foundations— political instability, economic crisis, and cultural decline—upon which the older

Weimar historiography was built. It has recently been suggested, to take one example, that constituencies hitherto considered uncompromising opponents of Weimar from the start—the military and members of the imperial civil service—had rather more complex and less antagonistic attitudes toward the Republic than previously thought.[44] Cultural conservatives, traditionally lumped in with these and other groups considered irreconcilably opposed to Weimar, offer still one more group, which merit our reconsideration.

This book is organized as a series of case studies that shed new light on the nature of cultural conservatism between Weimar and the Third Reich. Chapter 1 traces a kind of group biography of the music critics under discussion here through an examination of German music criticism in the wake of the First World War, a conflict that fundamentally altered German musical life no less than other facets of German society. While the war opened up a space for new critical voices in a newly democratic Germany, the inflationary pressures dating to wartime deficit spending unleashed contemporary anxieties about inflation's impact on the institution of the concert hall. Although historians have often seen the inflation as contributing in important, if elusive, ways to the collapse of the Weimar Republic, a closer examination of musical discourse in that period suggests that critics did not perceive that experience in solely negative terms. While many feared for the continued viability of key musical institutions and evinced great ambivalence over the advent of the so-called "new audience" into Germany's concert halls in the short term, some critics viewed the emergence of a less culturally sophisticated new public as a potential boon to the German classics in the long term.

Chapter 2 canvasses perceptions toward the radio in Weimar society and its relationship to classical music, arguing that while many culturally conservative critics misread the radio's impact on German society during the interwar period, Weimar radio cohered far more closely to conservatives' own conception of its proper relationship to society at large than radio under Nazism. Chapter 3 reexamines the musicological debate between "national" and "international" music over the period 1918–1925 with particular attention to the life and career of Hans Joachim Moser whose writings during the Weimar Republic have long been seen as preparing the ground for the xenophobic, anti-Jewish, anti-modern and nationalist scholarship which proliferated under the Third Reich. I argue that a close reading of his writings during Weimar reveals a bewildering array of contradictions in his work, only some of which points toward the Third Reich (and, indeed, anticipates his own subsequent work as a musicologist for Himmler's research outfit *Ahnenerbe*). Wagner and his reception both at Bayreuth and within the wider conservative press is the subject of Chapter 4. It is hard to think of another cultural figure more closely associated with Hitler and Nazism than Wagner, yet I argue that such an association has rested on a narrow focus within the Bayreuth circle and ignored the considerable debates that existed surrounding Wagner's legacy across the political spectrum in general and among cultural conservatives in particular. In Chapter 5, I turn toward notions of race and music performance under Weimar, arguing that while a considerable number of critics and musicologists dismissed analyses of the connections between race and music as "scientifically unsound," those who did emphasize the importance of race tended to celebrate the virtues of racial mixing and highlighted the Jews as the "race" best suited to musical performance. A concluding chapter offers some suggestions as to where the association between cultural and political conservatism comes from and why it persists in the popular and academic imagination alike.

A final note regarding terms and the scope of this study. First, this book does not pretend to be a comprehensive history of all classical music during Weimar. Modernist classical music has become synonymous with interwar culture, to say nothing of jazz and other idioms. Indeed, for many scholars these and other iconoclastic forms are the principal features of what has come to be termed "Weimar culture." Yet while modernist art occupied a central place during Weimar, it would be a mistake to believe that it completely displaced older music, or that composers of the eighteenth and nineteenth centuries ceased to be relevant in Germany's new century. One could argue that in the wake of a catastrophic world war, economic dislocation, social anxiety, and a widespread sense of uncertainty about the future, traditionalist culture mattered more than ever before to many Germans. It is the recognition of this fact that helped inform the orientation of the present study. While it is perilous to use the terms "conservative" and "progressive" to describe supporters of old and modern music, I have decided to retain them here for lack of more meaningful alternatives. My use of the term "musical culture" throughout the book refers exclusively to developments within classical music (i.e., not jazz, swing, folk, or other genres) and all translations from the original German are my own unless otherwise indicated.

Much recent writing on music during Weimar has tended to decenter the tradition while coupling it—explicitly or implicitly—with the politically conservative and socially reactionary. It is time we both re-centered tradition and reexamined the, at times, shaky historical foundation upon which this association has rested. It is worth noting that while Weimar critics focused their energies on cultural concerns unique to Germany after the First World War, their intellectual inheritances owed greatly to a critical tradition stretching back to the late eighteenth century. In order to understand the Weimar critic's role in society it is necessary as a first step to look at both the limits and aspirations of that tradition, which did much to shape both the ideological contours of the musical press at large and the critic's perceived social role in the cultural life of the nation after a lost war.

Notes

1. Thomas Mann's interest in the relationship between "good" and "bad" Germany is examined in Hans Rudolf Vaget, "National and Universal: Thomas Mann and the Paradox of 'German' Music," in *Music and German National Identity*, ed. Celia Applegate and Pamela Potter (Chicago: University of Chicago Press, 2002), 155–177.
2. For a stimulating discussion of this interpretation, see David Blackbourn and Geoff Eley, *The Peculiarities of German History: Bourgeois Politics and Society in Nineteenth-Century Germany* (New York: Oxford University Press, 1984).
3. See Fritz Stern, *The Politics of Cultural Despair: A Study in the Rise of the Germanic Ideology* (Berkeley: University of California Press, 1961) and George Mosse, *The Crisis of German Ideology: Intellectual Origins of the Third Reich* (New York: H. Fertig, 1964).
4. For a stimulating discussion, see Celia Applegate and Pamela Potter, "Germans as the 'People' of Music: Geneology of an Identity," in *Music & German National Identity*, ed. Celia Applegate and Pamela Potter (Chicago: University of Chicago Press, 2002), 1–35.
5. See, for example, Walter Laqueur, *Weimar: A Cultural History* (New York: Perigree Books, 1974), Peter Gay, *Weimar Culture: The Outsider as Insider* (New York: W. W. Norton & Company, 1968) and most recently, Wolf Lepenies, *The Seduction of Culture in Modern German History* (Princeton: Princeton University Press, 2006).
6. Georg Bollenbeck, "German Kultur, the Bildungsbürgertum and Its Susceptibility to National Socialism," *The German Quarterly*, 73 (1) (2000): 67–83 and Michael Meyer, *The Politics of Music in the Third Reich* (New York: Peter Lang, 1993).
7. Michael Kater, "The Revenge of the Fathers: The Demise of Modern Music at the End of the Weimar Republic," *German Studies Review*, 15 (2) (1992): 295–315. The generational approach between reactionary "fathers" and revolutionary "sons" was first articulated in Gay, *Weimar Culture*.
8. Eckhard John, *Musik-Bolschewismus: Die Politisierung der Musik in Deutschland, 1918–1938* (Stuttgart: Verlag J. B. Metzler, 1994), 9.
9. Of course, musicology was far from alone in this regard. Anthropology, too, had to reconcile with its own dark roots in racism and imperialism. See, for example,

Andrew Zimmerman, *Anthropology and Antihumanism in Imperial Germany* (Chicago: University of Chicago Press, 2001).

10 Pamela Potter, *Most German of the Arts: Musicology and Society from Weimar to the Third Reich* (New Haven: Yale University Press, 1998).

11 For Beethoven, see David Dennis, *Beethoven in German Politics, 1870–1989* (New Haven: Yale University Press, 1996). On Handel, see Pamela Potter, "The Politicization of Handel and His Oratorios in the Weimar Republic, the Third Reich, and the Early Years of the German Democratic Republic," *The Musical Quarterly*, 85 (2) (2001): 311–341.

12 Erik Levi, *Mozart and the Nazis: How the Third Reich Abused a Cultural Icon* (New Haven: Yale University Press, 2011).

13 Anders Rydell, *The Book Thieves: The Nazi Looting of Europe's Libraries and the Race to Return a Literary Inheritance* (New York: Viking, 2017), 35–40.

14 See, for example, Detlev Peukert, *The Weimar Republic: The Crisis of Classical Modernity* (New York: Hill & Wang, 1993) and Hans Mommsen, *The Rise and Fall of Weimar Democracy* (Chapel Hill: University of North Carolina Press, 1998).

15 Some classic historical accounts are Laqueur, *Weimar*, Gay; *Weimar Culture* and John Willett, *The New Sobriety: 1914–1933: Art and Politics in the Weimar Period* (New York: Da Capo Press, 1979). On music, see John Crawford and Dorothy Crawford, *Expressionism in Twentieth-Century Music* (Bloomington: Indiana University Press, 1993) and Nils Grosch, *Die Musik der Neuen Sachlichkeit* (Stuttgart: JB Metzler Verlag, 1999).

16 Pamela M. Potter, *Art of Suppression: Confronting the Nazi Past in Histories of the Visual and Performing Arts* (Berkeley: University of California Press, 2016), 34–47.

17 Gerwin Strobl, *The Swastika and the Stage: German Theatre and Society, 1933–1945* (Cambridge: Cambridge University Press, 2007).

18 Nicholas Attfield, *Challenging the Modern: Conservative Revolution in German Music, 1918–1933* (London: Oxford University Press, 2017).

19 Brian Cherney, "The Bekker-Pfitzner Controversy (1919–1920): Its Significance for German Music Criticism during the Weimar Republic (1919–1932)" (PhD Dissertation, University of Toronto, 1973), 3.

20 See Jessica Gienow-Hecht, *Sound Diplomacy: Music and Emotions in Transatlantic Relations, 1850–1920* (Chicago: University of Chicago Press, 2009).

21 This was a view voiced by Paul Marsop following a 1909 performance of Schoenberg's string quartet Op. 10 that occasioned a riot. Following the performance, Marsop wrote: "Whatever one likes to think about Schoenberg, like every artist not lost in the baseness of cabaret and the cesspool of operetta he has, at the very least, the right to be heard in peace before one judges his work." Quoted in Sarah Elaine Neill, "The Modernist Kaleidoscope: Schoenberg's Reception History in America, Germany and Austria 1908–1924" (PhD diss., Duke University, 2014), 43.

22 Martin Friedland, "Die 'Neue Musik' und ihr Apologet," *Zeitschrift für Musik*, 89 (15/16) (1922): 334–338 (here 338).

23 Alex Ross, *The Rest Is Noise: Listening to the Twentieth Century* (New York: Picador, 2007), 346.

24 For a wider discussion of this tendency toward binaries, see Tamara Levitz, "Review of Pamela Potter," *Most German of the Arts: Music and Society from Weimar to the Third Reich* in *Journal of the American Musicological Society*, 55 (1) (2002): 176–187.

25 Victor Klemperer, *I Will Bear Witness: A Diary of the Nazi Years, 1933–1945* (2 vols.) (New York: Random House, 1999).

26 See Bernd Sponheuer, "Beethoven in Auschwitz: Nachdenken über Musik im Konzentrationslager," in *"Entartete Musik" 1938—Weimar und die Ambivalenz*, ed. Hanns-Werner Heister (Saarbrücken: PFAU-Verlag, 2001), 798–820. As Sponheuer shows and the edited volume implies, however, such views toward music in the face of annihilation were only one among many responses toward culture in the camp system. While for some music served to heal and unite, it could just as easily, in other contexts, serve to divide and establish difference. See Shirli Gilbert, *Music in the Holocaust: Confronting Music in the Nazi Ghettos and Camps* (New York: Oxford University Press, 2007).

27 The phrase forms the title of Michael Brenner, *The Renaissance of Jewish Culture in Weimar Germany* (New Haven: Yale University Press, 1996).

28 Nadine Rossol, "Visualizing the Republic: State Representation and Public Ritual in Weimar Germany," in *Weimar Culture Revisited*, ed. John Alexander Williams (New York: Palgrave McMillan, 2011), 139–159.

29 Jay Winter, *Sites of Memory, Sites of Mourning: The Great War in European Cultural History* (Cambridge: Cambridge University Press, 1995). Traditionalist language here refers to the *form* of visual and plastic arts alternatively described as linear, static, and representational.

30 Gay, *Weimar Culture*, 106. Still, Gay implies the coupling of cultural modernism and political conservatism in the case of Nolde as the exception, which proves the rule.

31 Quoted in Ross, *The Rest Is Noise*, 352 (emphasis in the original).

32 Leonard Stein, ed., *Style and Idea: Selected Writings of Arnold Schoenberg* (Berkeley: University of California Press, 1984), 505.

33 Ross, *The Rest Is Noise*, 351.

34 Michael Haas, *Forbidden Music: The Jewish Composers Banned by the Nazis* (New Haven: Yale University Press, 2013), 209.

35 Gienow-Hecht, *Sound Diplomacy*, 20–39.

36 The *Reichskulturkammer* was among the organizations responsible for laying out the official party stance on cultural matters over the course of the regime. See Michael Kater, *The Twisted Muse: Musicians and Their Music in the Third*

Reich (Oxford: Oxford University Press), 1999. A recent treatment of the cultural coverage of the Nazi flagship press organ *Völkischer Beobachter* is found in David Dennis, *Inhumanities: Nazi Interpretations of Western Culture* (New York: Cambridge University Press, 2012). For a general discussion of the Nazi press, see Richard Evans, *The Third Reich in Power* (New York: The Penguin Press, 2005), 141–149. For an accounting of the function of art in Nazi circles, see Jonathan Petropoulos, *Art as Politics in the Third Reich* (Chapel Hill: University of North Carolina Press, 1999). On Hitler's personal artistic tastes, the best approach is offered in Frederic Spotts, *Hitler and the Power of Aesthetics* (New York: Overlook Press, 2003).

37 See, for example, Willett, *Art and Politics of the Weimar Period*. Anton Kaes, *Shell Shock Cinema: Weimar Culture and the Wounds of War* (Princeton: Princeton University Press), 2011.

38 See, for example, the excellent piece by Karl Christian Führer, "High Brow and Low Brow Culture," in *Weimar Germany*, ed. Anthony McElligott (New York: Oxford University Press, 2009), 260–281.

39 Benjamin Ziemann, "Weimar Was Weimar: Politics, Culture and the Emplotment of the German Republic," *German History*, 28 (4) (2010): 542–571.

40 Anthony McElligott, ed., *Weimar Germany* (New York: Oxford University Press, 2009). Kathleen Canning, Kerstin Barndt, and Kristin McGuire, eds., *Weimar Public/Weimar Subjects: Rethinking the Political Culture of Germany in the 1920s* (New York: Berghahn Books, 2010). John Alexander Williams, ed., *Weimar Culture Revisited* (New York: Palgrave McMillan, 2011).

41 An influential early reassessment is Jeffrey Herf, *Reactionary Modernism: Technology, Culture and Politics in Weimar and the Third Reich* (Cambridge: Cambridge University Press, 1984). For more recent treatments, see Roger Griffin, *Modernism and Fascism: The Sense of a Beginning under Mussolini and Hitler* (London: Palgrave McMillan, 2010) and Ruth Ben-Ghiat, *Fascist Modernities: Italy 1922–1945* (Berkeley: University of California Press, 2004).

42 Ehrhard Bahr, "Nazi Cultural Politics: Intentionalism vs. Functionalism," in *National Socialist Cultural Policy*, ed. Glenn R. Cuomo (New York: St. Martin's Press, 1995), 5–22.

43 Robert O. Paxton, *The Anatomy of Fascism* (New York: Vintage Books, 2005), 36.

44 On the rethinking of the civil service and military, see, respectively, Wolfgang Elz, "'Foreign Policy' and William Mulligan, 'The Reichswehr and the Weimar Republic'" in *Weimar Germany*, ed. Anthony McElligott (New York: Oxford University Press, 2009), 50–77 and 78–101.

1

(Re)Composing the Nation: Music, War, and the German Inflation, 1918–1924

"Sonate, que me vuex tu?"—"Sonata, what do you want of me?" This phrase, attributed to the musical essayist Bernard le Bovier de Fontenelle (1657–1757), is often taken as a logical starting point for any investigation into the origins of music criticism in Europe and with good reason. First, its French formulation serves as an important reminder of French and Italian dominance of musical Europe around 1800, both on the stage and within aesthetics and music criticism. Second, the phrase's frustrated tinge illustrates the rather low regard in which contemporaries held music, instrumental music in particular. Fired by the principles of Enlightenment philosophy, contemporary observers from Rousseau to Kant decried the non-representational quality of music that, unlike literature and visual art, left little for the listener to reflect upon. Music's uncertain sources of inspirational and ephemeral nature consigned it to a relatively lowly position in relation to the other arts. In a telling 1779 treatise on the arts, the French philosopher Boyé spoke for many when he declared music to be little more than "a pleasure of the senses and not of the intelligence."[1]

This was a situation that German music, Romanticism, and its supporters did much to change. Although its roots stretched back to the late eighteenth century, German music criticism experienced a golden age during the first half of the nineteenth century as writers such as E. T. A. Hoffmann, Adolph Bernhard Marx, and Robert Schumann blazed new trails in how contemporaries talked about and reflected upon music and established German as musical Europe's lingua franca. Their ideas were articulated and disseminated in music journals such as the *Allgemeine musikalische Zeitung*, established by Friedrich Rochlitz, which would become one of the century's most important venues for reviewing new music, announcing the discovery of hitherto lost letters and manuscripts of popular composers, and other affairs of interest to music lovers across German-speaking Europe, providing a model for subsequent journals to emulate. By the end of the nineteenth century many of Europe's most important figures in music criticism, from Eduard Hanslick and Heinrich Schenker to Guido Adler and Hermann Kretzschmar, were German speakers whose pupils would later figure prominently in Weimar's leading music journals. The turn of the century saw the appearance of new journals such as *Die Musik*, the most esteemed and widely respected music periodical of the new century, which featured contributions from an assortment of German-speaking Europe's leading critics, such as Julius Kapp, Adolf Weissmann, and Paul Bekker. Seeking to professionalize their field and insulate the ranks of full-time critics from outsiders, Bekker, together with Hermann Springer, Alfred Heuss, Wilhelm Klatte, and others, would join together in 1913 to help found the Society of German Music Critics (*Verband deutscher Musikkritiker*). Given that newspapers required no formal credentials or training on the part of their musical contributors, music criticism had long been vulnerable to dilettantes and amateurish interlopers. Thus, in addition to raising the profile of its members and the occupation of professional music critic more generally, the major impetus behind the *Verband*'s founding was to create a pool of qualified and perceptive writers from which newspapers could draw in the future.[2] During Weimar, as debates and conflicts between critics grew more heated and the tone more acerbic, the *Verband* founded a committee to intervene in cases where attacks crossed a line and did violence to a critic's professional reputation.[3] However, for the most part the body merely assumed an advisory role and efforts to further professionalize the organization along similar lines as organizations such as the Imperial Federation of German Journalists (*Reichsverband der Deutschen Presse*)—which took a leading role in securing legal protections and relief aid for its members—never fully got off the ground.[4]

As with every other facet of Germany society, the outbreak of war exacted a toll within the realm of music criticism. *Die Musik* was forced to cease publication altogether in September 1915 just as wartime disruptions to travel and solidarity severed ties between German critics and their colleagues in the wider world. Cooperative bodies such as the International Music Society were shuttered due to lack of funds and disruptions to international travel.[5] The war had a radicalizing effect on some leading figures such as the composer Hans Pfitzner, who emerged from the conflict as a full-blown nationalist and played a prominent role in Weimar's major cultural debates. Despite the war's real costs, however, some critics held out hope that the destruction of the old imperial order presented Germans with a clean slate and the opportunity to implement educational and civic reforms to the country's musical life. A 1919 article in the *Neue Musik Zeitung* suggesting a raft of proposals, such as overhauling the approach to music education in German schools and creating new government ministries with a special emphasis on cultural affairs, drew the signatures of several eminent critics, theater directors, and musicologists.[6] The critic Paul Bülow fantasized about a future where German youth would not only listen to the music of German masters but also read their prose writings that he romantically likened to "rich, neglected treasures lying in a forgotten castle waiting for a kingdom to bring them into the light to shine resplendently before the entire Volk."[7]

Still, 1918 marked a sea change within German music criticism from the world that came before for two overarching reasons. First, the war established Berlin as German-speaking Europe's unquestioned musical capital. In fin de siècle Europe, Vienna was arguably the most important musical center on the continent in art and literature as much as in music. As Carl Schorske showed in his seminal *Fin-de-Siècle Vienna: Politics and Culture*, Vienna was a hotbed of modernist movements and thinkers, from the dramatists Arthur Schnitzler and Hugo von Hofmannstahl to the artists Oskar Kokoschka and Gustav Klimt.[8] The city's musical life was no less iconoclastic as composers from Gustav Mahler and Anton Webern injected new musical languages into Europe's sonic landscape while Arnold Schoenberg's first forays into atonal and serialist methods of composition date from his pre–First World War years in Vienna. With the collapse of the Austro-Hungarian monarchy in 1918, countless artists and thinkers left this old world behind and saw Berlin as the city where Europe's musical and artistic future would be decided. Even the most celebrated performers hard-pressed to call one city "home" given their dizzying travel schedules had to admit Berlin's towering importance. The celebrated pianist Walter Gieseking, one of the most active touring artists across Europe and the United States in this period, recalled the gravitational pull of Berlin that remained, in his view, the "undisputed cultural epicentre of [musical life] in Europe."[9] A partial listing of the musical migrants alone who left Vienna for Berlin gives some sense of the monumental shift in Europe's musical center of gravity: Franz Schreker, Hanns Eisler, Erich Kleiber, Fritz Kreisler, Edmund Meisel, Arthur Schnabel, Ernst Toch, Mischa Spoliansky, and Arnold Schoenberg would all make Berlin their new home. Even composers who decided to stay in Vienna, such as Alban Berg, Erich Korngold, and Egon Wellesz, understood that if they were to keep abreast of modern musical currents and maintain contacts with music's leading lights, regular commutes would be necessary.[10]

Despite this broader shift, it is worth remembering that while Germany and a newly independent Austria remained separate political entities on the map, Europe's musical boundaries looked far different. Austrian composers—from Mozart and Schubert to Haydn and Bruckner—had long secured a place in the German canon. Many of Germany's preeminent musicologists had studied under Guido Adler, Max Graf, and other leading Austrian scholars while German and Austrian music critics alike read and engaged in lively debates within the major music journals of German-speaking Europe. Like Volga Germans, Sudeten Germans, and other members of the German diaspora, ordinary Austro-Germans retained a special affinity for their kindred neighbor to the North with large majorities favoring unification with Germany following the war. Although these collective hopes were quickly dashed by Allied policymakers wary of a resurgent supra-German state in central Europe so soon after the cataclysm of the First World War, cultural ties between the two states remained strong, prompting the Austrian writer Stefan Zweig to wonder whether it was the first time a state would be forced to be independent against the wishes of its own people.[11] Among music critics, many still saw Germany and Austria as part of the same *Kulturnation* and held out hope for a future where political fortunes might catch up with cultural realities. As the critic Anton Reichel remarked in an article titled "The Austro-German Cultural Mission," "without union with Germany, Austria can no longer remain 'Austria'; but Germany can also not abide permanent disunion without also allowing German culture as a whole to suffer!"[12]

Second, the newly liberalized atmosphere ushered in by the collapse of the imperial order saw a proliferation of new periodicals devoted to music of every stripe. Amid the economic dislocations and political violence of the interwar period, composers produced an astonishing amount of new and daring works requiring review and analysis by music critics. "All this material offered enough for glosses, longer notes and formal essays that accrued on my work desk," recalled the critic H. H. Stuckenschmidt.[13] Weimar democracy thus introduced a second important shift from the prewar world for the way in which it opened up a space for new voices within the ranks of German music criticism. Leading advocates of modernist music partnered with Universal Edition, a publisher of several contemporary composers, to launch the journal *Musikblätter des Anbruch* in 1919 whose editor Paul Bekker was a tireless devotee of modern music. Universal in particular went to great lengths to secure new music a proper hearing, partnering with Bekker to invite music critics who remained ambivalent to performances of new music.[14] Dedicated to championing modernist music and staffed with a number of leading Jewish thinkers and essayists—from Theodor Adorno and Paul Pisk to Rudolf Réti and Paul Stefan—the journal would contribute significantly to the association between Jewishness and musical modernism, as the Austrian composer Ernst Krenek later discovered.[15] In 1934 Krenek attempted to lay claim to the notion that the modernist aesthetic was "intrinsically Austrian" in nature, only to meet resistance from, among others, Josef Lechthaler, director of music within the Austrian Catholic Church, who claimed that public skepticism toward new music stemmed from the fact that it was "exclusively composed by Jews for Jews and therefore only purposeful in diverting 'an exotic minority.'"[16] Next to *Anbruch*, the other major periodical devoted to modern music was *Melos* founded in Berlin in 1920 by the conductor Hermann Scherchen. Both journals were devoted to reviewing performances of new music, publishing short biographies on young, emerging composers, and other issues relating to modern music before being shuttered following the Nazi "seizure of power" in 1933.

The coverage of modern music by *Anbruch* and *Melos* was more than balanced out by conservative journals committed to preserving the music of the more distant past.[17] These outlets, many of whose contributors were skeptical toward modern music and fearful of its implications for canonical composers whose music had long dominated the world's concert halls, had by 1919 already achieved preeminence as long-standing serials devoted to German music. The Leipzig-based *Allgemeine Musik-Zeitung* under the editorship of Paul Schwers launched fierce attacks against jazz and other forms of "decadent" art throughout the 1920s and into the 1930s.[18] The pages of *Signale für die musikalische Welt*, founded in Leipzig in 1843 and overseen during Weimar by the music critic Max Chop, took on a nationalistic slant over the course of Weimar and likewise held a contemptuous attitude toward the avant-garde. These two journals competed for readers' attention with the conservative *Neue Musik-Zeitung* under the direction of Wilibald Nagel from 1917 to 1921.

Perhaps the most important figure within the Weimar conservative press was Alfred Heuss. Born in Switzerland in 1877, Heuss studied music at the University of Leipzig and wrote for a broad spectrum of periodicals before the war, including a worker's journal titled *Sächsischen Arbeiterzeitung*, while also dabbling in composition. Like Pfitzner, the war appears to have a radicalizing effect on Heuss, engendering an anti-Semitism and staunch nationalism that would pour from his pen within the pages of the *Zeitschrift für Musik* upon his assuming the editorship in 1921. Next to the *Allgemeine musikalische Zeitung*, the *Zeitschrift*, founded by the composer Robert Schumann in 1834, was in many ways the flagship publication of the nineteenth-century musical press. Committed to taking on the pressing musical, philosophical, and aesthetic issues of the day, one of the journal's primary missions was to serve as a forum for the promotion of new German music and composers still standing in the shadow of French and Italian idioms. Under Heuss's leadership, the journal would assume a belligerent and acerbic tone over the course of Weimar; in 1923, its subtitle was changed from the benign *Semi-monthly for Musicians and Friends of Music* to the rather more bellicose *Combat Newspaper for German Music and Musical Culture*.[19] According to his biographer, Heuss would emerge as the "leader of the anti-moderns" who spent much of the thirteen years in his role attacking atonalists, Jews, foreigners, and others whom he held collectively responsible for the scourge of modernist music.[20] Although he died in July 1934 and thus did not live to see the full effects of Nazi policy at home and abroad over the 1930s, Heuss, by all accounts, found much to admire in the movement. By 1928, Heuss joined with the Nazi Party "philosopher" Alfred Rosenberg and Hans von Wolzogen, a member of the Bayreuth Circle and editor of the *Bayreuther Blätter*, to form the *Kampfbund für Deutscher Kultur*, an organization that served as an important vehicle for winning converts to the Nazi message of cultural decline and the need for Germans' spiritual and moral renewal.[21] In addition, he presided over the Nazi takeover of the *Verband deutscher Musikkritiker*—the association that he had helped found in 1913—that was renamed the *Arbeitsgemeinschaft deutscher Musikkritiker* (Working Group of German Music Critics) after 1933.

Certainly not all critics or journals could be pegged as straightforwardly modernist or conservative in outlook. The prestigious *Die Musik*, for example, assumed a more moderate stance throughout the Weimar years and regularly featured contributions by conservative and modernist critics alike. It was in many ways the perfect forum for a figure like Adolf Weissmann, one of the most highly respected and noteworthy critics of the interwar period whose editorial duties at the *Berliner Zeitung am Mittag* were overtaken by Stuckenschmidt after 1929. A regular contributor to journals across the spectrum, Weissmann's views on race and modernist music defy easy categorization—while he was unforgiving in his assessments of modernist composers like Arnold Schoenberg and Franz Schreker, he respected and, in some cases, championed the music of other modernists, such as Paul Hindemith and Ernst Krenek. Nor should we assume that modernist and conservatively inclined critics made enemies of each other based simply on aesthetic differences of opinion. Although the war radicalized certain figures like Pfitzner and Heuss, others maintained a friendliness and generosity toward colleagues with alternative musical viewpoints. The modernist critic Stuckenschmidt, for example, once recalled a row with an influential and deep-pocketed lawyer in Prague who called for the critic's sacking from the newspaper *Bohemia* following an unfavorable review of various compositions by young composers of a German conservatory, a demand that was only averted thanks to the intervention of the paper's culturally conservative editor Albert Wesselsky.[22]

While writing for specialized music journals might seem at first glance to be an esoteric undertaking reserved for an elite and narrow audience, most journals evinced an extraordinary variety in terms of coverage, subject matter, and perspectives. In addition to publishing reviews of recent concert performances, festivals, and recitals, journal writers tackled pressing contemporary questions about the impact of war and inflation on German musical life or how the advent of radio and film might reshape Germans' listening habits. Other writers took on issues that were more historical or philosophical in nature, such as the function of music in ancient Greek society or the place of music within the aesthetic hierarchies of Kant and Goethe. Newspapers announced the discovery of musical scores long thought to have been lost and published newly discovered letters and correspondence of famous composers, such as Beethoven, Wagner, and Schumann.[23] Alongside such serious matters, most journals made space for the feuilleton—a popular genre in which writers combined literary and journalistic modes to create an informal hybrid that alternatively mocked, enlightened, titillated, and sensationalized readers.[24]

While, as we will see below, figures from a broad range of backgrounds and professions made regular forays into German music criticism, professional music critics constituted the most important single group of contributors. Although many received formal training at university or dabbled in composition and performance themselves, what set them apart from musicians and musicologists was that they primarily earned their living through writing, whether as a chief music critic attached to a major newspaper or as a regular contributor to several at once. It is true that many journals were confined to a select group of regular subscribers—in the case of *Die Musik*, a scant 3300 copies were being produced monthly as late as 1933.[25] However, we should not take this as evidence of critics' irrelevance. Weimar's most illustrious critics such as H. H. Stuckenschmidt, Paul Bekker, and Ferdinand Pfohl regularly published essays and concert reviews in some of Germany's most illustrious newspapers with far larger audiences, from the *Vossische Zeitung* and *Hamburger Nachrichten* to the *Frankfurter Zeitung*.[26] In addition to penning longer reflections on the relationship between music and society or the impact of technology on the modern concert scene, critics also published regular reviews of performances that took place in cities across Germany. This often required attending evening performances before rushing home to write reviews long into the night in order to meet tight deadlines—a frenetic pace that, in hindsight, struck critics' themselves. H. H. Stuckenschmidt described a typical workday as follows:

> Most evenings, I sat down at my writing table at 11 pm with a bottle of Cinzano-Vermouth and a pack of cigarettes. If, as often happened, I finished [my work] by 2 am, I did so only after having emptied the bottle and smoked 20 cigarettes. Feeling buzzed, I then went to the overnight post office box and dropped the letter in.[27]

The critic Paul Stefan maintained such a dizzying pace attending concert halls and opera houses in Vienna that he was often rumored to be two places at once during his time as music editor of the newspaper *Die Stunde*.[28]

Next to critics, professional musicologists constituted a second important set of contributors to the leading journals of the day. Yet as a relatively new discipline at the turn of the century, *Musikwissenschaft* neither possessed a codified set of procedures for the systematic study of music, nor were its practitioners trained in a uniform set of methodologies. Early practitioners emerged from the musical directorships of leading opera houses and conservatories—figures such as Hermann Kretzschmar (1848–1924) who served as head of various ensembles in Leipzig before his appointment as Music Professor at the University of Berlin in 1904 or Guido Adler (1855–1941), deemed by some the founding father of Austrian Musicology, who studied under Anton Bruckner before taking over the post of ordinary professor of music at the University of Vienna, recently vacated by Eduard Hanslick.[29] While many critics developed warm relationship with their colleagues in the academy, turf wars did occasionally break out as to who was best equipped to pass judgment on new works and steer musical debate. The musicologists Hugo Leichtentritt and Arnold Schering, for example, viewed a doctorate in musicology as de rigeur for any music critic aspiring to the name.[30] And although German musicologists would participate unevenly and to varying degrees in music criticism, their general preoccupation with formal analysis—the study of harmonic, melodic, and other formalistic musical structures within the printed score—must be seen as complementing rather than supplanting older critical approaches tending toward the extramusical and metaphysical. While certain professional rivalries existed, several critics and musicologists developed warm personal relationships that continued over the course of Weimar. The eminent Jewish musicologist Alfred Einstein, who oversaw the first major revision to the Köchel catalogue of Mozart's complete works, maintained a friendly correspondence with the conservative critic Alfred Heuss even while living in a Germany that was fast becoming unrecognizable. Following the Nazi "coordination" (*gleichschaltung*) of the *Berliner Tageblatt* for which he wrote as chief music critic and suffering increasing harassment by Gestapo agents, Einstein lamented to Heuss in a July 1933 letter that the Germany that had surrendered itself to Nazism "no longer has the right to claim itself as the land of Mozart, Beethoven, Goethe and Schiller."[31] He would leave Germany in July 1933 for Britain before eventually settling in the United States as a professor at Smith College in Massachusetts.

Finally, musicians and composers constituted a final group of important contributors to music criticism over the course of Weimar. Given the fledgling democracy's perennial economic instability, contributions to music journalism served as an important source of income that could supplement unsteady earnings generated through commissions and academic employment. Composers such as Hans Pfitzner, Ernst Krenek, and Hanss Eisler made regular interventions into the pressing musical questions of the day, continuing the legacy of Schumann and Wagner whose prose writings were nearly as numerous as their musical compositions.[32] As for musicians, their demanding travel, practice, and performing schedules were such that they were less frequent contributors to music journals. One of the exceptions was the conservative pianist and composer Walter Niemann, a fierce critic of much of the modernist canon and advocate of Sibelius, Dvorák, and other composers of "national" music. Reflecting on the nature of music criticism within Weimar's iconoclastic soundscape, Niemann described the music critic's role in the following terms: "The difficult task of the music critic who writes for a large daily paper appears almost insurmountable—consisting, on one hand, of judging [music] from his own time and place while, on the other hand, preserving a healthy look backwards towards tradition."[33]

However differing their fates following the Nazi seizure of power in 1933, during Weimar, German musicologists, critics, and professional musicians alike were united in their commitment to restoring German music to the pride of place that it had enjoyed before the war, both at home and abroad. Prior to the conflict, Germany had achieved unparalleled dominance in seemingly every branch of the arts and sciences. While universities across the globe emulated the German model, German achievements in fields as disparate as physics and music were recognized the world over. From the period 1901–1933, 30 percent of all Nobel Prize winners were Germans, who showed particular dominance in medicine and physics.[34] Many Germans felt the nation's grasp as a world leader in the realm of culture and science slipping away as a direct consequence of the war. When, for example, the English conductor Leopold Stokowski received the Philadelphia Prize in his role as music director for the Philadelphia Orchestra in 1922, a writer in the *Neue Musik Zeitung* bitterly lamented, "German masters be gone! As for us in the vaunted country of thinkers and poets, scarcely a single artist receives first prize."[35] This was a tendency that German critics and musicologists desperately wanted to reverse. As the musicologist Hans Joachim Moser, who we will encounter at length in Chapter 3, recalled: "If Germany possesses *one* area and *one* profession that wield absolute influence, despite all of the enmity and distance we face in the world, these are German music and the composer … one must not allow this noble, truly peaceful weapon to rust from lack of use."[36] The critic Otto Schmitt lamented the "coarse shrieks being set forth in the foreign presses about our 'Hun-like' nature (*Hunnentum*)" yet reminded readers that "above all the wide-ranging fields of art, it is in music that [Germany] stands alone without peer—who [else] can claim to have a Johann Sebastian Bach, Mozart, Beethoven or a Wagner?"[37]

The restorative effects of German music were not for consumption by Germans alone but rather to be shared among people of all nations and, as Jessica Gienow-Hecht has shown, many German critics saw themselves as playing a central role as "sound diplomats" who sought to gain greater influence abroad by capitalizing on Germany's sterling reputation as a *Kulturnation*. The first generation of great American music critics often "took their cues from Germany at large," regularly read the German musical press, and judged the health—or, in the American case, just as often sickness—of local cultural efforts by the European standard.[38] German music critics themselves often wrote on the cultural affairs of other nations as foreign correspondents and were keen to report how deeply embedded the German classics were within the repertories of orchestras around the world. In 1923 Hermann Keller reported with unmistakable pride that "young America is a good and receptive land for art" where one could hear music by Bach, Handel, Schubert, Schumann, and other masters faithfully performed by Germans, from Fritz Reiner in Cincinnati to a German choir in St. Louis led by Hugo Anschuetz.[39] However, just as musical presses began humming once again in 1919 with this renewed sense of purpose and unprecedented opportunity for open critical expression, a potential threat loomed, which threatened to upend not only the world of music criticism but the institution of the public concert itself—the German Inflation.

The inflation and the rise of the "new audience"

The inflationary pressures that came to a head with the hyperinflation of 1922–1923 can be directly traced to the war years. Closed off from international markets and unwilling to raise taxes in wartime, the imperial government had embarked on a dangerous path of deficit spending to finance the war effort. While such a policy helped establish Germany on a wartime footing and secure domestic support for the war, it had the effect of profoundly altering social relations within German society and disrupting long-standing class structures. Still, German music journals joined with other newspapers to exhort their subscribers to buy war bonds almost a year after the formal cessation of hostilities in an effort to aid in the recovery. One October 1919 advertisement, seen in image 2 below, appealed to its readers' cultural sensibilities by depicting a somber Beethoven accompanied by passages from the famous choral finale of the Ninth Symphony: "If some day the 'beautiful spark of divinity' of peace is to blaze and 'be embraced you millions' is to ring out toward those returning home after the most devoted fulfillment of duties, you need not shamefully stand to the side so long as you also do your duty. Your duty: buy war bonds!"

Image 2 German War Bond Advertisement. *Neue Musik Zeitung*, 1919. Source: *Neue Musik Zeitung*, 40 (2) 1919, 21.

Yet it was not long before the inflation made its impact felt within the music publishing industry itself. As the German mark continued its precipitous fall against the dollar, the *Neue Musik Zeitung* felt obligated to explain to its shrinking list of subscribers why the quarterly costs of the journal had increased from 1,500 marks to 6,000 marks from January to August 1923. As seen below, the previous year had seen the editorial staff regularly publishing tables showing readers the skyrocketing cost of ink, paper, and other materials necessary to the publication process in 1922 compared to 1914:

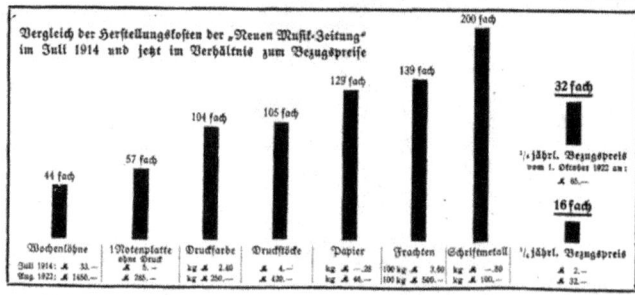

Image 3 Production costs of *Neue Musik Zeitung* July 1914 and present. Source: *Neue Musk Zeitung*, 43 (23), 1922, 388.

The journal was forced to close altogether in August 1923, followed shortly thereafter by Heuss's *Zeitschrift für Musik*, which curtailed its circulation from biweekly to monthly before being forced to halt publication for the months of September and October of the same year.

The economic origins and effects of the inflation are the subject of a rich historiography stretching back to the interwar period, having attracted the attention of such eminent historians as Charles Maier and Gerald Feldman.[40] More recently, historians have shifted their attention away from quantitative and statistical analyses toward a broader engagement with the way inflation penetrated deeply into German society and impacted the mental outlook and social psychology of ordinary Germans.[41] According to some scholars, the economic and social dislocations produced by the war were merely the first in a series of crises that wracked Weimar democracy, at once shattering cultural conservatives' faith in the state and making them susceptible to the darker forces of ethnic nationalism and anti-Semitism that the Nazis would later seize upon in their bid for power.[42] Indeed, the term *crisis* has become virtually synonymous with the Weimar Republic as a cursory glance at scholarship demonstrates.[43] Certainly within the world of classical music cultural conservatives in particular evinced deep concern with how the inflation threatened longstanding features of German concert life, from the social composition of concert attendees to orchestral programming decisions. They were likewise fearful of the inflation's impact upon long-established habits and decorum within the concert hall and were fervently committed to the educated middle class (*Bildungsbürgertum*)—of which they formed a part—and its self-styled role in shaping cultural taste. Yet alongside these concerns, critics also recognized the period following the First World War as an opportune moment to revitalize German culture from within. As Rüdiger Graf has argued, crisis must not be viewed simply as a teleological condition that predetermined the rise of Nazism and foreclosed untaken alternatives.[44]

Economic crisis and the rise of the new audience

While the postwar period witnessed the emergence of a new kind of concert attendee in the minds of German critics, the concert hall had long functioned as more than a purely musical space both on the continent and abroad. Since the beginning of the nineteenth century, the institution had loomed large as a place for reconfiguring social identities and asserting political ideals.[45] By the end of the war, however, contemporary observers had begun voicing concerns about the emergence of new social groupings for whom the war had been a blessing. While war profiteers and speculators were the subject of particular derision, it was the nouveau riche, whose rise to prominence threatened to upend well-established mores and traditions within the German concert hall, that was of gravest concern to music critics. Collectively referred to by critics as the "new audience," Gerald Feldman has nicely summed up the kinds of cultural faux pas to which they were prone:

> [He] was the sort of person whose wife regularly referred to their recently bought home as "ancestral" and confused *Oratorium* with a *Moratorium*, while he himself refused to pay the demanded price for a Rubens because it was a "used" picture, drank his beer out of a bottle even at the opera, and periodically took time off from the vulgarities of Berlin night life to taste what was passing for high culture. He bought Expressionist art for tax evasion or investment purposes and filled his house with unread books.[46]

In addition to printed testimonies, visual traces of the new audience can be found in contemporary satirical periodicals, above all in *Simplicissimus*, a popular weekly satirical magazine founded in 1896 that held particular appeal for middle-class audiences. On the eve of the First World War, it had 100,000 regular subscribers although, as Ann Taylor Allen has shown, its actual reach was probably significantly higher as editions were commonly recirculated in cafes, casinos, lending libraries, beauty parlors, and other popular establishments.[47] A 1920 image offers an early illustration of the *Raffke*, "or snatcher" as contemporaries called the newly wealthy, as well as the general Janus-faced quality of the early twentieth-century audience's attitude toward high culture, stood in for here by a highly stylized depiction of Botticelli's masterpiece *The Birth of Venus*.

The image captures the prudish conservative, who simply declares the work "disgraceful." A younger, though similarly conservative, bourgeois woman likewise exclaims, "Jesus, Mary and Joseph!" upon seeing such public displays of nudity. Meanwhile, an intellectual declares the piece to be simple "kitsch." These and other attitudes were, of course, well-established responses to art dating to the nineteenth century; however, the center frame in the middle row depicts the heightened danger posed by a new kind of patron given Weimar's current economic woes: the cultural charlatan. The couple bears all the trappings of the well-heeled, judging from the gentleman's suit and his wife's pearl necklace. Still, his unshaven face betrays the couple's social status almost as much as his juvenile reaction to the nude figure, which he declares to be "well-endowed!" Just below, two men appear who similarly eschew assessing the work on artistic

Image 4 "The Glass House Public and Picture 8611," *Simplicissimus*, 1920. Source: *Simplicissimus, 25* (27), 1920. Image retrieved from http://www.simplicissimus.info/index.php?id=5.

grounds in favor of a voyeuristic interest in the work's sexual qualities, in this case responding, "Oh boy, oh boy!"

Such caricatures resonated with writers such as Karl Blessinger (1888–1962), an early supporter of National Socialism whose cultural polemics have often been seen as anticipating the ideologically tainted scholarship of the Nazi period.[48]

While ensconced at the Münchener Akademie der Tonkunst in 1920, Blessinger wrote *Die musikalische Probleme der Gegenwart und ihre Lösung* ("The musical problems of the present and their solution"), lamenting that

> few among the public attend the concert for art's sake alone. Within a certain segment, the listener is indifferent and ill-prepared to take up certain new challenges while the other segment is [preoccupied] with excessive criticism and, consciously or not, competition based on envy [*Konkurrenzneid*] which will accept nothing new.[49]

The concert hall had come to assume a new function, one where artistic considerations took a back seat to both social and occupational ones; for Blessinger, "in the main, the concert-going public consists ... of people who arrange to see performances stemming from social motives or through personal relationships to the performers."[50] Nowhere was this more in evidence than in the lack of decorum and etiquette among the concertgoing public. According to the critic Edwin Janetschek writing in the conservative *Zeitschrift für Musik*, "The listeners' manners and dispositions in our concert halls have been worsened to a considerable degree by the war. Whoever has had to avoid the concert hall due to the onset of the war will scarcely recognize the current listenership."[51] Janetschek suggested a close connection between the rise of the nouveau riche and the new audience, as Germany's newly rich rushed to secure the kind of cultural capital commensurate with their newfound wealth:

> People who one used to never find in the theatres and concert halls now stream there in droves because for them the war and its happy occurrence effortlessly generated analogous piles of money, which they then used not only to splurge on diamonds and pearls, but also on spiritual beauty; that is, with whose aid they flaunted the outer appearance of musical appreciation and love and artistic advancement.[52]

High culture, according to this view, had become a mere accessory to what really mattered in Weimar Germany: money. *Kultur und Bildung* (culture and education)—the values that lay at the heart of educated Germans' middle-class identity—lost their luster as more and more Germans obsessed over money and capital whose holders were Germany's new masters. This was a view effectively captured in an image that appeared in the May 1921 edition of *Simplicissimus*.

It depicts a cafe setting where a bleary-eyed solo violinist can be seen playing before a room of inattentive patrons whose sole focus is the corpulent man mulling over the total cost of the evening's festivities. The man's capacity (or

Image 5 "Eight against One," *Simplicissimus*, 1921. Source: *Simplicissimus, 26* (8), 1921. Image retrieved from http://www.simplicissimus.info/index.php?id=5.

incapacity) to pay commands the entire room's attention, from the waitstaff in the background to the woman at the center of the image who, though facing right, is clearly preoccupied by the transaction. The violinist likewise shows greater interest in the money exchanging hands than what he is performing while German youth, we are told, are learning an important lesson on what really matters in life. This is a world where the whole of German life, from social status and interpersonal relationships to culture, has been utterly subordinated to money.

Within musical circles, Georg Göhler acknowledged that anxieties over "emergency situations" were seemingly omnipresent in Germany so much so that "one is satisfied with half measures—to put bandages where surgeries would be necessary and plug up every opening with the universal medium of the time—paper money."[53] The particular woes faced by the music world, like those faced in wider society, were of two kinds—an "inner and outer cause"—of which the first proved to be the most threatening. This was the "moral condition of the *Volk*, the prevailing view of life," for "without a moral renewal of the entire *Volk*, without a fundamental reorientation of this view, music cannot be saved, even with the support of millions."[54] As far as the outer cause was concerned Göhler cast blame at a likely suspect, matter-of-factly stating that "[all the deprivation] had come about as a consequence of the Versailles Treaty." For he and others, the shame of the Versailles Treaty left an indelible mark on musical life and while, under normal circumstances, art "certainly had nothing to do with politics," extraordinary times called for an altogether different relationship between politics and art. He pleaded:

> Everything that must be done in order to relieve the dire straits in which artists and all creative spirits find themselves is only a drop in the bucket and at best a chance effort, so long as the peace treaty of Versailles remains ... [if nothing is done], certainly it will slowly strangle everything, from elementary music instruction to public concerts and theater shows to music publication.

The second problem would take care of itself so long as Germany succeeded in its initial task of "securing the moral renewal of the *Volk*," but Göhler left little doubt what was at stake in this cultural effort: "Should the German people prove incapable of [achieving] moral renewal and unity through the forced revision of the Versailles Treaty, then the last hour of Germany as a musical as much as a world power has struck."[55]

But what did Göhler mean by "moral renewal" and why was it necessary in the first place? Alongside the new audience, the fracturing of the prewar cultural consensus threatened the existence of the autonomous artwork. Previously viewed, read, or listened to for its own sake, critics feared that high culture would now be treated like any purchasable commodity and governed more by social rather than purely aesthetic concerns. This was a world where the plea "L'art pour l'art" (art for art's sake) increasingly fell on deaf ears. The new patron attended the classical concert, not to *actually hear* Beethoven but *to be seen* as hearing him, and the German classics served merely to bolster the social standing of the concertgoer, who valued them only insofar as they endowed him with all the trappings of the culturally elite. This anxiety found expression in the following figure (Image 6):

Image 6 "The Book. The Books," *Simplicissimus*, 1926. Source: *Simplicissimus, 30* (47), 1926. Image retrieved from http://www.simplicissimus.info/index.php?id=5.

Here the artist juxtaposes German cultural life before and after the war through a representation of the book's place in German society. In the romanticized upper image, four figures ponder the contents of an unknown classic, aided by the solitary lamp located in the center of the image. The nuclear family is evoked through a depiction of the young man reading aloud to his wife and an older couple who look upon the reader with a certain wistfulness as he disseminates the book's hallowed contents for all to hear. The image below reflects the book's new function in a society rife with materialism and status. We are confronted with not one but many books that lay shut in tight rows on the built-in bookshelves lining the walls. Instead of a familial scene, here we find a man with a young woman—herself the embodiment of the "New Woman" with makeup, short hair, and a flapper dress—whose attention is focused exclusively on the music they are dancing too. The books serve merely as a backdrop, indexing the couple's well-to-do status but nothing more.

The economic impoverishment of the educated middle class had left that class, and by extension Germany, culturally impoverished in the minds of interwar critics, which was likewise the central theme of an essay by the Dresden-based critic F. A. Geissler. Writing for the journal *Die Musik* during the peak of hyperinflation, he sounded a note of great desperation as he considered the demise of German concert life, although the real culprits, in addition to the nouveau riche stressed by so many other critics, consisted of a surprising new group: the working class.[56] Like all classes, cultural elites were confronted with the realities of a dramatic reduction in their standard of living or, worse, the evaporation of their savings. Nevertheless, if the collapse of Germany economic capital remained outside of their control, the concert hall offered the *Bildungsbürger* a final preserve in which their cultural capital might remain intact. Now even this, according to Geissler, came under attack as the cultured elite found themselves crowded out by coarse organized workers, whose union membership offered better protection against the vagaries of the economy.[57] There was some truth to these accusations. Skilled workers were often better insulated from inflation's worst effects through salary adjustments and union activity compared to their unsalaried counterparts in the *Mittelstand*. Freelance writers, among whom many music critics counted themselves, independent lawyers, and other *geistige Arbeiter* (intellectual workers) on fixed incomes were all too often left with precious little money to spend on concert-hall visits and other cultural activities.[58]

In the minds of many critics, the debilitating conditions of a postwar German economy that had shattered both the savings and the prestige of culture's traditional defenders gave the impression of a society turned upside down, as Image 7 illustrates. As the "South Sea Islander" enjoys the fruits of European civilization, the "Sophisticated European" takes the place of the formerly colonized, a not-so-subtle reminder of just how deeply felt the wounds associated with the loss of Germany's overseas colonies as a result of the hated Versailles Treaty remained.

German critics were not alone in surmising that the war had fundamentally altered listeners' relationship to German music. The Polish violinist Bronislaw

Image 7 "Cultural Exchange," *Simplicissimus*, 1921. Source: "Cultural Exchange." *Simplicissimus*, 25 (47), 1921. Image retrieved from http://www.simplicissimus.info/index.php?id=5.

Huberman (1882–1947) offered some outside confirmation of critics' views in a 1921 short essay entitled "Artists and Concert Life as Affected by the War." As someone who had given concerts throughout Europe, Huberman was particularly well positioned to evaluate audience reception, noting particularly striking differences between concert life in England and that on the continent. "One of [musicians'] greatest joys," Huberman claimed, "was the feeling of giving pleasure and exhilaration to thousands by the reproduction of masterpieces ... we had contact with them, as it were by an electric current, and could make them feel our emotions."[59] As the title itself suggested, this idyllic world had been shattered by the war. While the rising influence of the working classes was making its impact felt, Huberman singled out the new middle classes as having an especially pernicious effect. Appearances could be deceiving, for "though the hall is often crowded, the best seats are taken chiefly by the 'nouveaux riches' of all sorts and conditions. Their minds are not cultured, and they come only because it is *bon ton* to have been to our concerts, which they swallow without digesting."[60]

In the minds of other critics, these listeners brought with them a particular characteristic of the interwar period—a love of all things foreign. Writing in the *Zeitschrift für Musik*, the critic Roderich Regidür lamented that while foreign artists thrived in Germany, German artists abroad suffered nothing but privation:

> German musicians, who before the war could practise their art all over the world, [have had] their employment hindered or entirely forbidden in most hostile countries. Only in Germany could these foreign, national musicians perform Jazz and other noise unhindered. How many Russian song and music societies travel now through Germany attracting an uncomprehending German *Volk* to the concert halls and theatres?[61]

For Regidür, this tendency was on full display during a performance by the Italian baritone Mattia Battistini (1856–1928), whose silky timbre won great acclaim all over Europe over a fifty-plus-year career and resulted in a corpus of 120 recordings spanning the operatic repertory from Mozart to Massenet. His performance of Beethoven's Op. 46 "Adelaide," however, was, in the judgment of Regidür, "simply catastrophic ... one is once again reminded that the innermost [feelings] of the German soul are neither felt nor understood by the representative of another *Volk*; of that, one has to always be clear."[62] Still, if the deficiencies in Battistini's rendition proved obvious to Regidür's trained ear, they appeared thoroughly lost on the German audience in attendance, which "characteristically" showed a "certain affinity" with the Italian singer while remaining "fully ignorant of what the famous Italian singer had done with the German song ... [O]ur musical culture once again lies in disorder; we do not even know ourselves."[63]

This impression of a Germany overrun by outsiders and obsessed with all things foreign was a rather incomplete one. On the one hand, inflation had prompted many foreigners to buy up German goods at prices that would have been unimaginable in their home countries. Border regions were particularly vulnerable with stories of Dutch farmers crossing into Germany to buy up entire herds of cattle, only to drive them right back across the border.[64] On the other hand, American novelties like Fordism and rationalization received a much more mixed reception with many Germans' attitudes alternating between feelings of admiration and disgust, curiosity, and repugnance.[65] Foreign artists could, on occasion, provoke violent responses from some members of the audience. In a 1923 review of a violin recital by Henri Marteau (1874–1934), the Munich-based critic J. E. Robert wrote:

> The hall filled up. Young lads had already in the wardrobe engaged in the most unpleasant pushing and shoving in an effort to be the first to check their coats. Then the violinist took the podium. But instead of the wonderful Adagio of the fifth solo sonata there came the sound of ear-splitting whistles, howls, hisses, roars and general romping throughout the hall over the customary applause. And just as the violinist began, several stink bombs were hurled, the first right at his feet. Young men sprang onto the podium, but not without first airing the cause of their grievance, which could be understood only after some minutes: "Marteau is a French citizen ... [D]uring the war he regularly committed espionage for France, was sentenced to death two times but repeatedly let go on the highest [military] orders. Whoever is really German—leave the hall!"[66]

The episode made for a shocking scene and had an ironic twist, for Marteau had arranged for the evening proceeds to go to a fund devoted to the care of German war invalids. In addition, despite his surname, Marteau was of mixed French-German ancestry and a Swedish citizen.[67] Still, critics did not take such breaches of etiquette lying down. Confronted with the new audience's improper decorum, critics unleashed a torrent of proposals that ranged from the practical to the comically absurd. Some critics insisted that Germans had to escape big cities like Berlin and Munich, where the penchant for modern, experimental art inspired such vitriol to smaller ones, where traditional fare flourished.[68] One critic suggested turning down the house lights as an effective means to combat all the unnecessary chatter and coughing, while another went so far as to insist that all malefactors' names be published in the local newspaper.[69] Yet another critic saw promise in the newly invented radio, which, as we will see in a later chapter, could "inspire the listener to active participation" and expand concertgoers' musical horizons. Music's special ability to transcend barriers imposed by education or occupation—a reach that neither literature nor visual art could ever hope to equal—meant that "in every place, a small germ cell should be created through municipal or state support which provides for the enjoyment of everyone."[70]

In sum, such evidence gives ample testimony to the pessimistic sentiment that ran through the conservative press during the inflation years. It should thus come as no surprise that scholars have turned to such evidence time and again as proof of the shattering effect the economic crisis had on Germans' commitment to Weimar democracy. Elias Canetti famously went so far as to posit a connection between the devaluation of currency during the peak years of hyperinflation and the later devaluation of human life during the Holocaust.[71] In musical life, too, some historians have detected a sharp increase in combative rhetoric, whether directed at Jews, foreigners, or modernists.[72]

Weimar critics: From resentment to recovery

It is important to note that the traumatic experience of inflation did not always provoke attacks on the usual suspects, nor did it elicit the uniform responses associated with crisis and reaction. Robert, who covered the Marteau concert, offers one useful jumping-off point: "In these times, we really have more important things to do than carry envy, hate and stink bombs into the concert hall." For him, the music hall was first and foremost a place where the aesthetic took precedence over the political, as in this case, when "900 people came out, not to see an alleged spy, but rather to hear the monumental fugue '*Komm, heiliger Geist, mit deinen Gaben*'"; they should, in his view, have been able to do so without having to bother with those "who indulge in conspiracy theories [*das Gras wachsen hören*]." While Robert believed that such incidents had been simply unimaginable before the war and were probably linked with the economic crisis through which Germany was passing, he left no doubt where he stood on the matter:

> National consciousness expresses itself not in cowardly loutishness against fellow countrymen; it reveals itself in noble, chivalrous attitudes, in courage and honorableness in loving devotion to the public good, as existed in August 1914. What we experienced in Munich on the night of December 13 in the *Bayrischer Hof* concert hall is the crassest opposite of the spirit of August 1914.

> It is arrogance; a brazen desire for dominance and cheeky interference in others' business which is thoroughly unworthy of the German name.⁷³

Fearing the damage such outbursts might have done to Germany's reputation, Robert suggested that those who attacked Marteau might indeed be the same as those engaging in more general violence on the streets:

> Who can guarantee us going forward that the methods used in Munich won't be repeated against Jewish musicians and conductors? [It is] Hiller's [sic] stormtroopers who wish to provoke such deeds ... What will the Swedes say if German musicians come there? They certainly won't throw stink bombs, but the concert agents will shy away from engaging German musicians if they have to fear an empty concert hall! ... [This incident shows] how much the soulful cultural condition of our comrades has sunk within certain circles, among whom civilized behaviour no longer prevails.⁷⁴

While it was hard to find any salutary effects on concert life provoked by inflation in the short term, some critics wondered whether there might not be unexpected long-term positive outcomes. According to the critic Geissler, it was simply asking too much to require the new concertgoing public to digest Schoenberg and Scriabin without having first had a firm grounding in Bach and Beethoven. By the interwar period it was established practice that concert programs themselves should proceed in chronological order, acclimating listeners with classic works by old masters before challenging them with more modern repertoire. Thus, for Geissler programming should first proceed,

> not from the bizarre and perplexed-sounding, but rather from the proportional and easy-going, so that the listener will not arrive too quickly at a fixed judgement concerning the modern [musical] trends. One must always remember not to expect too much too quickly of the new public; rather, it must first be cultivated as well as educated.⁷⁵

Although he remained uncertain of the extent to which the new audience might eventually be brought around to contemporary music, Geissler suggested a crucial relationship between the old German masters and the new audience. The decline in the general sophistication of the audience could paradoxically lead to a rise in the overall health of German concert life through a resurgence of the German classics.⁷⁶ This view was echoed by cultural conservatives and committed modernists alike. In a 1922 review for the conservative *Neue-Musik Zeitung*, the critic Otto Janowitz claimed it was counterproductive to devote too much programming to modern music, as

> the public does not love novelty, [as can be seen from] a recent cycle of chamber music performances. The all-Beethoven program played by a famous ensemble was a huge hit, the recital devoted to the Romantics a moderate success [ein halber]. Meanwhile, the recital devoted to modern music drew a blank.[77]

This vision of a German canon rejuvenated by the country's changed class structures was no mere a conservative fantasy but one that issued from voices within the modernist press as well, such as *Musikblätter des Anbruch*. The journal's former editor Paul Pisk, in spite of his staunch commitment to modern music as a founding member of the International Society for Contemporary Music, likewise had high hopes for what the rise of the new audience might portend for the operatic world, envisaging a return to "the old classical or romantic [opera]," which better suited the sensibilities of the novice listener.[78] Even creators of new music, such as the composer Hermann Wolfgang von Waltershausen, had to admit that the best concerts were ones that achieved a sense of unity consisting of old and new.[79]

Despite our sense of Weimar Germany as a society obsessed with the new and iconoclastic, matters appeared rather differently to contemporary music critics and musicologists who noted the traditional fare dominating Germany's concert scene. In a February 1922 letter to the great Austrian music theorist and musicologist Heinrich Schenker, the amateur musician Moriz Violin described Hamburg's concertgoing public as "thoroughly conservative, [one] that will walk out of the concert hall when an excessively [modern] work is performed."[80] In city after city, it was not the nightmarish modern and foreign classical music of conservative fantasy but traditional and German classical music that predominated, as statistical surveys of programming in towns and cities showed. As the following table of performances in Mannheim and Berlin shows, big cities and small towns alike maintained a strong emphasis on the German classics.[81]

As the table illustrates, in Mannheim, of the ten most performed composers, nine were German (Chopin is the sole exception); in the case of the Berlin Philharmonic, not a single non-German is to be found among the ten most performed composers. Moreover, closer inspection of both lists reveals that, taken together, the thirty-nine most performed masters included only six modern composers.[82] Measured differently, the difference is even more striking: in Mannheim and the Berlin Philharmonic over the years in question, total performances of eighteenth- and nineteenth-century masters exceeded those of their twentieth-century counterparts by a staggering 1,114 to 189. These numbers would seem to confirm what historians have identified in other cultural domains, namely that the interwar period witnessed a far greater interest in traditional idioms than has often been recognized.[83]

Table 1 Concert statistics: Mannheim and Berlin Philharmonic, 1922–1925

CITY OF MANNHEIM, 1923–1925		BERLIN PHILHARMONIC, 1922–1925	
Composer	Performances	Composer	Performances
Schubert	156	Beethoven	18
Beethoven	130	Brahms	13
Brahms	122	Mozart	8
Mozart	102	R. Strauss	8
Schumann	95	Handel	6
Reger	74	Schumann	5
R. Strauss	66	Haydn	5
J. S. Bach	65	J. S. Bach	5
Wolf	61	Pfitzner	4
Chopin	52	Bruckner	4
Mendelssohn	45	Mahler	3
Liszt	43	Tchaikovsky	3
Wagner	37	Schubert	3
Handel	32	Berlioz	3
Cornelius	31	Stravinsky	2
Bruckner	30	Braunfels	2
J. Strauss	30	Liszt	2
Pfitzner	29	Wagner	2
——-	—————	Reger	2
——-	—————	Weber	2
——-	—————	Schoenberg	2
——-	—————	Various	1

While the economic catastrophe of 1923 elicited some hostile reactions from journals like the *Zeitschrift für Musik* and *Allgemeine Musik-Zeitung*, others redoubled their efforts to reach out to the international music-loving community by proclaiming that the storm had passed. In the October 1923 issue of the *Musikblätter des Anbruch*, the Austrian critic Paul Stefan noted just how tied German-speaking Europe was to the oscillating fortunes of Weimar Germany's music press, while issuing a plea for continued international cooperation and outreach:

> The catastrophe in the German Reich has interrupted or impeded altogether the German music periodicals … Still, we can at least take up the burden of our task even if we are alone. We want to give an appraisal, whilst also speaking for others, of how this fact hampers and condemns us to silence. In the last few years, our newspaper has been esteemed ever more warmly. The lone criticism which we have received was for being a publisher's newspaper. But that has always been vouched for. [The paper] has no blinders and is associated with no party, no person, and is against no party, as the term 'universal' indicates, not

only on paper but in practice … As we have readers from all over the world, we would like to accrue our reports from all over the world.[84]

Conservative periodicals, too, sounded a note of hope and promise in the months following the inflation. The *Neue Musik-Zeitung*, forced to close in August 1923, reopened in January 1924 having overhauled the paper's format and abandoned the *Fraktur* typeface of the pre-inflation period in favor of a newer, fresher script. In a message to subscribers, it pledged "[to] take up once again its beneficial work on behalf of German art and its supporters newly adorned and with fresh strength."[85] Max Chop, editor of the conservative *Signale für die Musikalische Welt*, offered a similarly hopeful prognosis about Germany's (and the paper's) future:

> Does it seem that the close of the year 1924 and the beginning of 1925 appear differently than the year before? For the person who involuntarily puts this question to himself as a conscientious recorder and observer of the weather within the artistic sky, the answer must be a joyful "Yes!" It is in fact entirely different; the foam from a time of ferment has been gradually disposed of, the extremes were pushed back to their own borders; cultural progress has once again taken its place in the foreground, and balance is being achieved in wholly natural ways. At the present, we hardly any longer find ourselves in a cultural crisis.[86]

As many historians have noted, hyperinflation did not impose universal misery on all Germans but rather produced winners and losers across different social strata, and among musicians it was no different. While unsalaried freelance musicians confined to domestic performances were particularly hard-hit, artists able to book international engagements had crucial access to currencies undamaged by inflation. Thus, the wife of the violinist Adolf Busch was remembered for having showered family members and friends with imported chocolates, expensive clothing, and holiday travel during the worst months of the hyperinflation.[87] Reflecting years later on life in Germany in the early 1920s, the pianist Arthur Schnabel remembered the inflation years in surprisingly nostalgic, even glowing terms: "the disunity of the Germans had completely disappeared and inflation established perfect unity. Everybody was gay and alert, in the best of spirits. Music went on absolutely undisturbed during the period, animated and stimulated as never before."[88] As we saw earlier, while some Germans maintained a laser-like focus on money during inflation in an effort to weather the storm, others reached the opposite conclusion and gave up trying to understand the vicissitudes of Germany's economic fortunes. Among this group, money came to matter less, not more, over time as the novelist Stefan Zweig vividly illustrated in his memoir *The World of Yesterday*. Domiciled in

Salzburg, directly on the Austrian-German border, Zweig was ideally situated for observing inflation's sociocultural effects both within his native Austria and in Germany. His memorable account merits inclusion here in its entirety:

> I will never forget what operatic performances were like in those days of our greatest need. You groped your way through dimly lit streets ... and paid for your seat in the gallery with a bundle of banknotes that would once have allowed you to hire a luxurious box for a year. You sat in your overcoat, because the auditorium was unheated, and pressed close to your neighbors for warmth—and the theatre itself, once brilliant with uniforms and expensive gowns, was so dismal and grey! ... Everything seemed doubly desperate in this scene of former luxury and imperial extravagance ... But then the conductor raised his baton, the curtains parted, and it was more wonderful than ever before. The singers and musicians gave of their best, for they all felt that this might be the last time they performed in the theatre they loved. And we listened with bated breath, more receptive than ever, knowing that for us, too, this might be the last time. Thousands of us, hundreds of thousands, lived like this. We all strained ourselves to the limit in these weeks and months and years on the brink of downfall. I never felt the will to live in a nation and in myself as strongly as I did then, when the end of everything, life and survival itself, was at stake.[89]

The wistful tone of Zweig's recollection stood in stark contrast to the circumstances in which he found himself at the time of writing. He left Europe permanently in 1934 following the Nazis' seizure of power and lived first in England and then the United States before settling in Brazil in 1941. A broken man by the time he sat down to complete his memoirs, Zweig took poison, together with his second wife, Charlotte, only two weeks after finishing the manuscript. Still, his romantic description of concert life during the inflation years, experienced in such spare surroundings stripped of all the "glitter," "costly gowns," and other social accoutrements that for many purists had always distracted from the true meaningful purpose of the public concert, illustrates some of economic crisis's positive, if unintended, consequences for cultural life.

A burning question remains: was the new audience a real historical phenomenon or merely a figment of critics' imaginations? It is a hard question to answer. The vast majority of concerts throughout Germany in this period were probably attended by a rather small circle of regular attendees, particularly in the years following the hyperinflation. Although we lack precise statistics for 1914–1928, the figures for annual theater subscribers in 1928 in several major German cities are illuminating: the Städtische Bühnen in Cologne, a city with a population of 730,000, managed just 2,544 subscription holders. Bremen and

Oberhausen, with populations of 320,000 and 190,000, secured only 1,297 and 890 annual ticket holders, respectively.[90] Still, these figures tell us little about the social composition of the audiences, much less the oscillations between ongoing and newly minted concert subscribers. Statistical data on the fluctuations in old versus new patrons would in any case tell us next to nothing about the motivations of a new class of subscribers and whether their patronage was driven by social rather than aesthetic considerations.

There can be no question that the inflation years and their perceived relationship to the rise of the new audience unleashed fears about the continued viability of Germany's concert halls, opera houses, and other cultural institutions, as well as anxieties about the intrusion into concert life of new social climbers, whose presence manifested itself in diverse ways. Perceived as lacking etiquette befitting the concert hall and appropriating culture solely with base social considerations in mind, the new audience elicited concern from some contemporary observers. As the musicologist Hans Joachim Moser put it in a 1921 article,

> Germany's current dismal situation has often been compared with the time of the Thirty Years' War, and with good reason … not least owing to the suffering of the German musical profession in the broadest sense under the thousands of hardships endured in wartime and afterwards, stemming from the currency devaluation, the confusion in taste, the general moral and economic prostration and the most pronounced threat of further decay.[91]

As we have seen, the economic crisis elicited hostile responses from certain conservative circles, some of whom channeled their anger in the direction of Germany's "cultural enemies," whether modernists, Jews, or foreigners. Indeed, some of these disillusioned "culture warriors" would ultimately become an important constituency for the Nazis who pledged to protect culture and restore it to its rightful place in German society.[92] At the same time, it is worth remembering that although an individual or collective sense of crisis may have diminished faith in Weimar democracy among some, it just as often opened up new vistas of recovery and possibility in the eyes of contemporaries from across the political, cultural, and social spectrum.[93] Economic distress and political instability were rampant, a direct consequence of Germany having lost the war, but this experience also underwrote the possibility of reimagining promising "new historical conditions" that accompanied defeat.[94] Crisis, in other words, is best viewed not as a symptom of Weimar Germany's slow and inevitable death but rather in ways that come closer to the original Greek *krisis*, which simply means "turning point" or "moment of decision."[95] As Wolfgang Schivelbusch has observed, after overcoming an initial sense of loss and devastation following defeat in the First World War, many Germans viewed the immediate postwar years as an opportunity to cleanse the nation and sweep away the artificiality and emptiness of the old order. In its place would stand a Germany newly committed to the arts and more certain than ever before of the place of music in the cultural life of the nation.[96]

Inflation in Germany and the larger anxieties to which it gave rise has often been seen as presaging Germany's gradual descent into dictatorship. The relentless attention scholars often give to experimental and iconoclastic trends in Weimar's cultural scene has sometimes risked masking the fact that traditional culture continued to dominate German stages for much of the period.[97] And although German critics cast a wary eye on the new audience's lack of cultural experience and taste, they also looked on the postwar years as a potential clean slate where their ability to shape public taste mattered more than ever before. Even amid the economic anxieties produced by hyperinflation, critics in the conservative press remained hopeful about the continued dominance of the old masters in concert programming, whose works held greater appeal among new listening publics making their way into German concert halls. At the same time, as Germany's economic situation stabilized in 1924, progressives and conservatives alike doubled down on their cosmopolitan appeals to friends of music the world over. Perhaps most important, the introduction of the *Rentenmark* and the relative stabilization of Germany's economy that followed pumped much-needed funds into the country's cultural institutions, leading to the resumption of a more or less well-functioning concert scene. Theaters and concert halls, which from the outset of the republic had relied heavily on public funds to make ends meet, became even more dependent on the state, whose share of financing grew to more than half of the total operating expenditures by 1928–1929.[98] It was in large measure thanks to this public assistance that cultural institutions were able to weather the storm. When a second, even more severe economic crisis hit in 1929, they would not be so fortunate.

Notes

1 Mary Sue Morrow, *German Music Criticism in the Late Eighteenth Century* (Cambridge: Cambridge University Press, 1997), 6.
2 Lucian Kamienski, "Der Verband deutscher Musikkritiker," *Die Musik*, 12 (47) (1913–1914): 316–320.
3 See "Ehrengerichtsordnung," 1925, Box 16 Folder 199, Paul Bekker Papers MSS 50, Yale Music LIbrary, Yale University.

4 "Verband deutsche Musikkritiker," *Neue Musik Zeitung*, 44 (16) (1923): 286.
5 Pamela Potter, *Most German of the Arts: Musicology and Society from the Weimar Republic to the End of Hitler's Reich* (New Haven: Yale University Press, 1998), 35.
6 Waldemar v. Baussnern et al., "Gesellschaft und Musik in der Neuzeit," *Neue Musik Zeitung*, 40 (22) (1919): 275.
7 Paul Bülow, "Das Schriftum unserer deutschen Musiker in Zeit und Schule," *Neue Musik Zeitung*, 43 (8) (1922): 113–116.
8 Carl Schorske, *Fin-de-Siècle Vienna: Politics and Culture* (New York: Vintage, 1981).
9 Walter Gieseking, *So wurde ich Pianist* (Wiesbaden: F. A. Brockhaus, 1964), 55–56.
10 For a larger discussion of this shift from Vienna to Berlin, see Michael Haas, *Forbidden Music: The Jewish Composers Banned by the Nazis* (New Haven: Yale University Press, 2013), 99–112.
11 Stefan Zweig, *The World of Yesterday* (Lincoln: University of Nebraska Press, 2009), 305.
12 Anton Reichel, "Deutsch-Oesterreichs künstlerische Sendung," *Neue Musik Zeitung*, 42 (14) (1921): 213–214.
13 H. H. Stuckenschmidt, *Zum Hören geboren: Ein Leben mit der Musik unserer Zeit* (München: Deutscher Taschenbuch Verlag, 1982), 77.
14 In a 1926 letter to critic Adolf Weissmann, Bekker expressed real regret for failing to arrange a visit to a dress rehearsal of the modernist Italian composer Alfredo Casella's ballet *La Giara* but declared that he "would make up for it at the next opportunity" when the critics' paths crossed again. See Paul Bekker to Adolf Weissmann, March 27, 1926, Box 18 Folder 231, Paul Bekker Papers MSS 50, Yale Music Library, Yale University.
15 Haas, *Forbidden Music*, 119–120.
16 Ibid., 114.
17 There is a broad consensus on the journals that constituted the conservative music press in this period. For more, see Fabian Lovisa, *Musikkritik im Nationalsozialismus: Die Rolle deutschsprachiger Musikzeitschriften, 1920–1945* (Laaber: Laaber-Verlag, 1993) and Marc-André Roberge, "Focusing Attention: Special Issues in German-Language Music Periodicals of the First Half of the Twentieth Century," *Royal Music Association Research Chronicle*, 27 (1994): 71–99.
18 See, for example, Jonathan O. Wipplinger, *The Jazz Republic: Music, Race and American Culture in Weimar Germany* (Ann Arbor: University of Michigan Press, 2017), 151–152.
19 Joel Sachs, "Some Aspects of Musical Politics in Pre-Nazi Germany," *Perspectives of New Music*, 9 (1) (1970): 74–95 (here 75).
20 Oliver Hilmes, *Der Streit ums "Deutsche": Alfred Heuss und die Zeitschrift für Musik* (Hamburg: Bockel Verlag, 2003), 113.
21 For a longer discussion of the *Kampbund* and its appeal, see Alan E. Steinweis, "Weimar Culture and the Rise of National Socialism: The Kampfbund für deutsche Kultur," *Central European History*, 24 (4) (1991): 402–434.
22 Stuckenschmidt, *Zum Hören Geboren*, 108.

23 See, for example, Wilhelm Altmann, "Bisher unveröffentlichte Briefe Robert Schumanns," *Die Musik*, 15 (2) (1923): 865–869 and Sebastian Röckl, "Unveröffentlichte Schreiben Richard Wagners," *Zeitschrift für Musik*, 91 (1924): 230.

24 However, not all critics were enthused with a genre that they deemed ill-suited for and distracted from the business of serious music criticism. For one critique, see Hilda Mena Blaschiz, "Gegen den Feuilletonstil in Musikkritik und Musikbetrachtung," *Neue Musik Zeitung*, 42 (16) (1921): 245–247.

25 Lovisa, *Musikkritik im Nationalsozialismus*, 22.

26 Bekker was the music critic at the *Frankfurter Zeitung* 1911–1922 while Pfohl served as chief music editor at the *Hamburger Nachrichten* from 1892–1931. Stuckenschmidt began making regular contributions to the *Vossische Zeitung* beginning in 1927.

27 Stuckenschmidt, *Zum Hören geboren*, 113.

28 Ibid., 75.

29 Potter, *Most German of the Arts*, 32–37.

30 Ibid., 127.

31 Alfred Einstein to Alfred Heuss, July 17, 1933, Box 5 Folder 454, Alfred Einstein Papers 1835–1985, Jean Hargrove Music Library, University of California, Berkeley. Throughout the letter, Einstein addresses Heuss with the informal "Du."

32 Christopher Hailey, *Franz Schreker, 1878–1934: A Cultural Biography* (New York: Cambridge University Press, 1993), 130–131.

33 Walter Niemann, *Mein Leben furs Klavier: Rückblicke und Ausblicke* (Düsseldorf: Staccato-Verlag, 2008), 95. Much of Niemann's self-serving memoir is devoted to establishing his self-image as an artist above all else and to defending his notoriously harsh criticisms of the composer Max Reger during Weimar.

34 Fritz Stern, *Dreams and Delusions: The Drama of German History* (New Haven: Yale University Press, 1999), 32.

35 "Unterrichtswesen," *Neue Musik Zeitung*, 43 (14) (1922): 232.

36 Quoted in Potter, *Most German of the Arts*, 4.

37 Otto Schmitt, "Der deutche ausübende Künstler nach dem Kriege," *Zeitschrift für Musik*, 88 (1921): 329.

38 Jessica Gienow-Hecht, *Sound Diplomacy: Music and Emotions in Transatlantic Relations, 1850–1920* (Chicago: University of Chicago Press, 2009), 122–126.

39 Hermann Keller, "Amerikanisches Reisetagebuch," *Neue Musik Zeitung*, 44 (16) (1923): 284–285.

40 See Constantino Bresciani-Turroni's *The Economics of Inflation: A Study of Currency Depreciation in Post-war Germany, 1914–1923* (London: Allen & Unwin, 1937), "The Politics of Inflation in the Twentieth Century," in *In Search of Stability: Explorations in Historical Political Economy*, ed. Charles Maier (Cambridge: Cambridge University Press, 1987); and Gerald Feldman's monumental classic,

The Great Disorder: Politics, Economics, and Society in the German Inflation, 1914–1924 (New York: Oxford University Press, 1993).

41 Jürgen Freiherr von Kruedener, "Die Entstehung des Inflationstraumas: Zur Sozialpsychologie der deutschen Hyperinflation 1922/1923," in *Konsequenzen der Inflation*, ed. Gerald Feldman et al. (Berlin: Colloquium, 1989), 213–286. See also Bernd Widdig, *Culture and Inflation in Weimar Germany* (Berkeley: University of California Press, 2001) and Martin Geyer, *Verkehrte Welt: Revolution, Inflation, und Moderne: München, 1914–1924* (Göttingen: Vandenhoeck & Ruprecht, 1998).

42 See Sachs, "Some Aspects of Musical Politics," 74–95; and Michael Kater, "The Revenge of the Fathers: The Demise of Modern Music at the End of the Weimar Republic," *German Studies Review*, 15 (2) (1992): 295–315.

43 Detlev Peukert, *The Weimar Republic: The Crisis of Classical Modernity* (London: Penguin, 1991), but also Ehrhard Bahr, *Weimar on the Pacific: German Exile Culture in Los Angeles and the Crisis of Modernism* (Berkeley: University of California Press, 2008); Todd Herzog, *Crime Stories: Criminalistic Fantasy and the Culture of Crisis in Weimar Germany* (New York: Berghahn Books, 2009); and Juergen Freiherr von Kruedener, *Economic Crisis and Political Collapse: The Weimar Republic, 1924–1933* (New York: Berg, 1990).

44 Rüdiger Graf, "Either-Or: The Narrative of 'Crisis' in Weimar Germany and in Historiography," *Central European History*, 43 (4) (2010): 592–615.

45 See Leon Botstein, "Listening through Reading: Musical Literacy and the Concert Audience," *19th-Century Music*, 16 (2) (1992): 129–145. For Germany in particular, see Sven Oliver Müller, "Distinktion, Demonstration und Disziplinierung: Veränderungen im Publikumsverhalten in Londoner und Berliner Opernhäusern im 19. Jahrhundert," *International Review of the Aesthetics and Sociology of Music*, 37 (2) (2006): 167–187; and Sven Oliver Müller, "Cultural Nationalism and Beyond: Musical Performances in Imperial Germany," in *Imperial Germany Revisited: Continuing Debates and New Perspectives*, ed. Sven Oliver Müller (New York: Berghahn Books, 2011), 173–185.

46 Feldman, *Great Disorder*, 553.

47 Ann Taylor Allen, *Satire and Society in Wilhelmine Germany: Kladderadatsch and Simplicisssimus, 1890–1914* (Lexington: University Press of Kentucky, 1984).

48 See Potter, *Most German of the Arts*, 108–109.

49 Karl Blessinger, *Die musikalische Probleme der Gegenwart und ihre Lösung* (Stuttgart: Benno Filser, 1920), 57.

50 Ibid., 56.

51 Edwin Janetschek, "Konzertsaalunarten," *Zeitschrift für Musik*, 87 (9) (1920): 99–101 (99).

52 Ibid., 99.

53 Georg Göhler, "Die Notlage der deutschen Musik," *Zeitschrift für Musik*, 88 (19) (1921): 487.

54 Ibid., 487.
55 Ibid., 488–489.
56 F. A. Geissler, "Das Neue Publikum," *Die Musik*, 15 (12) (1923): 873–876 (876).
57 For insight into the plight of the "intellectual worker" during the hyperinflation, see Widdig, *Culture and Inflation*, 169–195.
58 Feldman, *Great Disorder*, 527–554.
59 Bronislaw Huberman, "Artists and Concert Life: As Affected by the War," *Music and Letters*, 2 (2) (1921): 121–129 (122).
60 Ibid., 122.
61 Roderich Regidür, "Das deutsche Publikum und die ausländischen Musiker," *Zeitschrift für Musik*, 94 (6) (1927): 357–358 (357). Roderich Regidür was the pen name of the Dutch composer and writer Theo Rüdiger.
62 Roderich Regidür, "Battistini, 'Adelaide' und das deutsche Publikum," *Zeitschrift für Musik*, 94 (6) (1927): 356–357 (356).
63 Ibid., 357.
64 Recounted in Eric Weitz, *Weimar Germany: Promise and Tragedy* (Princeton, NJ: Princeton University Press, 2007), 139.
65 Mary Nolan, *Visions of Modernity: American Business and the Modernization of Germany* (New York: Oxford University Press, 1994).
66 J. E. Robert, "Bach, Beethoven und Stinkbomben," *Zeitschrift für Musik*, 90 (1) (1923): 6–7 (6).
67 Although Marteau indeed eventually acquired Swedish citizenship, he was of mixed parentage, born in Reims, France, to a German mother and French father. Upon the eminent violinist Joseph Joachim's death in 1907, he assumed the directorship of the violin department at the prestigious Berlin Hochschule für Musik before being expelled to Sweden during the First World War. "Henri Marteau," Internationale Musikbegegnungsstätte Haus Marteau, n.d., http://www.haus-marteau.de/files/02_Informationen/Henri_Marteau/henrimarteau.php?nav=8&subnav=51 (accessed June 21, 2017).
68 Robert Hernried, "Neues Publikum," *Allgemeine Musik-Zeitung*, 49 (1922): 903–904.
69 Modern rituals concerning proper etiquette at public concerts were largely inherited from practices established by the early nineteenth century, though in the Weimar period they often doubled nicely as cost-saving measures. See Celia Applegate, "Culture and the Arts," in *Germany, 1800–1870*, ed. Jonathan Sperber (New York: Oxford University Press, 2004), 119–128. Janetschek, "Konzertsaalunarten," 101.
70 W. Buschmann, "Über den Kulturwert der 'Konzertvereine' für die Kleinstadt," *Zeitschrift für Musik*, 95 (3) (1928): 148–149.
71 Elias Canetti, *Masse und Macht* (Frankfurt am Main: Fischer, 1960).
72 Sachs, "Some Aspects of Musical Politics," 74–95.

73 Robert, "Bach, Beethoven und Stinkbomben," 7.
74 Ibid., 7.
75 Geissler, "Das Neue Publikum," 876.
76 Geissler, "Das neue Publikum," 876–878.
77 Otto Janowitz, "Musikhunger und Konzertprogramme," *Neue Musik-Zeitung*, 43 (10) (1922): 145–146. It is important to note, however, that Janowitz viewed the return to the classics among the new audience as stemming more from "lazy listening" (*Hörstfaulheit*) than from true audience appreciation for the classics. In the above-mentioned case, Janowitz sarcastically asked, "Who really believes that [the turnout for Beethoven] stemmed from true appreciation for the composer and not, in more than 90% of cases, from laziness?" See ibid., 145–146.
78 Paul Pisk, "Das Neue Publikum," *Musikblätter des Anbruch*, 1 (9) (1927): 94–96.
79 H. W. v. Waltershausen, "Konzert-Programme," *Neue Musik-Zeitung*, 46 (1) (1925): 1–4.
80 Letter from Moriz Violin to Heinrich Schenker, February 2, 1922, Schenker Documents Online, http://www.schenkerdocumentsonline.org/documents/correspondence/OJ-14-45_13.html (accessed June 2017).
81 For Mannheim, see Karl Stengel, "Statistisches aus Konzertsaal und Theatre," *Zeitschrift für Musik*, 93 (12) (1926): 680–681. It should also be noted that the term *modernists* for the above-mentioned composers refers to their birthright, not their compositional style. Some, like Max Reger, composed in older forms (e.g., fugues and variations), while the composer Richard Strauss's musical style arguably belongs more to the late Romantic than the modern tradition. Hans Pfitzner, in contrast, was a self-declared anti-modernist who would later become the most notorious of the so-called Nazi composers. See Michael Kater, *Composers of the Nazi Era: Eight Portraits* (New York: Oxford University Press, 2002), 144–183. For Berlin, these figures are found in Peter Wackernagel, *Wilhelm Furtwängler: Die Programme der Konzerte mit dem Berliner Philharmonischen Orchester, 1922-1954* (Wiesbaden: F. A. Brockhaus, 1965), 7–13. Composers within the "various" category included César Franck, Modest Mussorgsky, Alexander Scriabin, Alexander Glazunov, Max Trapp, Jean Sibelius, Bernhard Sekles, Arcangelo Corelli, Domenico Cimarosa, Feruccio Busoni, Felix Mendelssohn, Frédéric Chopin, Bela Bartok, Ottorino Respighi, Antonin Dvorak, Johann Christian Bach, Paul Hindemith, and Christoph Willibald Gluck.
82 These included Max Reger (1873–1916), Richard Strauss (1864–1949), Hans Pfitzner (1869–1949), Walter Braunfels (1882–1954), Igor Stravinsky (1882–1971), and Arnold Schoenberg (1874–1951). This is all the more striking given that the years listed here coincided with the newly installed Wilhelm Furtwängler's directorship at the Berlin Philharmonic. Though by no means disinterested in works by older masters—the Romantic repertory from Beethoven to Brahms lay at the heart of his oeuvre—Furtwängler had already shown considerable interest in new music during his residency at Mannheim from 1914 onward and played

an important role in programming in his capacity as the musical director of the philharmonic. See Raymond Holden, *The Virtuoso Conductors: The Central European Tradition from Wagner to Karajan* (New Haven, CT: Yale University Press, 2005), 203–224.

83 The most influential voice here has been that of Jay Winter, *Sites of Memory, Sites of Mourning: The Great War in European Cultural History* (Cambridge: Cambridge University Press, 1995). This point is driven home in the superb review essay Benjamin Ziemann, "Weimar Was Weimar: Politics, Culture and the Emplotment of the German Republic," *German History*, 28 (4) (2010): 542–571.

84 Paul Stefan, "Zum nächsten Jahrgang," *Musikblätter des Anbruch*, 5 (10) (1923): 282.

85 "Zum Geleit," *Neue Musik Zeitung*, 45 (1) (1924): 3.

86 Max Chop, "Musikalisches Neujahr," *Signale für die Musikalische Welt*, 83 (1) (1925): 7–9 (9).

87 Quoted in Tully Potter, *Adolf Busch: The Life of an Honest Musician*, vol. 1: *1891–1939* (London: Toccata, 2010), 340.

88 Arthur Schnabel, *My Life and Music* (New York: St. Martin's, 1963), 92.

89 Zweig, *The World of Yesterday*, 319–320. To be sure, Zweig was describing conditions as they appeared in 1919–1920—well before the period of hyperinflation—and in his native Austria, whose experience of inflation was "shabby child's play" compared to that of Germany. Still, his rather nostalgic recollection of this trip to the theater in the immediate postwar period is revealing.

90 Karl Christian Führer, "German Cultural Life and the Crisis of National Identity during the Depression, 1929–1933," *German Studies Review*, 24 (3) (2001): 461–486 (464).

91 Hans Joachim Moser, "Deutschlands Tonkunst in alter und neuer Kriegszeit," *Sonderabdruck aus den Preussischen Jahrbüchern*, 184 (1921): 353–373.

92 Sachs, "Some Aspects of Musical Politics," 74–95.

93 See, for example, the collection of essays in Moritz Füllmer and Rüdiger Graf, eds., *Die "Krise" der Weimarer Republik: Zur Kritik eines Deutungsmusters* (Frankfurt am Main: Campus, 2008).

94 Peter Fritzsche, "The Economy of Experience in Weimar Germany," in *Weimar Publics/Weimar Subjects: Rethinking the Political Culture of Germany in the 1920s*, ed. Kathleen Canning et al. (New York: Berghahn Books, 2010), 161–182.

95 Graf, "Either-Or," 599.

96 Wolfgang Schivelbusch, *The Culture of Defeat: On National Trauma, Mourning and Recovery* (New York: Picador, 2004), 230–232.

97 Karl Christian Führer, "High Brow and Low Brow Culture," in *Weimar Germany*, ed. Anthony McElligott (New York: Oxford University Press, 2009), 260–281.

98 Führer, "German Cultural Life."

2

Radios and Records: Image and Reality in Weimar Technology

"What withers in the age of the technological reproducibility of the work of art is the latter's aura ... *the technology of reproduction detaches the reproduced object from the sphere of tradition. By replicating the work many times over, it substitutes a mass existence for a unique existence.*"[1] These remarks, taken at face value, might at first be mistaken as those of a cultural conservative wary of modernity and its effects on traditional culture. Indeed, Hanz Heinz Stuckenschmit once observed that the primary opponents of radio during Weimar tended to emit from artists and critics of a "conservative mentality."[2] They are, in fact, the words of the neo-Marxist cultural theorist Walter Benjamin who penned them in Paris in 1936, by then already in exile following the Nazi rise to power in 1933. Yet Benjamin did not see the rise of the radio, film, and other modern media in a wholly negative light, for although the shattering of the work's "aura" destroyed any basis for genuine authenticity, it also served to "emancipate" the work from "its parasitic subservience to ritual" while expanding the possibility for broader social democratization. It provides a particularly useful jumping-off point for this chapter's discussion of the views of cultural conservatives toward radio and other modern media—ones that often reflected the same mixture of praise and hostility found in Benjamin's writings. In many ways, Benjamin's Marxist reading of radio echoed critiques articulated by some cultural conservatives a decade earlier, and historians and other scholars have sometimes struggled to reconcile the embrace of radio and other modern technologies by conservative forces with an otherwise traditionalist cultural and social agenda. As Jeffrey Herf has shown, far right political groups launched ferocious rhetorical attacks against modernity just as they adapted modern media and technology to suit their own purposes over the course of Weimar and into the Third Reich.[3] Herf and others have attempted to square the circle by labeling such figures "reactionary modernists," "modernizing traditionalists," or "modernist classicists" to take only three prominent examples.[4]

Historians have long recognized some of the profoundly anti-modern aspects of Nazism that found expression in a whole set of cultural and social ideals, ranging from attacks against "degenerate" art and artists to the valorization of traditional modes of familial and social organization.[5] Yet it would be wrong to see Nazism as opposed to modernity *tout court*. In a pioneering study, Detlev Peukert highlighted the state's modern encroachment into the affairs of society through the administration of welfare and public health policy as a necessary precondition for the massive efforts at social engineering under the Nazi dictatorship, a view that has greatly shaped subsequent work locating modernity as the linchpin that explains the sheer murderousness of the Holocaust.[6] In cultural matters, Nazi elites trafficked heavily in traditional and modernist art alike to win allies and curry favor, while Nazi authorities—from city planners and engineers to civil servants—worked tirelessly to create a "purified" Germany unmoored from its past and rushing headlong into a glorious new age according to the designs of its new masters.[7] Taken together, these insights have caused us to reconsider the extent to which the road to Nazism was paved with anti-modern anxieties and sentiments. The reception of German radio among Weimar's cultural conservatives offers still another case worthy of reconsideration given the persistent belief in that group's hostility toward modern technology. In the magisterial first volume of his trilogy of the Third Reich, for example, Richard Evans recalls that during Weimar "new means of communication added to the sense of old cultural values under threat."[8] Corey Ross, in an excellent survey of mass media in twentieth-century Germany, avows that while conservative attitudes toward commercial culture could hardly be described as an example of a "politics of cultural despair," "it is nonetheless fair to say that mass communications and commercial culture were generally viewed with skepticism … and regarded by many as a social and cultural 'problem' that required urgent solutions."[9]

While there is much to recommend this view, a close examination of music and radio between Weimar and the Third Reich suggests a need to revise our understanding of traditionalists' attitudes toward radio as well as the cultural affinities between Weimar conservatives and National Socialists within this crucial area. As one of the foremost scholars of Weimar has recently argued, in the case of radio "there was no clear divide between modernists and traditionalists" and from the outset many Germans of different political persuasions saw radio as a blank slate on which they could project their greatest hopes: a tool for greater political participation and democratization on the left and the spread of edifying cultural content on the right.[10] As the conservative critic Fritz Lauhöfer wrote in the conservative *Neue-Musik Zeitung*, "Is not the lack of criticism …

characteristic of a lack of sensitivity today and symptomatic of how much we today are consumed by the progress of technology?"[11] This chapter reexamines the conservative reception of recorded music (i.e., music transmitted via radio, phonograph, and gramophone) in an effort to highlight the wide range of attitudes that existed among Weimar's cultural conservatives. As we will see below, some welcomed the opportunity to extend the reach of high culture to new audiences through the medium, while others feared its negative impact on public concert life. Some lauded its potential to rejuvenate declining music-making activities (e.g., *Hausmusik*) as well as open up new compositional possibilities among composers writing with its particular strengths and weaknesses in mind, while for others radio could never hope to replicate the experience of live performance.[12] All too often, individual observers often remained torn on the issue of the radio's general suitability for the classical repertory. The conductor Wilhelm Fürtwangler offers a typical case in point:

> [Radio offers] the previously unimagined possibility presented by mechanical reproduction for the popularization of music. Alongside this, the boundaries clearly emerge once more. Extremes of pitch and levels of volume are reproduced very partially and often not at all; in the case of larger ensembles, particularly orchestras and choirs, a self-contained and uniform sound cannot be accomplished simply by setting up various recording devices. As a result of all this ... the correct impression of the whole, is distorted, twisted, indeed in most cases practically a forgery.[13]

In what follows, I argue that Weimar traditionalists considerably misjudged the impact of radio on German society during the 1920s and that the function of radio during Weimar—both in theory and practice—cohered far more closely to conservative demands than it would under National Socialism. Thus, the first section maps out positive and negative critiques of recorded music among Weimar critics before turning, in section two, to measure the ways in which these collective hopes and fears were (and just as often were not) realized in German society at large. The final section discusses the fate of radio under Nazism.

The advent of radio: Promise or tragedy?

If German cultural elites held Bach, Mozart, and Handel as the Old Testament prophets from the turn of the nineteenth century, the concert hall served as their house of worship. As Sanna Pederson has shown, the symphony concert was an important early space where nationalist and aesthetic priorities came together and played a crucial role in identity formation at the turn of the nineteenth century.[14] Upon its debut in 1923, radio seemed destined to disrupt this state of affairs and whatever critics thought of its long-term effects, there was broad consensus that recorded music would profoundly transform German classical music culture. Among cultural conservatives, certain critics were fearful of what this portended for the future of Germany's concert halls. Here the conservative and Marxist critique were one and the same—in addition to threatening the livelihoods of German musicians, recorded sound served at best as a cheap imitation of live performance. In a line of thinking that continues to this day, some critics invested live listening with a quasi-sacred, metaphysical meaning and looked on efforts to mediate performance through recording technologies as an affront to genuine aesthetic experience. The conservative critic Fritz Stege typified this view in his reporting on the musical situation in Silesia in 1926, lamenting that the region continued to suffer from "an epidemic of recorded discs [Schallplatten]" and yearned for a future when "all of this will be swept out with an iron broom."[15] The critic Reinhold Zimmermann predicted that Germans' increasing reliance on recorded music threatened musical instruments such as the piano with the prospect of extinction. An initial blow in the form of a Germans inflation that had rendered large instruments unaffordable was exacerbated by new technology, which turned formerly active, vigorous German lay performers into passive, lazy listeners. While conceding that "it is undoubtedly true that the Beethoven piano sonata played by a competent artist on record, for listeners desirous of a better reading, is botched in person by somebody or another," Zimmermann feared that the general decline in amateur music-making would have severe repercussions on the future of the piano and with it the keyboard literature itself. As more Germans relied on others to make music for them, Zimmermann wondered, "What will happen to the limitless treasures of our piano literature if the piano truly dies out?"[16]

Other critics pointed to the sensory limitations of sound technology. According to Wilhelm Heinitz, trained as an oboist and from 1915 a researcher at the *Phonetischen Laboratorium* at the University of Hamburg who would become a fervent Nazi supporter, the radio's greatest handicap lay in the didactic constraints it imposed on an audience of varied physical and cognitive predispositions. Heinitz viewed music-making as primarily a motor activity and the resultant sounds as merely the aural outcome of this fundamentally motor-based pastime, a view that would find full realization in his 1931 treatise *Strukturprobleme in Primitiver Musik* (Structural Problems in Primitive Music).[17] For Heinitz, radio disrupted the holistic nature of music-making—and just as importantly, musical listening—by separating performers from listeners. The overall effects on the latter group were certain to prove uneven; motorists (*Motoriker*) responding to the natural world through physical engagement and visual learners (*Optikern*) accustomed to forming impressions through visual stimuli were left in the lurch, leaving aural learners the sole beneficiaries of the new technology.[18] Operatic works drawing on the visual and textual in addition to the purely musical—a category that, Heinitz was quick to point out, included Wagner's esteemed *Gesamtkunstwerke* (total artworks)—would surely fall into obscurity since "the continued performance of such works could hardly [be expected] to produce much gratification. By this means, an entire genre of lapidary works for *artistic enjoyment* will have ceased to exist."[19] Such views found visual expression in *Simplicissimus* in a 1924 piece entitled "Tannhäuser on the Radio" (Image 8). The image depicts a singer standing before a microphone

Image 8 "Tannhäuser on the Radio," *Simplicissimus*, 1924. Source: *Simplicissimus, 29* (8) (1924). Image retrieved from http://www.simplicissimus.info/index.php?id=5.

singing Wagnerian arias with his hands casually thrust into his pockets. His fellow artists, who in stage productions would normally be found driving the drama along in their acting roles, are engaged in anything but the high-minded performing for which Wagner's works were intended. The soprano can be seen reclining on a divan, casually reading a newspaper next to a man resting his eyes in between numbers. In the background, a performer can be seen vulgarly picking his nose while a sinister-looking figure looks on. The cast, of course, need not concern themselves with stage costumes and props—everyday dress will do for a medium that places no demands on looking the part.

Recording technologies likewise met with a dubious reaction among some major artists suspicious of their artistic value. Indeed, whatever their personal political views, some critics viewed musicians as inherently conservative in cultural matters. According to Stuckenschmidt, there was "no more conservative mentality, none more disinclined to innovation, than the musician's" who saw in radio and other recorded music "a betrayal of sacrosanct traditions, vain decadence, and brazen iconoclasm."[20] Indeed, echoing some of their conservative peers, select performers lauded music's ephemerality before the age of recorded sound and evinced profound fascination with the ways in which recorded music threatened their agency in terms of establishing when, where, and how audiences might enjoy "their" music. According to pianist Artur Schnabel, recorded music was doubly damned, for it was hard to countenance making music "not knowing how [the audience] would be dressed, what else they would be doing at the same time, how much they would listen." Echoing conservative sentiments about aesthetic experience, Schnabel "also felt that recordings are against the very nature of performance, for the nature of performance is to happen but once, to be absolutely ephemeral and unrepeatable."[21] Schnabel's contemporary, the Chilean pianist Claudio Arrau who also performed throughout German concert halls at the time, drew a similar distinction between a performer's "live" and "recorded" self. He recalled the case of the virtuoso Edwin Fischer who, in Arrau's view, often appeared "possessed" when he performed live, but whose passion could "very seldom [be detected] on his records."[22] In the end, however, it did not always take long to bring artists around to the promise of recording; in Schnabel's case, in 1929 the music company HMV Group approached him with the Herculean task of recording the complete Beethoven piano sonatas, which he did from 1932–1935 at Abbey Road studio in London, the first pianist to have done so.[23]

Undoubtedly part of the reason behind this cool reception in certain circles was due to the technical complexity of early models, which made listening to and performing for the radio a bewildering experience for many users. While the mystery surrounding the gramophone's reproducibility could at least be seen and touched in the form of the record, the properties governing radio transmission appeared infinitely more mysterious and bizarre, a fact routinely satirized by contemporary magazines. Early designers made no effort to mask the complex mechanical apparatus behind the wood-grained paneling or other facades characteristic of later models with the result that early radio sets often resembled a tangled mess of cables and wires. Knobs were highly sensitive, prone to breakdown, and hard to manipulate, a source of ceaseless frustration for listeners whose desired program was often interrupted by transmissions from other frequencies. A 1930 letter from Schoenberg's daughter to the composer surrounding the latter's one-act opera *Von heute auf morgen* captures the trepidation and inevitable frustration that characterized many listeners' experiences with radio:

> I am so excited about the opera that I have to write to you right away. Unfortunately we were a bit nervous when tuning in and there was a lot we did not hear very well. But what we heard was marvelous! … In spite of the poor transmission one had the impression that it was a wonderful performance, especially toward the end. The duet was unfortunately almost inaudible; it seems to have been tuned into another frequency because of the other German station.[24]

Not only audiences but performers too commented on the fragile nature of the early efforts to broadcast chamber music and works for solo piano, as the pianist Walter Gieseking recalled in his memoirs: "It was in England, November 1924 that I played on the radio for the first time. In these early years of the radio the transmission was a delicate, complicated undertaking."

Naturally, not all cultural observers were ready to dismiss recorded music's potential. While it threatened to further diminish public attendance at concert and opera halls among listeners who could now enjoy performances at home, it granted access to new listenerships for whom the opera house and concert hall remained distant and foreign entities. This was certainly a welcome prospect for many modernist critics eager for new music's potential to tap into audiences. "Radio makes opera a reality for everyone," Frank Warschauer wrote, "[and] will undermine the artistocratic prerequisites of the opera and thereby pose the question of its fate." According to this view, radio heralded a reckoning for the opera world as more and more Germans assessed the artistic merits of works artificially propped up by a narrow circle of listeners too often motivated more by the social rather than artistic dimensions of opera attendance. To the horror of conservatives such as Heinitz, Warschauer fantasized in the pages of *Musikblätter des Anbruch* of Germans listening to opera "with beer and house slippers" in the comfort of their own living rooms.[25] Other conservatives held a more sanguine outlook. Writing in the conservative *Neue Musik-Zeitung*, the critic Rudolf Cahn-Speyer envisaged radio as a means for German musicians to reach new audiences and secure musical engagements and called for the abandonment of strict state control over radio and the embrace of a freer, more open system along the lines of the American model.[26]

Indeed, criticism of the radio and its suitability as a medium of transmission for classical music does not admit to a simple bifurcation between hostile cultural conservatives on the one hand and progressive musical modernists on the other as the cases of Max Butting and Alfred Heuss reveal. Following the completion of his studies at the Akademie der Tonkunst in Munich in 1914, Butting was deemed unfit for military service on health grounds and entered his father's ironworking business until 1923, whereupon he linked up with several fellow artists to form what came to be known as the November Group, a radical group whose socialist views informed their attitudes toward social and cultural policy. There he worked side by side with fellow modernist and socialist-minded composers Hanns Eisler and Kurt Weill before setting off to further his career as the main music journalist for the *Sozialistischen Monatsheften* (Socialist Monthly Magazine). Though among the later defenders of the radio, in some cases going so far as to compose works with the new technology and its possibilities exclusively in mind, Butting was less than enthusiastic with state control of radio and its function among the musical public. Unlike the traditional concertgoing public, "most [radio] listeners are at the mercy of the broadcast station. It is not what the listener wants that is heard, but rather is up to the transmitter—in any case, what the listener wishes to hear, we do not know."[27] This was all the more remarkable given that five years had transpired since the appearance of the first radios into German homes—more than enough time to adjust to the new circumstances introduced by the technology, in Butting's view. And yet composers' compositional efforts did not reflect this fact. Most continued to compose for the modern concert hall, failing to recognize that "the acoustics of the study in relation to the best music heard over the radio [*Lautsprechermusik*] is different than the hall is for the orchestra."[28] *Rundfunksmusik*, according to Butting, was emerging as a new kind of musical genre unto itself, the conventions for which were to be considered as carefully as those to be found in long-established idioms like the symphony, the oratorio, and the opera. It could not be left to mere technicians to work out the kinks in the new technology, for the radio posed challenges that could only be overcome by the composer. Performance practices, which worked for the concert hall, were likely to fall flat when transmitted over the airwaves—a fact that especially revealed itself in the works of composers such as Wagner and Brahms. According to Butting, in the case of Wagner's *Der Ring der Nibelungen*, "the many horns and tubas blur and confuse the tone [whilst] the doubled thirds of the woodwinds in Brahms' symphonies lose most of their characteristic color value when they are broadcast, because of the dissolution of timbre."[29] All of this went to show that "no matter how careful and technically correct a broadcast may be, the tones issuing from the loudspeaker are different from the original."[30]

For his part, the conservative editor Alfred Heuss emerged as an unapologetic defender of radio during the 1920s. Although he viewed the emergence of new approaches to composition in the interwar period with deep skepticism if not outright hostility, the general situation of music during Weimar compared rather favorably, in his view, with that which obtained under the *Kaiserreich*. "After all," he declared, "were not the 500 soloist concerts in Berlin before the war also attended by a mere 5000 paying listeners? ... That concert life—where it is healthy and viscerally (*innerlich*) constituted—suffers through the coming of the radio is an unfounded presumption."[31] For Heuss, the advent of radio into German homes did not signal cultural decline or calls for a return to some imagined prewar Belle Epoque and took fellow traditionalists to task for suggesting a connection between modern technology and Weimar decadence. Far from presaging German cultural decline, the radio held great promise as an instrument of cultural recovery and rebirth. Wedded to the "universal" appeal of the German classics, the theoretically universal reach of the radio could, in Heuss's view, bring German culture to countless millions hitherto excluded from it:

> Through this medium, millions of people, for whom the names of the masters of the classics have until now scarcely existed, can, for the first time, become acquainted with serious music. And what, among other things, it will mean to bring things of cultural worth to the most distant cottages and villages, let us not even ponder. But today one thing already seems clear to me: if there is a medium through which to somewhat close the gap which has opened up between "educated" and "uneducated" since the late Middle Ages and with which to again make the concept of the "Volk" a living entity, it is the radio.[32]

If Heuss's invocation of the *Volk* calls to mind right-wing nationalist ideology and its vision of an organic, cohesive nation epitomized in the Nazi conception of the *Volksgemeinschaft* (people's community), it is worth remembering the extent to which appeals to a German *Volk* resonated across all segments of German society after the First World War. While the Nazi idea of the Volk was distinctively defined as much by who did not belong—above all, Jews—as who did, Germans across the political spectrum found much to admire in the idea of a collective *Volk*. Political leaders, from socialists to liberal democrats, incorporated the notion into their party platforms and made regular appeals to a German *Volksgemeinschaft* in public speeches over the course of Weimar.[33] Indeed, for some Germans otherwise turned off by what they saw as the Nazis' vulgar anti-Semitism and inclination to violence, the Nazi *Volksgemeinschaft* was one of the few messages that held any real appeal.[34] This appeal was not limited to politics. Within artistic circles, the 1920s likewise saw modernist reformers seize upon on a new aesthetics that wedded art to new conceptions of the collective, which broke with older conservative emphases on the individual cultivation of *Bildung* and *Geist*.[35]

Heuss would seem to be the quintessential "reactionary modernist" of the kind Jeffrey Herf has described, namely one who "incorporated modern technology into the cultural system of modern German nationalism, without diminishing the latter's romantic and antirational aspects."[36] He was joined by others who saw in radio a solution to other perceived ills plaguing German concert halls. As we saw in Chapter 1, by the second half of the nineteenth century the new audience had introduced new distractions for musical purists, which radio seemed ideally suited to combat. One much–remarked-upon virtue of radio lay in its ability to provide access to classical music outside of the distracting confines of the public concert hall, for which no greater symbol existed than the virtuoso. Celebrated and at the same time endlessly satirized since the early nineteenth century by satirists such as Wilhelm Busch (see image 9 below), the virtuoso occupied a prominent place within both an expanding repertory and the wider public's imagination, a prominence that the First World War had done nothing to curtail. From the time of its great early exponents Paganini and Liszt, whose uncanny dexterity allowed for the composition and performance of works of increasing complexity and difficulty hitherto deemed unplayable, virtuosos had attracted large numbers of admiring followers to concert halls throughout Europe. Characterized in broad terms, which ranged from "heroic" and "conquering" to "demonic" and "otherworldly," the virtuoso also attracted equal numbers of detractors who looked upon their performances as little more than vain exercises in showmanship. According to some critics, virtuoso performers too often evinced more concern with sensationalist fireworks than the serious business of musical cultivation.[37] Commenting on the musical scene in fin de siècle Vienna, the great nineteenth-century critic Eduard Hanslick never tired of reminding his audience that it was impossible for a Liszt work to be anything other than acclaimed irrespective of the actual musical merits of the work in question, given the composer's unsurpassed flair and charismatic stage presence.[38]

Image and Reality in Weimar Technology 65

14. Finale furioso

Image 9 "Finale Furioso," Wilhelm Busch, 1860s. Source: Wilhelm Busch, "Finale Furioso," Wikimedia Commons. Image retrieved from https://commons.wikimedia.org/wiki/File:Busch_Werke_v1_p_404.jpg.

This was not the first time that recorded music had been identified as a viable substitute for live performance. Next to radio, the gramophone made wide inroads into German homes only in the interwar period despite having been invented in the late nineteenth century. The technology overcame the ephemeral and abstract nature of music by raising the prospect for musical performances to be recorded for posterity. With the introduction of the lateral cut record in 1889, the didactic potential for Germany's aspiring soloists and conductors did not go unnoticed as they now had opportunities to compare different renditions of a work to arrive at its deeper meaning. Despite his misgivings about German radio outlined earlier in this chapter, the Hamburg critic Wilhelm Heinitz invested one of the first major gramophone companies, the *Deutsche Grammaphon-Aktiengesellschaft*, with a potential for "limitless enrichment ... young, budding *Kapellmeistern* hidden behind in the background of the concert stage or opera gallery will now find rich material to work with that stands ready to be utilized with unlimited use."[39] Even among nonperformers records stood ready to have an important function beyond their intended use, for they "could play a great role among broad circles of the musically cultivated as an illustration of [the development] of music history."[40]

The heuristic appeal of the gramophone likewise resonated strongly with Fritz Sporn, city music director and music instructor of the *Realschule* of the town of Zeulenroda since 1920. A committed pedagogue, Sporn saw the gramophone as a technology, which held great promise for its ability to overcome the special challenges presented by formal music instruction—ones not present, for example, among those seeking to cultivate in German youth an appreciation of poetry and drama. Unlike these sister arts, which merely required the sound of the human voice to spring to life from the printed page, "when one lays a Beethoven symphony, a Bach cantata or fugue before the students—all remains dead and stays that way until it can be rendered as music. And the students cannot do it ... here only one instrument can help—the modern gramophone."[41] Given the inaccessibility of the concert hall among youth—which, apart from its prohibitive cost, remained a hallowed space upon which the uninitiated dare not tread—the heuristic possibilities of the invention seemed virtually limitless. Until now, after all, youth engagement with the classics was limited to the repertory for keyboard; symphonies, concerti, opera, and chamber music remained either closed off entirely or in the much-diminished form of arrangements and reductions for piano.[42] The unsuitability of the concert hall as the ideal transmitter of the classics did not end there—had youthful concertgoers possessed the requisite degree of cultivation, concert halls continued only to perform a small and increasingly standardized selection of works at the expense of the much larger corpus of works which made up the Western tradition. A fervent Baroque enthusiast, Sporn viewed the gramophone as injecting new life both into neglected composers such as Buxtehude and Schütz as well as the sparsely performed works of established masters, the cantatas, and chamber works of J. S. Bach foremost among them.[43]

Other devices such as the phonograph made similarly bold promises to transform society for the better. In 1905, an entry in the *Phonographische Zeitschrift* proclaimed that "thanks to this invention and its undreamt-of improvement in quality and reduction in price ... the phonograph in its modern perfection can nowadays become 'universal' music for the home ... easily accessible to everyone, even to the less well off."[44] After the war, music found itself competing for Germans' time as other leisure institutions made wide inroads into German society. Modern sports such as tennis, boxing, and track and field, for example, had convinced many Germans to reconsider their previous attitudes toward physical fitness, a fact that Ludwig Koch both grudgingly admired and fiercely resented.[45] Director of a record company called the Lindström-Konzern since 1929, Koch made great efforts to position his company's product as an indispensable tool among music pedagogues, educators, and others within the *Schulreform* movement.[46] In 1927, he had attracted the ire of nationalist critics like Alfred Heuss for his part in organizing and curating the international Frankfurt exhibition *Musik im Leben der Völker* (Music in the Life of the People) with the German Chancellor Gustav Stresemann's full support, the first of its kind to appear in Germany since the end of the First World War.[47] Koch proved just as adept, however, at ingratiating himself with both cultural conservatives and German nationalists, who, in 1930, went to great lengths to proclaim the record as the potential savior of serious art music, under assault since the end of the war by jazz and *Schlagermusik* (pop music).[48] In 1934 in his role as director of the Lindström *Kulturabteilung*, he presented President Paul von Hindenburg with a pair of *Tonbücher*, who accepted them on behalf of the military, which contained the following prefatory dedication: "Our army and navy carry in themselves the spirit of the past and work to further cultivate it for the future. On this basis, these 'Songbooks of the German Military' are a gift of the German *Volk*."[49]

An astute businessman, Koch was thus eager to market the technology to as wide an audience as possible and made regular appeals within contemporary music journals. "Nobody would deny," he claimed in a 1931 article for *Die Musik*,

> that sport and recreation promote community health. But sport and recreation in the lives of children as well as adults should never so have the upper hand that no time remains leftover for spiritual life. The leather ball brings thousands upon thousands into ecstasy while the performance of a string quartet or accredited ensemble of the highest order manages to reach scarcely 300 to 400 people.[50]

The stakes could not be higher for, as Koch wryly reminded, what culture-minded Germans did to redress the imbalance would ultimately answer the question as to whether Germany "would remain in the eyes of the world the land of Schmeling's fist [*Faust Schmelings*] or revert back to that of Goethe's Faust [*Faust Goethes*]."[51] Given this situation in which musical culture threatened to be crowded out by other social enticements competing for the German public's attention, critics invested more faith than ever in technology's potential to reach new audiences hitherto excluded from the realm of high culture. Some observers went further still and, with an eye toward Weimar's hopelessly fractured politics, viewed radio as an instrument ideally suited for fostering not only greater cultural but also political democratization and social cohesion within German society. In his opening address to the seventh annual German radio exhibition in 1930, for example, the physicist Albert Einstein proclaimed the radio as a harbinger of "true democracy" though by this late date the Republic was arguably living on borrowed time.[52]

Radio proponents eager to deliver on promises of greater "social leveling" and "cultural standardization" were similarly disappointed.[53] For whatever its effects in the political sphere, radio was far from democratic in Weimar Germany, whether measured by who had access to the technology or what they heard over the airwaves. As Karl Christian Führer has pointed out, radio programming proved remarkably unresponsive to popular taste as radio stations—owned and administered by the state—programmed what they deemed high minded and worthy at peak listening hours and restricted *Gebrauchsmusik* (popular music) to less desirable slots even in the face of a declining listenership and public calls for programming reforms.[54] Contemporary satiricals mocked both the state's heavy-handed control of radio and pointed out that the mere ability to transmit content across social and cultural divides said nothing about success in finding intelligible and receptive audiences on either side. Image 10 depicts an indigenous woman with a gramophone at her feet next to an ape listening to a loudspeaker with the simple caption "though we can't understand, at least we can hear each other." Image 11 poked fun at the mysterious nature of radio transmission as radio waves move across the page while a stylized Prussian official warns, "Careful. Radio waves!"[55]

Image 10 "Two Corners of the World," *Simplicissimus*, 1924. Source: *Simplicissimus*, 29 (8) (1924). Image retrieved from http://www.simplicissimus.info/index.php?id=5.

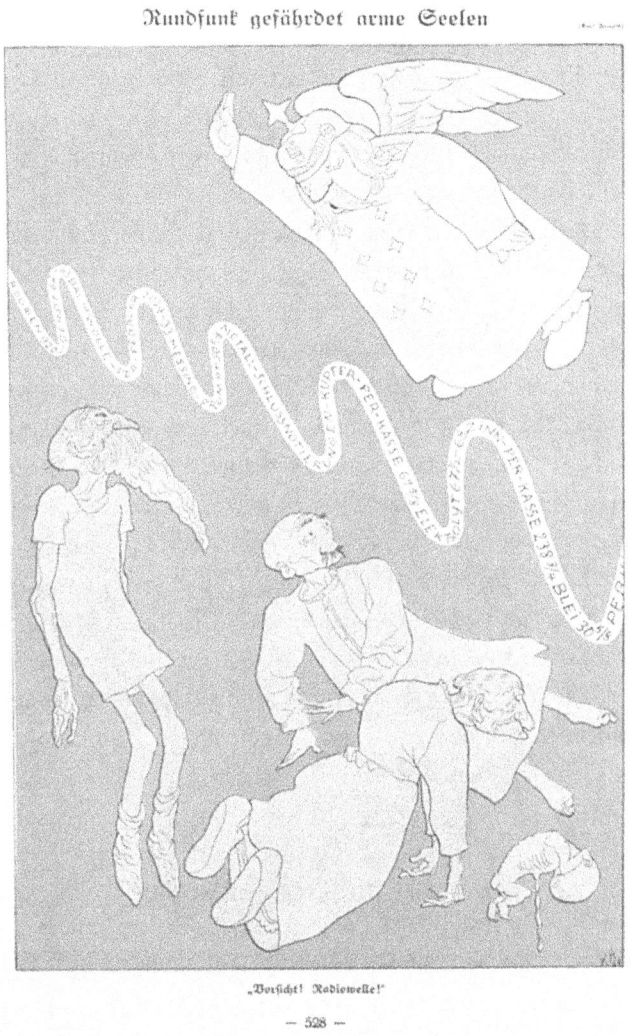

Image 11 "Radio Endangers Poor Souls," *Simplicissimus*, 1924. Source: *Simplicissimus, 28* (43) (1924). Image Retrieved from http://www.simplicissimus.info/index.php?id=5.

Contemporaries, too, noted the false premises upon which an association between cultural and political democratization rested. It was true, according to Fritz Lauhöfer writing for the *Neue Musik Zeitung*, that whereas other countries had tended to seize on radio for less high-minded purposes, Germans could harness high culture for the benefit of the entire *Volk*: "In contrast to other countries—especially America where this invention has been made less to serve community-minded purposes than advertisement-minded ones—[in Germany] doubtlessly one finds among us earnest efforts to employ the radio in the service of the people's cultural needs."[56] According to the reviewer, music had traditionally served to underline class difference, for "up to this point, one has seen music as a privileged site of certain classes whose property and social class made possible the numerous trips to the concert hall and theatre." As this older function threatened to be dislodged, some in Germany had "gone so far as to designate the widening of the radio as the necessary precondition for the 'democratization of music,'" though Lauhöfer left little doubt where he stood on the matter. "The transferability of a concept borrowed from the political sphere to denote the collective tendency of the new invention is dubious. Democratization of music!"[57] Why, he asked, should critics of his ilk necessarily greet the advent of the radio as such a positive development? For Lauhöfer, radio separated what belonged together, namely, "the spatial and the corporeal," both for the individual listener as well as society at large. In other words, radio witnessed the aesthetic being sacrificed in the name of increased accessibility. "Is this alone not proof," he asked, "that the radio—in spite of its much talked about universalizing main features—has a strong individualizing streak [*einen stark individualistischen Einschlag*], a tendency towards isolation, separation and confinement?"[58] According to this critique, far from leading to greater democratization and cultural engagement, radio threatened Germany with further social fragmentation and atomization.

The radio and German society

As the above discussion has illustrated, conservative opinion on the virtues and vices of the radio and other modern media varied greatly. But to what extent were such attitudes grounded in a historical reality and where can we look for answers to those questions that loomed largest in the minds of contemporary critics: did the radio, in fact, foster greater musical democratization during the Weimar Republic? To what extent did the technology spread classical music to audiences historically beyond its remit in the age before radio technology? Can radio and the gramophone, as some critics feared, be said to have led to a decrease in live performance in general and that performed within the home (*Hausmusik*) in particular? What of the claim that radio invariably led toward the atomization and cultural isolation of German society? This section seeks to offer tentative answers to these and other questions. The widespread view—one that lingers still today—of modern media as culturally democratizing mediums has rested in large measure on the perception that music was now accessible to audiences hitherto excluded from the concert hall due to expense and their status as social outsiders. Radio ownership statistics over the course of Weimar certainly attest to an explosion in accessibility to new kinds of musical programming: in 1923, the year broadcasting was first introduced in Germany, there were a total of 1,580 registered sets. Only six years later, in 1929, there were 3,066,682.[59] Yet, if we look more closely at both the distribution (geographically and socially) of those sets as well as the content of concert programming, these technologies' democratizing impulses appear in a different light.[60] As Corey Ross has shown, the vast majority of gramophone owners, especially before the First World War when the technology was considerably more expensive than in the 1920s, were in the middle classes and thus remained prohibitively expensive for many lower-class groupings. In 1929, for example, a simple tabletop model was priced at 50 *Reichsmarks*, which placed it beyond the reach of the typical working-class family whose average weekly income ran to only 39 RM.[61]

As we saw above, many critics praised the radio for its ability to bring German *Kultur* to the uncultivated and uninitiated, particularly those living outside the major cities. Nevertheless, such high hopes do not appear to have been borne out for much of the 1920s. For the Berlin-Funk Stunde, the primary transmission station for Berlin and surrounding areas, 531,000 (83.5 percent) radio subscribers lived in the capital and Stettin whose overall population ran to some 4.3 million. The rest of the territory, by contrast, contained only 105,000 subscribing households, or 16.5 percent of the subscription total, despite having roughly 600,000 more inhabitants (4.9 million).[62] The democratization of radio is further called into question when measured in still a different way, namely by looking at the extent to which the state-directed radio transmissions responded to audience demands and preferences. Despite being formally open to private investors, radio was from its inception under state control with representatives of the *Reichspostministerium* (Reich Postal Ministry) serving as the body responsible for operational and programming duties.[63] As Karl Christian Führer has shown, radio companies—themselves staffed and directed by members of the *Bildungsbürgertum*—held great promise in the radio's ability to foster deeper audience engagement with high culture. In order to achieve this, concert broadcasts were not only frequently accompanied by academic lectures designed to give listeners' greater historical and aesthetic insight into the works being performed, but also given priority in the arrangement of programming, often securing the peak listening periods of the day, especially the 8:00 to 10:00 p.m.

slot.⁶⁴ It was no mere coincidence that for several months during 1925–1926, the *Sender* for the Stuttgart area aired the series "Mozart: His Life and Work" between the hours 8:00 and 11:00 p.m.⁶⁵ The death centennials of eminent German composers, three of which fell in the later years of the Weimar Republic, also drew special programs devoted to the lives and works of established masters. The years 1927 and 1928—which marked the *Jahrfeier* of Beethoven and Schubert, respectively—were especially noteworthy occasions in this respect.⁶⁶ However, such efforts to steep the masses in German high culture increasingly, and quite literally, fell on deaf ears. According to a 1933–1934 survey, only 7.9 percent of unskilled workers and 10.5 percent of skilled workers evinced any interest whatsoever in classical concerts.⁶⁷ Sharp divisions emerged between rural conservatives and their urban counterparts, the former of whom remained wary of urban culture—hotbeds of degeneracy, *Schund* and *Schmutz* (trash and smut) as they saw it—and resisted educated elites' efforts to export urban *Bildung* and *Kultur* through radio to an idyllically conceived, purified countryside.⁶⁸ In the end, given a choice between the three domains for which radio was intended—"entertainment," "information," and "education"—radio planners under Weimar, free from having to rely on advertising income and the attendant pressures which all too often accompanied it, clearly singled out "education" as the function most deserving of their attention whether audiences liked it or not.

What of the claim that radio contributed to a complacent, passive audience increasingly disinterested in amateur performance, whether in the home or as part of the country's robust free associations? Such a view, which might at first glance make intuitive sense, is not borne out when we look more closely for supporting evidence. Participation in choral singing societies offers an instructive case in point. Since the early nineteenth century, choral societies had loomed large as a pillar of German associational life and had grown considerably over the course of the nineteenth and early twentieth centuries. The largest such group, the *Deutscher Sängerbund* (DSB), boasted 186,434 members in 1912.⁶⁹ By 1931, by which point radio had firmly established itself in cultural life, membership in the DSB exploded to 938,043 members.⁷⁰ Workers' organizations took an even more active role in fostering amateur participation in choral singing activities over the same period. Membership in the flagship workers' singing organization, the German Workers' Singers' League (*Deutscher Arbeiter-Sängerbund*), nearly doubled across the pre- and post-radio era, from 230,000 members in 1920 to 440,000 in 1928. When other singing groups, such as church-affiliated organizations, are taken into account, by 1931 the total number of German citizens participating in amateur singing approached some 2 million members.⁷¹ It is rather harder to measure the degree to which music-making in the home declined (or not) in the post-radio age, though the number of periodicals devoted to *Hausmusik*—two dozen of which were established between 1918 and 1932—suggests that this institution continued to prosper.⁷² Whether radio had something to do with the "reawakening of Hausmusik," as one critic thought, is difficult to assess, but the evidence here militates against the idea that Germans in the age of radio were ever content to allow others to make their music for them.⁷³ Indeed, a group of young, nationalist musicians calling themselves the Finkensteiner Bund imagined *Hausmusik* as an organic German cultural practice that Weimar's loathed asphalt culture had displaced. Although it remains perilous to infer reactionary political motives among its practitioners, there can be no question that Weimar technology, far from stamping out the theory and practice of amateur music-making, revitalized dormant public debates about *Hausmusik* and its perceived role in German cultural life.⁷⁴

Did the radio atomize German society and erode public interest in and support of public performance as many critics feared? Fritz Läuhofer spoke for many when he wrote in 1927 that radio "has a strong individualizing streak, a tendency towards *isolation, separation* and *confinement*."⁷⁵ In reality, radio was often very much a group activity in which families and friends engaged collectively. Early models of the radio, in addition to imposing considerable financial costs on purchasers, were rather cumbersome for early users both in terms of appearance and practical use. The earliest models, which cost between 250 and 300 *Reichsmarks* (the average monthly salary of a skilled worker or office clerk), meant that the decision to acquire a radio was not to be taken lightly but rather one which demanded a careful consideration of the family budget. Family friends, whose budget precluded the purchase of a radio or who lived outside the urban areas, which comprised the bulk of the 1920s radio listenership, often welcomed the chance to try out their friends' newly acquired technology.⁷⁶ Critics' scuffles over the collectivizing tendencies of radio listening were often merely a matter for academic debate, for ordinary Germans really had little say in the matter whether they welcomed such group listening or not. The home itself afforded little protection from the constant intrusion of radio traffic, prompting one critic to go so far as to predict "the end of the private sphere." In M. M. Gehrke's unflattering depiction, a typical Weimar *Altbau* was one in which

> the neighbor down the hall has a radio, and the one across the hall, the one below, above, and next door. All of them have speakers, all of them open their windows well into the autumn, and if they are closed in the winter, the speakers,

so very good at reproductions, penetrate the walls of old and new buildings alike into the home that was once my castle. I am steadfastly a pirate listener, although it was not in the least my intention to become one.[77]

While early models required listeners to individually wear headsets, later models greatly improved on this, successfully transforming the radio from a foreign, unwieldy technical apparatus to just another piece of furniture within the middle-class home.

What of the claim that radio invariably led to decrease in public performance? Modernist critics such as Stuckenschmidt certainly thought so and welcomed the prospect given the continued inaccessibility of concert halls and technical promise of recorded sound.[78] Yet despite these predictions, public performance in the interwar period showed little sign of declining, much less disappearing, following the advent of radio. First, in the case of the gramophone, recording technology was severely limiting with respect to classical music. During the interwar period (and well into the 1950s) companies continued to rely on the 78 rpm disc, which allowed for only three to four minutes of uninterrupted music. Needless to say, such limitations and the ceaseless rotation of discs that they necessarily required did not lend itself to Beethoven symphonies, Wagnerian operas, or other large-scale musical works ill-served by such constant interruption.[79] In nonclassical genres, the radio paradoxically seems to have spurred the growth of live performance, for while it did much to fuel demand for certain hit tunes, early technology was ill-equipped to fully placate listening audiences, who looked to dance halls and live clubs instead to satisfy their musical appetites.[80] The 1933 occupational census, according to which nearly 100,000 Germans continued to earn their primary income as performing artists and musicians—more than practicing doctors and lawyers put together—paints a similar picture of Germany as one that can hardly be characterized by a declining interest in live musical performance.[81] In terms of orchestral ensembles, the radio again appears not to have done much to diminish Germany's clout, which continued to be the envy of the world in terms of the number of symphony orchestras, opera houses, and other performing entities on offer. One historian has even spoken of a "glut" in certain cities such as Mainz and Wiesbaden, whose 250,000 inhabitants could choose between two independent opera companies and three symphony orchestras.[82] For its part, Berlin, admittedly an exceptional case, boasted no less than four opera houses and three symphony orchestras, including perhaps the world's leading orchestral ensemble, the Berliner Philharmoniker.[83]

Questions of continuity and rupture between Weimar and the Third Reich have occupied historians' attention since the advent of the Nazi regime itself, and while real areas of continuity continue to be uncovered, it is hard to imagine an area of German cultural life in which rupture emerges more clearly and forcefully than in the case of radio between these two periods in German history. As we will see below, if Weimar cultural conservatives harbored illusions that the Nazis' cultural conservatism dovetailed nicely with their own artistic views, they would be sorely mistaken as would become clear from the regime's first months in power.

Radio, music, and Nazism

In December 1925 a young Joseph Goebbels, having just returned home from a performance of the play *Peer Gynt*, finally got around to penning his observations on a device that had made its first German broadcast just over two years before.[84] Whether he was prompted to do so by the appearance of the new technology in his own home remains unclear, yet his remarks might initially come as a surprise: "Radio! Radio! Radio in the house! With radio, the German forgets about work and fatherland! Radio! The modern medium of the petty bourgeois [*Verspießungsmittel*]! Everyone get to the house! The ideal of the petty bourgeois!"[85] Such biting criticism comes in stark contrast to Goebbels's later attitudes toward the medium as Reich Minister for Propaganda. By 1933, Goebbels was proclaiming the radio the "eighth wonder of the world" and that "[it] will be for the twentieth century what the press was for the nineteenth century."[86] The seismic shift in Goebbels's attitude toward radio becomes understandable when examining the intervening seven years and the changes they had witnessed within Germany's sonic landscape.

First, such attitudes on Goebbels's part become less surprising when we remember the relationship between radio and the nascent National Socialist German Workers' Party in the 1920s. If state control of radio during Weimar had rendered the radio rather inflexible and unresponsive to public taste, such a policy was not entirely without benefit, for throughout the course of the Weimar Republic, the Nazis and other extremist organizations were banned from using it.[87] What was a blessing in the 1920s, however, quickly became a curse by 1933, for the same concentration of control made the *Gleichschaltung* of radio a rather more straightforward process compared to other areas of social and political life. Second, by 1933 the radio was no mere bourgeois novelty. In the eight years separating Goebbels's December 1925 dismissal of the radio as a "petty bourgeois" instrument and the eve of the Nationalist Socialist seizure of power, radio ownership more than tripled from 1,376,564 to 4,307,722.[88] Still, this left fully three-quarters of German households without a radio, a gap Goebbels sought to overcome by way of the vaunted *Volksempfänger* (People's Receiver). Such a device was not a Nazi invention—popular interest in a commercially cheap radio set dated from the mid-1920s—but there is reason to believe that Gobbels's efforts to bring the Führer's voice into people's homes met with some success. By 1941, only 35 percent of German homes lacked a radio.[89] The substantial Nazi effort in this vein was not unique, however; as Wolfgang König has pointed out, Germany's own considerable jump in radio ownership over the course of 1934–1942 (a 174 percent increase) was, in some cases, nearly matched (Sweden, 138 percent; Belgium 137 percent) and in others outpaced (Norway, 231 percent; France, 286 percent) by several neighbors over the same period.[90]

The climate changed almost overnight. By January 30, 1933, mere hours after Hindenburg had appointed Hitler Reich Chancellor, Goebbels issued the first Nazi broadcasts—a series of speeches and celebratory proclamations dedicated to the "new Germany" over the entire country with the exception of Bavaria, which managed to hold out a short while longer.[91] A flurry of activity followed only three days later as Goebbels sought to assume control over personnel and programming decisions from the Interior Ministry while managing to wrest certain responsibilities from the radio's previous masters at the Postal Ministry. Within a matter of weeks, up to 40 percent of the Weimar radio workforce had been purged both voluntarily and under the threat of force on racial or political grounds. Clearly, the cultural dispositions of existing managers counted for very little, as the case of Ludwig Neubeck, manager of the *Mitteldeutscher Rundfunk* based in Leipzig, illustrates. Intendant since 1929, Neubeck championed the radio as a didactic tool and saw the new regime as being a potential boon to the regeneration of the German classics and *Hausmusik*. In June 1933, he did not see the new regime's goals as at all incompatible with this ongoing renewal, not least as he believed the Nazi view of radio as:

> the most important instrument for the cultivation of *Bildung* and the people's education ... the German government has taken [the radio] in hand with this knowledge and one should fully expect that it will employ it in the closest cooperation with all other institutions of artistic cultivation to work for systematic, spirited cultural improvement in the interest of the entire *Volk's* education.[92]

In the end, such praise made no difference. Though it was published in the September issue of the *Zeitschrift für Musik*, Neubeck had penned the essay three months prior, in June. Later that summer he was incarcerated in a Leipzig prison where he ultimately perished under shadowy circumstances in August 1933. By the end of that same month, of the ten radio managers responsible for broadcasting over their respective *Länder*, only one remained from the Weimar years.[93]

In the space of a few months, Goebbels managed to swiftly and decisively bring the radio firmly under Nazi control—but to what end? More importantly, for our purposes, what place would music occupy on National Socialist radio? On the one hand, it would appear that if cultural conservatives were wary of what, exactly, the Nazis would ultimately broadcast, there was broad agreement among most on the Nazis' clear thinking on what they *would not*. Many found themselves in agreement with the official party position on forbidden music, which demanded "nothing atonal, nothing of foreign influence, no swing, no Latin-American dance music, no nigger Hottentot rhythms."[94] Likewise, later on there were reasons for cultural conservatives to find comfort as regards the kind of music that the regime supported. According to a October 1934 speech by Eugen Hadamovsky, newly installed by Goebbels in the summer of 1933 as *Reichssendeleiter* (Reich Broadcasting Chief) in which capacity he liaised between the Propaganda Ministry and the individual *Sendern*, National Socialist radio would promote "the most popular and beloved works of our great masters among the *Volk*. By that I mean Richard Strauss, Mozart, Liszt, Haydn, Pfitzner, Beethoven, Brahms, Hugo Wolf, Vollerthun, Händel, Schumann, Bach."[95]

In practice, however, as we will see below, cultural conservatives would not be entirely pleased with the fate of German classical music under National Socialism for two overarching reasons. First, Nazi conceptions of the radio as a political tool meant to serve political ends ran counter to many cultural conservatives' attitudes, who looked on radio as an instrument to serve culture rather than politics. As Carolyn Birdsall has shown, for much of the 1930s Nazi cultural authorities used radio to mobilize the *Volk* and found imaginative ways to encourage ordinary Germans to participate in the celebration of the nation through festival broadcasts and public commemorations.[96] Such efforts had the effect over time of normalizing the regime and inscribing Nazi ideology into the minds of radio listeners in ways many were not even aware, as the Jewish diarist Victor Klemperer was later to observe. Writing in 1938 on a trip Leipzig during which he and his wife stopped in a truck stop, Klemperer recalled,

> The Party Rally was coming over the loudspeaker. Announcement, the arrival of Field Marshal Goering. Introductory march, roars of triumph, then Goering's speech, about the tremendous rise, affluence, peace and workers' good fortune in

Germany, about the absurd lies and hopes of its enemies, constantly interrupted by well-drilled roars of applause. But the most interesting thing about it all was the behavior of the customers, who all came and went, greeting and taking their leave with "Heil Hitler." But no one was listening ... Truly: not one of a dozen people paid attention to the radio for even a single second, it could just as well have been transmitting silence or a foxtrot from Leipzig.[97]

Second, the Nazis proved far more permissive toward "degenerate" and "bolshevist" music than their rhetoric would have us believe, much to the dismay of cultural traditionalists. From the outset it was clear that the radio first and foremost was to be made to serve the regime, not the other way around. As the manager of the Cologne *Reichsender* declared in 1934, "The main task of the German radio is to hold the German people close at attention for those times when the *Führer* wishes to go before the *Volk* and speak to it."[98] Clear proof of this can be seen in the immediate establishment across all radio jurisdictions of the so-called Hour of the Nation in the 7:00–8:00 p.m. time slot previously devoted to the broadcast of classical music.[99] While the prospect of unremitting political broadcasts rankled many listeners and caused Goebbels to gradually shift airtime away from political content and toward lighter music preferred by German listeners over the course of the 1930s and into wartime, the theoretical Nazi promise of a radio purged of degenerate music and musicians left some room for optimism.[100] In practice, things were rather different, as the case of jazz illustrates. Apart from the inability of Nazi authorities to completely banish jazz due to ingenious methods of deception and smuggling within the record industry as well as bureaucratic oversight on the part of inept customs officials, in the early years of the regime such hoodwinking on the part of jazz enthusiasts was not even necessary in the first place. Despite having banned jazz in March 1933, prior to the reorganization of radio under Nazi auspices Goebbels demonstrated a considerable degree of laxity toward the genre for fear of ostracizing certain segments of the German population, which might turn to foreign (enemy) broadcasts in order to satisfy their cultural appetites. As a result, at Goebbels's urging the so-called Golden Seven jazz orchestra was formed, headed by the committed National Socialist Willi Stech and began broadcasting approved jazz across Germany in December 1934. The experiment proved to be short-lived, however, as a backlash among certain die-hard opponents compelled the regime to cease jazz broadcasts altogether by summer 1935.[101] However, even if the regime did not itself wish to provide a safety valve for jazz music in the form of its own ensemble, the task of ridding the airwaves of "degenerate music" remained no easy task. Contractual complications, for example, emerged in the form of radio broadcasts of film music and the producers and investors with partial stakes and ownership rights in them.[102]

If policing radio was a rather straightforward matter for cultural authorities (when, as we saw above, they were not sacrificing ideological purity for a more pragmatic approach), the record industry presented altogether different challenges. For one thing, record contracts established before 1933 could not simply be done away with. Even if they could, the backlash against the classical branch of the German record industry, which continued to flood international markets with recordings of Beethoven, Mozart, and Schumann by German ensembles—including the Berlin Philharmonic under the direction of Hitler's favorite conductor, Wilhelm Furtwängler—would undoubtedly be ferocious. For its part, the recording industry itself was far from willing to toe the party line without putting up a fight. Dance, swing, and other forms of popular music were among the best-selling kinds of music throughout the late 1920s and well into the Third Reich and therefore among the most profitable from the standpoint of record companies. Benny Goodman, Richard Tauber, and other musicians of Jewish ancestry were enormously popular with German audiences irrespective of the regime's official stance toward such artists on either aesthetic or racial grounds. In sum, Nazi rhetoric surrounding culture bore little resemblance to the reality on the ground. As Corey Ross succinctly put it, "In spite of the rhetorical attacks on musical 'asphalt culture', the commercial imperative that so irritated conservative critics during the Weimar era remained paramount throughout the 1930's."[103]

In the final analysis, perhaps we need to look no further than the respective parties responsible for broadcasting between Weimar and the Third Reich for the most dramatic evidence of the competing visions toward radio between the two. Hans Bredow, often referred to by contemporaries as the "Führer" of German radio during Weimar, euphorically envisioned that with radio, "love of the arts, public spirit, and thirst for knowledge come to life again and create the basis for intellectual sowing and ripening ... we will and must preserve our intellectual level [*geistige Höhe*] ... While foreign nations strive for a wider range [of transmission stations], we strive for deepening [*Vertiefung*]."[104] Despite the early lip service paid to the cultural mission of radio by Reich Broadcasting Director Hadamovsky, Goebbels revealed the regime's real attitude toward radio in 1936 at the opening speech of the 13th Great German Broadcasting Exhibition: "The overwhelming majority of all radio listeners lead hard and unrelenting lives characterized by a daily nerve and strength sapping struggle, and only the desire to have a few hours of peace and leisure to achieve real relaxation and recovery.

Compared to them, the numbers that wish to nourish themselves on Kant and Hegel are of scarcely any importance."[105]

Indeed, as Konrad Dussel has argued, the general disposition toward radio between Weimar Nazi cultural authorities could not have been more different: under Weimar as one geared, above all, toward its heuristic, educative potential and, under the Nazis, as a propagandistic tool valued above all for its ability to, alternatively, win political supporters and entertain and distract the masses.[106] The content of radio's first broadcasts under Weimar and Nazism would appear to bear such priorities out: on October 29, 1923, Weimar radio debuted with an hour-long program consisting of chamber pieces, chamber arrangements of symphonic works, and operatic arias.[107] The National Socialist era of radio officially opened late in the evening on January 31, 1933, with a speech entitled "Appeal to the German Nation," the first of many, which would be delivered in the years ahead by the new Führer, Adolf Hitler. Whatever their contempt for Weimar democracy, on the one hand, or their political affinities toward National Socialism on the other, there were good reasons for conservatives to be nostalgic over radio's new role in German society, even if this recognition came as a belated one.[108] What under Weimar had functioned as a bourgeois, tightly regulated, *anspruchsvoll* (demanding) instrument, the Nazis transformed into a truly mass, more loosely regulated, *unterhaltungsvoll* (recreational) device. When it came to ridding Germany of "cultural degeneracy," for some traditionalists there was more to admire about Nazi policing of the streets than of the airwaves.[109]

In all the conservative debate about radio during Weimar, which dwelled so ponderously on the virtues and vices of the technology *in and of itself*, few evinced the perspicacity of a Cardinal Pacelli (the future Pope Pius XII), on full display in a famous encounter recalled by the jurist Arnold Brecht at one of the first experiments with early live broadcasts in 1921:

> I met him on the top floor of the Vox House in Potsdamer Strasse, where he, Ebert's secretary Meissner, and I had been invited to one of the first radio tryouts. I was at the time head of the division in the Ministry of the Interior which was in charge of radio affairs, and I listened, absorbed, to this new technical wonder. When we got up, Pacelli said to me quietly but urgently: "But *what* will the people be told by means of this new medium?" I have never forgotten that.[110]

If, as we have seen, conservative critics' views toward the radio or the impact of inflation did not always unfold in altogether predictable ways, the reader could be forgiven for thinking herself on safer terrain in the case of the next subject on our historical itinerary—nationalism. Yet as we will see below, here too conservative opinion throws up surprising twists and turns that challenge our conventional understanding and expectations. It is to these debates that we must now turn.

Notes

1. Walter Benjamin, "The Work of Art in the Age of Its Technological Reproducibility," in *The Work of Art in the Age of Its Technological Reproducibility and Other Writings on Media* (Cambridge: Harvard University Press, 2008), 19–55 (emphasis in the original).
2. H. H. Stuckenschmidt, "Mechanische Musik," in *The Weimar Republic Sourcebook*, ed. Anton Kaes, Martin Jay, Edward Dimendberg (Berkeley: University of California Press, 1994), 599.
3. Jeffrey Herf, *Reactionary Modernism: Technology, Culture and Politics in Weimar and the Third Reich* (Cambridge: Cambridge University Press, 1986).
4. In addition to Herf, see Adam Stanley, *Modernizing Tradition: Gender and Consumerism in Interwar France and Germany* (Baton Rouge: Louisiana State University Press, 2008) and Roger Griffin, *Modernism and Fascism: The Sense of a Beginning under Mussolini and Hitler* (New York: Palgrave Macmillan, 2007).
5. See Eric Michaud, *The Cult of Art in Nazi Germany* (Palo Alto: Stanford University Press, 2004) and Claudia Koonz, *Mothers in the Fatherland: Women, the Family and Nazi Politics* (New York: St. Martin's, 1988).
6. Detlev Peukert, *The Weimar Republic: The Crisis of Classical Modernity* (London: Penguin Press, 1991). On the connection between modernity and the Holocaust, see Zygmunt Bauman, *Modernity and the Holocaust* (Ithaca: Cornell University Press, 2001).
7. Griffin, *Modernism and Fascism: The Sense of a Beginning under Mussolini and Hitler* offers one of the best guides.
8. Richard Evans, *The Coming of the Third Reich* (New York: Penguin Press, 2003), 123.
9. Corey Ross, *Media and the Making of Modern Germany* (New York: Oxford University Press, 2008), 53.
10. Eric Weitz, *Weimar Germany: Promise and Tragedy* (Princeton: Princeton University Press, 2007), 244. Yet even here, Weitz's next statement belies the extent to which a conservative hostility and progressive embrace of radio is often taken for granted by scholars. The next sentence reads, "The modernist composer Arnold Schönberg was a harsh critic of radio."
11. Fritz Lauhöfer, "Rundfunk und musikalische Kultur," *Neue Musik-Zeitung*, 48 (24) (1927): 529–532. Lauhöfer generally eschewed writing for the mainstream right

musical press (e.g., Zeitschrift für Musik and Allgemeine Musik-Zeitung) in favor of centrist publications like the *Neue Musik-Zeitung* and *Die Musik*. But there is no mistaking his conservative leanings; in addition to the essays cited here, see, for example, Fritz Lauhöfer, "Vom Kunstverstand bei Mozart," *Die Musik*, 20 (7) (1928): 495–501.

12 In the early 1930s and into the Third Reich, reactionary critics made great efforts to decouple *Hausmusik*'s nineteenth-century association with bourgeois culture and repackage it as something revolutionary and modern. For a wide-ranging discussion, see Celia Applegate, "The Past and Present of *Hausmusik* in the Third Reich," in *Music and Nazism: Art under Tyranny, 1933–1945*, ed. Michael Kater and Albrecht Riethmüller (Laaber: Laaber-Verlag, 2003), 136–149.

13 Wilhelm Fürtwangler, *Notebooks, 1924–54* (London: Quartet Books, 1989), 54.

14 Sanna Pederson, "A.B. Marx, Berlin Concert Life, and German National Identity," *19th-Century Music*, 18 (2) (1994): 87–107.

15 Fritz Stege, "Schlesiche Funkstunde," *Zeitschrift für Musik*, 99 (11) (1932): 1036.

16 Reinhold Zimmermann, "Stirbt das Klavier aus?" *Allgemeine Musik-Zeitung*, 58 (1931): 223–224.

17 Wilhelm Heinitz, *Strukturprobleme in Primitiver Musik* (Hamburg: Friederichsen, de Gruyter & Co., 1931).

18 Wilhelm Heinitz, "Soziale und kulturelle Probleme der Musik im Zeichen der Radioübermittlung," *Die Musik*, 16 (7) (1924): 489–492.

19 Ibid., 490 (emphasis in the original).

20 Stuckenschmidt, "Mechanische Musik," 599.

21 Artur Schnabel, *My Life and Music* (New York: St. Martin's Press, 1963), 97.

22 Joseph Horowitz, *Conversations with Arrau* (New York: Knopf, 1982), 89.

23 César Saerchinger, *Artur Schnabel: A Biography* (New York: Dood, Mead & Company, 1957), 221–225. Seventy-five years later, Schnabel's authoritative Beethoven cycle has yet to go out of print.

24 Quoted in Christopher Hailey, "Rethinking Sound: Music and Radio in Weimar Germany," in *Music and Performance during the Weimar Republic*, ed. Bryan Gilliam (Cambridge: Cambridge University Press, 1994), 23.

25 Frank Warschauer, "The Future of Opera on the Radio," in *The Weimar Republic Sourcebook*, ed. Anton Kaes et al. (Berkeley: University of California Press, 1994), 609.

26 Rudolf Cahn-Speyer, "Was nützt der Rundfunk dem Künstler?" *Neue Musik-Zeitung*, 46 (10) (1925): 233–235.

27 Max Butting, "Rundfunkmusik—wie wir sie brauchen," *Die Musik*, 21 (6) (1929): 443–447.

28 Ibid., 445.

29 Max Butting, "Music of and for the Radio," *Music & Letters*, 8 (3) (1931): 15–19.

30 Ibid., 16–17.

31 Alfred Heuss, "Über Rundfunk und andere zeitgenössische Musikfragen," *Zeitschrift für Musik*, 93 (10) (1926): 561–564.
32 Ibid., 562–563.
33 For a discussion of the origins of the *Volksgemeinschaft* and its legacy during Weimar, see Michael Wildt, *Hitler's Volksgemeinschaft and the Dynamics of Racial Exclusion* (New York: Berghahn, 2012), 15–49.
34 This was the case, for example, with the liberal Marianne Weber, cousin of the famous sociologist Max Weber, and her circle of friends. See Eric Kurlander, *Living with Hitler: Liberal Democrats in the Third Reich* (New Haven: Yale University Press, 2009), 26–28.
35 Stefan Jonsson, "Neither Masses nor Individuals: Representations of the Collective in Interwar German Culture," in *Weimar Public/Weimar Subjects: Rethinking the Political Culture of Germany in the 1920s*, ed. Kathleen Canning, Kerstin Barndt, and Kristin McGuire (New York: Berghahn Books, 2010), 279–301.
36 Herf, *Reactionary Modernism*, 2. Herf cites Ernst Jünger, Carl Schmitt, Werner Sombart, and Martin Heidegger as other examples.
37 See Dana Gooley, "Warhorses: Liszt, Weber's 'Konzertstück' and the Cult of Napoleon," *Nineteenth-Century Music*, 24 (1) (2000): 62–88.
38 Dana Gooley, "Hanslick and the Institution of Criticism," *The Journal of Musicology*, 28 (3) (2011): 289–324.
39 Wilhelm Heinitz, "Musikpädagogik und Grammophon," *Die Musik*, 17 (3) (1924): 203–204.
40 Ibid., 204.
41 Fritz Sporn, "Das Grammophon im modernen Musikunterricht," *Zeitschrift für Musik*, 11 (92) (1925): 643–646.
42 Ibid., 644.
43 Ibid., 645.
44 Quoted in Corey Ross, "Entertainment, Technology and Tradition: The Rise of Recorded Music from the Empire to the Third Reich," in *Mass Media, Culture and Society in Twentieth-Century Germany*, ed. Corey Ross and Karl Christian Führer (New York: Palgrave, 2006, 25–43) (here 29).
45 Erik Jensen, *Body by Weimar: Athletes, Gender and German Modernity* (New York: Oxford University Press, 2010).
46 Stefan Gauss, *Nadel, Rille, Trichter: Kulturgeschichte des Phonographen und des Grammophons in Deutschland, 1900–1940* (Köln: Böhlau Verlag, 2009).
47 Alfred Heuss, "Musik im Leben der Volker: Eroffnung der internationalen Ausstellung," *Frankfurt Allgemeine Zeitung*, August 1927: 433–434.
48 Ludwig Koch, "Schallplattenindustrie, Staat und Volkbildung," *Die Musik*, 22 (7) (1930): 515–519.
49 Quoted in Gauss, *Nadel, Rille, Trichter*, 210–211.
50 Ludwig Koch, "Die Schallplatte als Widererweckerin der Hausmusik," *Die Musik*, 23 (5) (1931): 351–352.

51 Ibid., 353.
52 See Bryan Gilliam, *Music and Performance during the Weimar Republic* (Cambridge: Cambridge University Press, 2005), 14.
53 Corey Ross and Karl Christian Führer, "Mass Media, Culture and Society in Twentieth-Century Germany: An Introduction," in *Mass Media, Culture and Society in Twentieth-Century Germany*, 4.
54 Karl Christian Führer, "A Medium of Modernity? Broadcasting in Weimar Germany, 1923-1932," *The Journal of Modern History*, 69 (4) (1997): 722-753.
55 *Simplicissimus: eine historische Zeitschrift*, 1924, http://www.simplicissimus.info/index.php?id=5.
56 Lauhöfer, "Rundfunk und musikalische Kultur," 529.
57 Ibid., 530.
58 Ibid., 531.
59 Führer, "A Medium of Modernity?" 731.
60 Konrad Dussel, *Deutsche Rundfunkgeschichte: Eine Einführung* (Konstanz: UVK Medien, 1999), 19-39.
61 Ross, "Entertainment, Technology and Tradition," 28. This, of course, also does not account for the cost of the records themselves, which ranged in cost from 3.50 RM for popular music to as much as 7.50 RM for classical recordings.
62 Führer, "A Medium of Modernity?," 737.
63 For more on the establishment of radio in Germany as well as the prehistory of the Edison phonograph and other technologies at the turn of the century, see Dussel, *Deutsche Rundfunkgeschichte: Eine Einführung*, especially 19-39.
64 Ibid., 53.
65 Joachim-Felix Leonhard, *Programmgeschichte des Hörfunks in der Weimarer Republik* (Band II) (München: Deutscher Taschenbuch Verlag, 1997), 745-746.
66 Ibid., 374.
67 Führer, "A Medium of Modernity?" 750.
68 See especially Florian Cebulla, *Rundfunk und ländliche Gesellschaft, 1924-1945* (Göttingen: Vandenhoeck & Ruprecht, 2004), 84-101. Alongside Führer, Cebulla gives detailed evidence of early radio distribution throughout Germany, which evinces further sharp differences across geographic, class, and population lines, 31-45.
69 Dieter Dowe, "The Workingmen's Choral Movement in Germany before the First World War," *Journal of Contemporary History*, 13 (2) (1978): 269-296.
70 Leo Kestenberg, *Jahrbuch der deutschen Musikorganisationen 1931* (Berlin: Max Hesse, 1931), 1920.
71 Quoted in Pamela Potter, *Most German of the Arts: Musicology and Society from the Weimar Republic to the End of Hitler's Reich* (New Haven: Yale University Press, 1998), 5-6.
72 These included *Die Laute: Monatsschrift zur Pflege des deutschen Liedes und gutter Hausmusik; Die Gitarre; Zeitschrift zur Pflege des Gitarren-und Lautenspiels und*

der Hausmusik; Lauten-Almanach; Ein Jahr- und Handbuch für alle Lauten- und Gitarrenspieler; Muse des Saitenspiels: Fach- und Werbe-Monatsschrift für Zither-, Gitarren- und Schossgeigenspiel; Münchner Zither-Zeitung: Fachblatt für Zitherspiel; Die Volksmusik; Die Zupfmusik; Der Lautenspieler; Schallkiste: Illustrierte Zeitschrift für Hausmusik; Budeszeitung des Deutschen Mandolinen- und Gitarrenspieler-Bundes; Der Blockflötenspiegel; Arbeitsblatt zur Belebung historischer Instrumente in der Jugend- und Hausmusik and *Zeitschrift für Musik*. Quoted in Potter, *Most German of the Arts*, ff. 17, 270.

73 Ludwig Koch, "Die Schallplatte als Widererweckerin der Hausmusik," *Die Musik*, 23 (5) (1931): 351–352.
74 Celia Applegate, *The Necessity of Music: Variations on a German Theme* (Toronto: University of Toronto Press, 2017), 266–274.
75 Lauhöfer, "Rundfunk und musikalische Kultur," 531 (emphasis mine).
76 Ross, *Media and the Making of Modern Germany*, 182–183.
77 M. M. Gehrke, "Das Ende der privaten Sphäre," *Die Weltbühne, 26* (2) (1930): 61–64. Quoted in Anton Kaes, Martin Jay, Edward Dimendberg, eds., *The Weimar Republic Sourcebook* (Berkeley: University of California Press, 1994), 613.
78 Stuckenschmidt, "Mechanische Musik," 598.
79 Ross, "Entertainment, Technology and Tradition," 29.
80 Ibid., 36.
81 Alan Steinweis, *Art, Ideology & Economics in Nazi Germany: The Reich Chambers of Music, Theater and the Visual Arts* (Chapel Hill: The University of North Carolina Press, 1993), 7. The 100,000 can be further broken down as follows: 84,362 musicians, music teachers and Kapellmeistern, 9,499 singers and voice teachers, and 5,129 dancers and dance teachers.
82 Karl Christian Führer, "High Brow and Low Brow Culture," in *Weimar Germany*, 260–281.
83 The other two orchestras were the *Kapelle der Staatsoper* and the *Rundfunk-Sinfonieorchseter Berlin*. The opera houses included the *Deutsche Oper-Charlottenburg*, the *Staatsoper-Unter den Linden*, the *Komische Oper* and, until its closing in 1932, the experimental *Kroll Oper* led by Otto Klemperer. For a fuller discussion of Berlin musical life between Weimar and the Third Reich, see Pamela Potter, "Musical Life in Berlin from Weimar to Hitler," in *Music and Nazism: Art under Tyranny, 1933–1945*, 90–101.
84 The first broadcast took place at 8:00 a.m. on October 29, 1923, and consisted of an hour-long program of classical fare, followed by the German national anthem played by the Reichswehr band. See Leonhard, *Programmgeschichte des Hörfunks*, 23.
85 Joseph Goebbels, *Die Tagebücher von Joseph Goebbels* (Band 1/II) (München: K.G. Saur Verlag, 2005), 33.
86 Joseph Goebbels, "Der Rundfunk als achte Großmacht," *Signale der neuen Zeit*, 1933, http://research.calvin.edu/german-propaganda-archive/goeb56.htm.

87　Winifred Lerg, *Rundfunkpolitik in der Weimarer Republik* (München: Deutscher Taschenbuch Verlag, 1980).
88　Führer, "A Medium of Modernity?" 731.
89　Wolfgang König, "Der Volksempfänger und die Radioindustrie: Ein Beitrag zum Verhältnis von Wirtschaft und Politik im Nationalsozialismus," *VSWG: Vierteljahrschrift für Sozial- und Wirtschaftsgeschichte*, 90 (3) (2003): 269–289.
90　Ibid., 273–274.
91　Hans Sarkowicz, "'Nur nicht langweilig werden … ' Das Radio im Dienst der nationalistischen Propaganda," in *Medien im Nationalsozialismus*, ed. Bernd Heidenreich and Sönke Neitzel (Paderborn: Ferdinand Schöningh, 2010), 205–234.
92　Ludwig Neubeck, "Die kulturelle Sendung des Rundfunks," *Zeitschrift für Musik*, 100 (12) (1933): 1205–1207 (here 1207).
93　Ibid., 206–207. Alfred Bofinger, director of the Stuttgart-based *Süddeustcher Rundfunk*, was the sole exception.
94　Jörg Koch, "Das NS-Wunschkonzert," in *Medien im Nationalsozialismus*, 253–271.
95　Eugen Hadamovsky, "Der grosse Magnet des Rundfunks heisst Musik," in *Quellen zur Programmgeschichte des deutschen Hörfunks und Fernsehens*, ed. Konrad Dussel and Edgar Lersch (Göttingen: Muster-Schmidt Verlag, 1999), 130.
96　Carolyn Birdsall, *Nazi Soundscapes: Sound, Technology and Urban Space in Germany, 1933–1945* (Amsterdam: Amsterdam University Press, 2012).
97　Victor Klemperer, *I Will Bear Witness: A Diary of the Nazi Years, 1933–1941* (New York: Random House, 1999), 267.
98　Quoted in Sarkowicz, "'Nur nicht langweilig werden …,'" 216.
99　Konrad Dussell, "Radio Programming, Ideology, and Cultural Change: Fascism, Communism and Liberal Democracy, 1920s-1950s" in *Mass Media, Culture and Society in Twentieth-Century Germany*, ed. Karl Christian Führer and Corey Ross (London: Palgrave McMillan, 2006), 80–94 (here 84).
100　From 1933 to 1937, in fact, the overall amount of airtime devoted to music increased from 58 to 69 percent. See Kate Lacey, *Feminine Frequencies: Gender, German Radio, and the Public Sphere, 1923–1945* (Ann Arbor: University of Michigan Press, 1996), 102.
101　Michael Kater, *Different Drummers: Jazz in the Culture of Nazi Germany* (New York: Oxford University Press, 1992), 46–52.
102　Ross, *Media and the Making of Modern Germany*, 291.
103　Ibid., 291–292.
104　Führer, "A Medium of Modernity?," 728.
105　Joseph Goebbels, "Rede zur Eröffnung der 13. Grossen Detuschen Rundfunk-Austellung 1936," in *Quellen zur Programmgeschichte des deutschen Hörfunks und Fernsehens*, 136.
106　Dussel, "Radio Programming, Ideology and Cultural Change," 80–94.

107 Brian Currid, *A National Acoustics: Music and Mass Publicity in Weimar and Nazi Germany* (Minneapolis: University of Minnesota Press, 2006), 19. In addition to these classical offerings, which dominated the broadcast, one "gypsy" song was played along with the "Deutschlandlied" played by the *Reichswehr* military band.
108 Adolf Hitler, "Appeal to the German People, 31 January 1933," http://germanhistorydocs.ghi-dc.org/sub_document.cfm?document_id=3940.
109 This was the case, for example, in the aggressive crackdown on "swing youth." See Detlev Peukert, *Inside Nazi Germany: Conformity, Opposition and Racism in Everyday Life* (New Haven: Yale University Press, 1987), 197–207.
110 Arnold Brecht, *The Political Education of Arnold Brecht: An Autobiography 1884–1970* (Princeton: Princeton University Press, 1970), 200 (emphasis in the original). Retrieved on May 24, 2012, from http://germanhistorydocs.ghi-dc.org/sub_document.cfm?document_id=3871.

3

Internationalism, Nationalism, and the Case of Hans Joachim Moser

In the summer of 1915, almost one year into a war that would prove so fateful to the course of twentieth-century European history, an article appeared in the journal *Die Tonkunst* titled "On National vs. International Music."[1] In it, the music critic H. Ruah suggests how Germany might utilize its great musical tradition in the midst of world war, a conflict that had done nothing to reduce the appeal of German music abroad. Lamenting British control of the seas that prevented German goods from entering or exiting the country, he shared stories of French copyists rumored to be circulating pirated editions of German masterworks. For Ruah, the lesson was clear: "Even our enemies cannot do without it—not even during the war ... One can see: there is simply no doing without German music." Whatever the intentions of the French, Ruah saw this episode as evidence of a German cultural hegemony that might be harnessed to his country's advantage. By severing music from its sentimental moorings, the classics could be turned into a weapon of war and made to serve the fatherland. While Germany could ill-afford to cut itself off altogether from the wider world,

> to be musically independent from abroad should prove to be far easier. Then we won't need to ration Beethoven and Richard Wagner so much, as we are already forced to do with potatoes and pastries (*Schweineohren*). Let us be free of the caviar of our enemies and they, in turn, from our musical caviar. Then they won't have our "*Eroica*" [Beethoven's 3rd Symphony] anymore; neither in music nor on the battlefields.[2]

In the same year, an essay by Wilibald Nagel in the conservative *Neue Musik Zeitung* took up the same theme in a piece entitled "Kosmopolische oder nationale Musik?"[3] "Nothing," he writes, "would give greater proof of a limited intellect than to speak the words of an extreme nationalism."[4] His view of true artistry was similarly cosmopolitan: "To be artistic, is to be created as a free, independent spirit. Whoever binds and restricts himself to the national formulas will soon be cut off." He envisioned a future where musicians and composers would roam freely, unencumbered by political strife and hostility between nations. The artist belonged, like the businessman and the scientist, "to the world and when the borders closed off by the war open, they will have their freedom again." The logic undergirding Nagel's views was simple: just as global finance and modern science were interdependent and depended on transnational collaboration art, too, was international for there was scarcely "any land with a completely pure national art music … there has never been any country whose artistic creations remained outside the influence of another people." To stifle the free exchange of styles would, in short, be to stifle the very foundation upon which *all* great art was based to the impoverishment of all.[5]

In comparing these two essays, the difference in tone is evident. While Ruah sees potential benefit in sequestering off German music from the rest of the world, Nagel views the consequences of such an effort as nothing short of devastating for European cultural life, Germany included. Ruah's bellicose rhetoric evinces a fierce nationalism and commitment, above all else, to Germany's war aims, while Nagel's more tempered tone reveals greater concern with preserving culture in the midst of war while anticipating how to meet the challenges of a postwar world. In Ruah's short piece, references to Germany's enemies (*Feinde*) appear five times; in Nagel's—more than three times in length—we find not a single reference. Although both wrote as conservative nationalists—with Nagel's views, in particular, hardening over the course of the war—what each author has to say about the overall position of German music in the world might initially strike us as somewhat surprising. While Nagel claimed that all art was nationally constrained, he envisioned an authoritarian postwar world where a leader would emerge to safeguard the conditions necessary for the flourishing of all national idioms. The leader "would never try to anxiously ward off foreign advances to sources of art, for genuine and honest art is not the privilege of one *Volk* alone."[6] For his part, Ruah believed that "music, like all true art, belongs to all of humanity. Certainly! And yet there is German music and here we can proudly say: **German music is the music of humanity, of all peoples of the Earth**."[7] Although as a committed nationalist Ruah calls for the need to ration if not altogether restrict German music from the rest of the world in wartime, he appears as a committed internationalist when it comes to the power of German music to speak to all peoples of the world, irrespective of their linguistic, ethnic, or cultural background.

In short, both Nagel and Ruah embody a kind international nationalism. At one level it is rather simple to explain the appeals to universalism behind Ruah's rhetoric, for it is clear that his is not an egalitarian form of internationalism; while the German classics were endowed with a special power to reach the disparate peoples of the world, the same could hardly be said of the national musical idioms deriving from those same cultures. "German music," he wrote, "is international while French, Russian, Italian, and certainly English [music] is not."[8] For Ruah, German musical universality was itself a sign of German cultural superiority. Secondly, Ruah was hardly alone in privileging German music above all others, and his declaration of German music as "the music of humanity" was not a particularly unique view but rather one that many if not most contemporary observers—even during the Great War—would have taken as a matter of course. In a 1915 cultural history survey, for example, the British musicologist Donald Tovey reached a similar conclusion: the entire Western tradition, in his view, was little more than a chronicle of artists' efforts to create universally admired cultural touchstones. And yet, while the nations of the world could put forward countless works to compete for the title cultural "touchstone," in music the task was far simpler: there, he wrote, "all our 'touchstones' [are] German."[9]

We are accustomed to viewing internationalism and nationalism in stable, binary terms. While the former has long been associated with the political left, their rightist counterparts frequently railed against the dangers of cosmopolitanism and the sinister threat it posed to national culture. Prior to the First World War, these sentiments sprang both from right-wing institutions, such as the Pan-German and Naval Leagues, and nationalist politicians and intellectuals, from Karl Lueger and Oswald Spengler to Houston Stewart Chamberlain.[10] Calls for action directed against "International Jewry" responsible for, among other things, stabbing Germany in the back in the final stages of the First World War or the "cosmopolitan artists" who lurked behind the abstract, atonal excesses of modernist art were standard fare within right-wing circles throughout the years of the Weimar Republic. For this reason, expressions of internationalist sentiment have tended to be viewed as incompatible with nationalist ideals and the reason why the terms "international nationalist" might seem contradictory. In musical discourse the perspectives of Ruah and Nagel present a useful starting point for uncovering the relationship between the national and international in music, one fraught with innumerable tensions and contradictions. There can be little question that cultural pessimism contributed to a crisis of faith in Weimar democracy and even anticipated Nazi views toward modernist art in important ways. For this reason, however, scholarship on musical culture between the years 1918 and 1945 has sometimes resembled, to borrow Helmuth Walser Smith's memorable phrase, a "hearse in reverse" whereby scholars have started with the catastrophe of Nazism and worked their way backward in search of origins.[11] In the first part of this chapter, I examine the debates surrounding "cosmopolitan" versus "national" music in the early years of the Weimar Republic with a particular focus on the writings of conservative opinion. I argue that many critics' sentiment toward the canon and the uses to which it might be put after the war suggest a need to rethink the nature of German cultural nationalism. For unlike German political nationalism, which one classic study defined as "exclusivist" and "differentialist" in character, German musical nationalism was highly malleable and, in the hands of some critics, proved capable of serving different masters.[12] Perhaps no figure better embodies these tensions than the conservative musicologist Hans Joachim Moser. The second part of this chapter thus examines his writings over the course of the Weimar Republic and early Nazi period, calling into question a linear continuity in his career between Weimar and the Third Reich.

Nationalism and internationalism in music

Nagel and Ruah were merely among the first to fire the initial salvos in a debate that would continue well into the early years of the Weimar Republic. What accounts for the proliferation of music articles devoted to the question of nationalism and internationalism at this particular historical moment? Part of the answer unquestionably lies in the broader transformation of Europe then taking place at the end of the First World War, a war that would see the collapse of the great multinational empires and the creation of new states, above all in Eastern Europe. Many observers then and since who perceived an increasingly shrill atmosphere of nationalism as one of the primary factors that pushed Europe over the precipice to war viewed the creation of new nation-states as an important precondition for securing the peace. However, the incomplete nature of this transformation left substantial minorities enclosed within newly redrawn national boundaries and the principle of national self-determination, enshrined as a hallmark of the Versailles settlement, appeared at times to conflict with calls for international protections by a plethora of advocacy groups committed to ensuring that states did not renege on their promises to secure minority rights for their citizens. International projects and initiatives sprang up all over Europe to redress these and other issues following the war, and it was within these and other larger debates that musical exchanges surrounding the "national" and "international" took place.[13]

A second reason the immediate postwar period seemed a particularly opportune time for German observers to reassess the place of music in its national and international contexts was due to the perceived damage done to Germany's reputation during the war, whose consequences extended to musical life in important ways. The experience of German music in America offered an instructive case in point. Owing to the perceived absence of a sufficiently cultivated native musical tradition of their own, patriotic-minded American organizations were well aware of their country's continued reliance on German musical imports. Nine of the nation's top orchestras were led by German conductors and it has been estimated that fully two-thirds of the music performed by American orchestras between 1890 and 1915 was German.[14] Prior to the First World War, such an overwhelming presence of German culture undoubtedly constituted, to use Jessica Gienow-Hecht's term, an "emotional elective-affinity" by which Americans' profound esteem for Germany's musical tradition translated into admiration for Germany in general.[15] It was an esteem captured by one of Germany's greatest nineteenth-century musical scholars and a pioneer of modern musicology, Hermann Kretszschmar, who in 1881 observed:

> The natural musical talent of the Germans has been a favorite academic question from time immemorial … we did not possess an innate genius [for music] but rather have to thank, above all, the application of our industriousness. [By the late eighteenth and nineteenth-century] we proudly toasted our own musical emergence [Ausbruch] and modestly accepted the sense that through extraordinary cultivation [of our talent] we had obtained leadership over all musical peoples due to what we had experienced in our country in the eighteenth and nineteenth-centuries. Among other peoples, one finds nothing against which to compare the excellence of the Germans, from the age of the bards and hornblowers to the advent of Italian Opera.[16]

During the First World War, thanks in large measure to heavy doses of Allied propaganda characterizing Germans as "warmongering Huns," this esteem had been severely damaged. The war saw Beethoven banned in several American cities, from Pittsburgh and Boston to New York.[17] German conductors and musicians found themselves pushed out of America's leading orchestras with two of the most prominent, Karl Muck and Ernst Kunwald, ending up imprisoned in a German internment camp at Fort Ogelthorpe, Georgia.[18] In the wake of such damage, German critics sought at the very least to rehabilitate Germany's musical preeminence, if not its hegemony, within musical circles in the rest of the Western world.

Reestablishing this international appeal would not come easy and immediately came under siege among select German critics. Some perceived the campaign of support for internationalism in music—a benign enterprise in and of itself—as a Trojan horse for securing commitment to a broader internationalist agenda. In 1921, the nationalist composer and critic Robert Hernried offered an early assessment, sarcastically observing, "if there is an international art, it stands to reason that there are 'international people' as well." Hernried admitted that while people "[are] a product of our education and our environment," no amount of exposure to other cultural experiences could ever hope to overcome the influence of inherited traits, traits stemming from "race, our tribe and our strictly personal hereditary characteristics derived from our forefathers." For proof, one only needed to compare the lives of three composers, only one of whom had succeeded in his effort to compose proper national music. It was only the music of an Edvard Grieg (1843–1907), according to Hernried, which "can simply only be observed from the standpoint of the national in music." While his use of dissonant harmonies and settings of texts by Goethe, Heine, as well as his fellow countryman Henrik Ibsen clearly indicated the "Norwegian-national" character of his music, one could also trace evidence of his Scottish ancestry in "recumbent tuning and bagpipe-like accompaniment" in many of his works, which "derived from the folk-national source of his muse."[19]

The other two, however, offered proof of what lay in store for the composer who attempted to compose "national music" for a nation he could not properly call his own. Many of Johannes Brahms's works, such as his Symphony No. 1 in C Minor, exhibited strong elements of that composer's North German heritage, while his much-admired Lieder betrayed Low German influences. While these works and others had earned the composer well-deserved fame, his forays into other national genres—such as with the *Zigeunerlieder* Op. 103 or the Hungarian Dances—were, according to Hernried, less deserving of praise whatever their commercial successes: "Even if Brahms has become endlessly popular through these pieces, they nevertheless do not rank among the most prized creations … this is only to point out where his national character emerges most powerfully: in his songs and his deeply felt development of German folk tunes." Finally, there was the composer Giacomo Meyerbeer. Though he "was raised, loved and later supported German art" as a German Jew, he possessed a "latent racial singularity" (*ruhenden Rasseeigentümlichkeiten*), which compelled his decision to seek his musical development first in Italy and then Paris where he settled to compose Grand Opera in the French manner. "Hence, was his music also possibly international?" Hardly, according to Hernried, for "one finds the core of real French music [in his work] just as little as one finds the core of the German. The consequence of this internationalism was and must be as much a complete absence of inner expressiveness as of an outrageous outer method." Meyerbeer's music was doomed to remain "neither French nor German ... an example of anational artistry ....greatness is art is always only to be found in the *expression of the national* and in this alone."[20] As his analysis of Grieg, Brahms, and Meyerbeer had shown, composers who styled themselves cosmopolitan and self-consciously strove for the universal could never hope to find success. For Hernried, the Western canon consisted of little more than the fruits of creative national self-awareness. To study the history of Western musical achievement within it was to study the history of national—and above all German—achievement.

Naturally one can find evidence of a general tendency within progressive music journals toward upholding internationalism alongside a countervailing conservative trend toward the national. Immediately after the war, musicologists such as Hugo Riemann were sounding the alarm about ongoing politicization surrounding the question of internationalism in art. In the foreword to his reissued *Kleines Handbuch der Musikgeschichte* (Short History of Music), the influential musicologist hoped for a resumption of the kind of healthy international exchange in scholarly musicological research that had been disrupted by the Great War. As we will later see with Hans Joachim Moser, Riemann also recognized the international foundation that had always figured prominently in German and, indeed, all modern musical traditions. Tracing the emergence of national self-awakening in musical traditions across Scandinavia and Europe over the course of the nineteenth century it was "doubtless, the case" he wrote,

> [that] the Romantics—through their quaint obsession with the foreign and exotic—gave an impetus for the concentration of composers on the musical peculiarities of their own nation or race. Schubert's [Hungarian Divertimento?], Liszt's Hungarian Rhapsodies, Brahms' Hungarian Dances and Gypsy Songs indicate the rising interest in Germany for the music of Hungarian Gypsies (while) the collecting of Polish Dances goes back still further.[21]

Although this interest in and cultivation of foreign music could, in the right hands, only enrich native idioms and foster greater cultural understanding between nations, Riemann was clear about one negative consequence of such interest in the national. "Some parochial idiots [attempt] to develop from these natural roots a national music ... and so the international universally human character of music was negated for the first time and the national principle—the question of race—inserted itself into art."[22]

This line of thinking was taken up by Paul Bekker in an essay for the *Musikblätter des Anbruch*. Bekker admitted that while one could certainly find ample instances, if not a basis, for the labeling of individuals as "international" or "reactionary" in the daily newspapers or within the declared principles of the political pamphlets, "what in the world are the elementary, organic differences between national vs. international music? Do the Germans have tonality as a part of their inheritance, or somewhere within a certain art form? Are there national and international C scales or violins?"[23] Admittedly, he claimed, each nation possessed certain characteristics traceable to "race, climate and natural ability." Yet even if it was possible to definitively show some kind of national style or character in music, Bekker asked,

> What would be gained from it? That we can stand before the mirror and proclaim to be "the fairest of them all?" In the end, we would fare as badly as the evil stepmother in the fairy tale; indeed, we must also hear that "Snow White" was "a thousand times more beautiful." Then perhaps we would share the fate of this stepmother who is not helped to triumph despite all her appearances before the mirror. We do not find beauty composed after national principles questioned before a national-aryan mirror, but rather where nature plants genius.[24]

The bellicosity of certain conservatives, whose contempt for internationalism anticipates Nazi rhetoric in certain ways, was striking. In 1921, Alfred Heuss, editor of the *Zeitschrift für Musik*, offered a more pessimistic assessment of internationalism in music in an article entitled "*Weltbürgertum und Internationalität in der Tonkunst*." Echoing Robert Hernried's earlier 1921 assessment, he perceived far more nefarious influences afoot in the rhetoric surrounding internationalist—which he took as modernist—art, for the term *internationalist* did not simply reflect a straightforward call for international solidarity through art but rather "has instigated immense bewilderment" and concealed unspoken agendas behind which lurked "international (Jewish) attitudes."[25] The term *Weltbürger*, which implied an exclusively narrow civic attachment and hopelessly broad universal one, was itself a contradiction in terms. One could, like J. S. Bach, theoretically function as a "Weltkomponist" through deep immersion in past musical conventions and forms of every tradition. But the composer of modernist music, who according to Heuss was among the strongest proponents of internationalism in art, "works entirely in the opposite manner as Bach. [He desires] to be acclaimed as soon as possible, devotes more time to propaganda than his work; which gives one a dim feeling that an art which has no proper rooting ... has no chance at all of spreading."[26]

By contrast, Händel, Haydn, Gluck, Mozart, and Beethoven—all these men were "Weltbürger" in the sense that they created

> something open, strong and indeed universally human from the most varied European musical styles through a firm anchoring in a specifically German core ... and if from them German music has acquired the ability to go further than the music of other peoples, this, again, is because of the specific way in which the German soul revealed and connected itself to the great masters of art music.

The composer Hans Pfitzner found himself in broad agreement with this assessment, perceiving musical modernism as the by-product of a "Jewish-international spirit that implants into the German the completely alien madness of demolition and destruction. [It] is a symptom of decay."[27]

Such prescriptions, however, do not always admit to clear correspondences between politics and culture, as critics who were committed nationalists within the realm of politics found themselves articulating a vision of German music, which took on a transnational and cosmopolitan appearance. Increasingly, the most fervent supporters of Germanness in music found themselves subscribing, perhaps inadvertently, to a kind of musical internationalism. Notwithstanding the many differences between the conservative Alfred Heuss and the modernist Paul Bekker, both subscribed to a view of Beethoven, for example, as a universal composer, whose heroic style resonated with all the peoples of the world.[28] Furthermore, if we recall Ruah's dictum mentioned earlier in this chapter—that "greatness in art is always only to be found in the *expression of the national and in this alone*"—a potential paradox emerges if we take a logical next step in Ruah's assertion, for if it reminds us that greatness always rests in the hands of the most nationally minded, it says nothing whatever about which nation that might be. Superiority simply rests with those whose national consciousness is most fully realized, whether German, French, Italian, or Russian. This was the conclusion drawn by Martin Friedland in a 1922 essay for the conservative *Allgemeine Musikalische Zeitung*.[29] "The art of another nation," he wrote, "is not less meaningful, worthwhile or legitimate just because it appears foreign-derived from the standpoint of the observer, because it sprang from foreign sentiments or because it emerged under a different sun and climate or was conceived for other minds, eyes or ears." For this reason, Friedland ridiculed efforts to marginalize Verdi due to his Italianness or Gounod on account of his Frenchness. Cultural taste should not proceed from some blind adherence to national identity but rather from an even-handed analysis of which composer "has rendered the national conditions and factors both more often and strongly to artistic fruition and outperformed the others as measured by his role as the originator and shaper and ethical personality of *his* national particularity."[30]

German music critics were not the only group eager to tackle the question of internationalism in music. Musicologists, too, took great interest in these ongoing debates, above all Guido Adler (1855–1941), one of the most important music historians of the modern period and considered by many to be the founder of Austrian Musicology. By 1924 Adler had already demonstrated a strong commitment to internationalism based on a long record of initiatives to foster international cooperation and scholarly exchange, culminating in the founding of the *Internationale Gesellschaft für Musikwissenschaft* in 1927 of which he remained honorary president until his death.[31] In addition, he organized several international congresses devoted to the life and works of the First Viennese School in whose music he sustained the greatest interest, over the course of his professional life. Unlike Moser, who throughout his writings in the Weimar period often appeared to oscillate between the national and international dimensions of Western music in general and its German branch in particular, Adler remained firmly committed to the decisive role international exchange played in driving musical development, though he, too, acknowledged the importance of national considerations. Rather than seeing internationalism and nationalism in mutually exclusive terms, Adler saw these forces as complementary. His remarks as the 1924 keynote address on "Internationalism in Music" before the International Music Congress in Basel, Switzerland, give some sense of this view:

1. Artistic activities vibrate between nationalism and internationalism. The one is as necessary as the other is indispensable.
2. There is in progress a reconciliation of these opposing factors, which is favorable, salutary, and inevitable in and for the evolution of musical art.
3. This reconciliation is not to be effected by external compromise but through organic combinations and solutions of elementary scope.
4. The mission of each and every nation participating in musical advancement is to be fulfilled within the bounds of the alternate ebb and flow of the several schools as they take up and elaborate their own specialties, each taking rank according to its vocation, that is, its qualification.
5. Whereas the potentialities of internationalism would seem to be unlimited as regards duration, the rank of any nation is limited in time.
6. Neither hatred nor love, neither advantage nor sympathy, determines national rank but an indwelling love and longing for art.

7. A comparison of these phenomena in the development of music with political and general conditions of culture might aid in clarifying our conclusions. History teaches us that the wholesome evolution of musical art is altogether dependent upon a rightly proportioned blending of nationalism and internationalism.[32]

Adler's essay contained many of the elements often used to take on a question that occupied the attention of a number of musicologists and critics in the years after the First World War, namely the question of Germanness in music. Although attempts to account for Germans' seeming propensity for musical composition can be traced as far back as the seventeenth century and the end of the Thirty Years' War, the matter took on a new urgency in the postwar period as Germans sought to recover cultural prestige in a world more familiar with stories of German barbarism than *Kultur*. In addition, as Pamela Potter has shown, German musicologists eager to demonstrate their utility to wider society and win credentials for the new discipline of musicology concentrated more than ever before on finding an answer to the question: what was Germanness in music?[33] Here, the widely understood international (narrowly defined and limited to within Europe) ties that marked German musical development from the time of Heinrich Schütz presented a contradictory picture.

As many would soon find out, answers were not readily forthcoming. One explanation located Germanness in music as stemming from a particularly German strength for adapting foreign models. If Germany's geographic location at the center of Europe, which had made it particularly vulnerable to foreign invasion, accounted for the nation's political misfortunes from the Thirty Years' War to the most recent conflict, this same geographic *Sonderweg* had at the same time been responsible for the development of an especially rich musical tradition in the German lands. Alfred Heuss, for one, held this view and his writings reflected this understanding, including one of his final essays comparing the Germanness of Bach and Händel in commemoration of the 175th *Todestag* of the latter.[34] Finding his native Germany too politically and artistically restrictive, Händel had, rather paradoxically, to leave Germany in order to give his Germanness full expression—first, by way of a sojourn through "art friendly and hospitable" Italy before eventually settling in England where, though a German composing primarily Italian opera, he also worked from French models. The end result was that unlike other foreign composers such as Piccini, "[Händel] achieved a higher unity for French Opera as much on the basis of his German attachment as from his French and Italian experiences

[*Schulung*]." For this reason, according to Heuss, a Händel Oratorio was nothing more than "an English artwork [composed] in the German spirit."[35]

A second strategy by which musicologists attempted to define Germanness in music involved identifying certain musical characteristics as particularly German, including a greater use of counterpoint, richer use of harmony, and greater feeling for instrumental voice writing. Conservative musicologists pored over orchestral scores in search of these and other "German" devices, notably in Hans Joachim Moser's 1923 *Geschichte der deutschen Musik*, which attempted—rather unsuccessfully it turns out—to arrive at definitive conclusions by looking not at Germany's universally renowned masters but through an examination of compositions by so-called *Kleinmeister* or secondary figures.[36] These attempts to locate Germanness in music were not confined to right-wing circles. Paul Bekker admitted in 1924 that "there are differences traceable to race, climate or natural inheritance which to a certain degree [manifest themselves] in artistic attachments. The Italian will rather content himself primarily with the vocal, the German primarily with the instrumental and the Frenchman primarily with formal instincts."[37] Of course, as Bekker later had to acknowledge, there was little empirical basis for making such sweeping generalizations.

Whatever the political and cultural differences between these critics, their efforts to locate Germanness in music shared a tendency that can be found in vastly different historical contexts and in commentators ranging from the early J. S. Bach biographer Johann Nicholas Forkel to Theodor Adorno—that is, a striving for "idealized self-description." Unable to draw upon characteristics broad enough to encompass German music from Bach to Brahms while also accounting for all the disparities in between, the "German" in music all too often emerges, as Bernd Sponheuer has argued, "in a historical process through a confused web of events, circumstances, decisions and intentions." As a result, German music could find itself cast as exclusivist and universalist, depending on the inclinations of its investigator.[38] Given this tendency, perhaps it should come as no surprise that essays on the national and international often betrayed a striking degree of contradiction and tension. For taken to one logical end, if German musical greatness rested on adapting and improving upon foreign models, it stood to reason that Germany's musical past—and future, according to some—depended in crucial ways on the continued vigor of those models and Germany's access to them. This was the conclusion reached in many of the writings of one of Weimar's most esteemed musicologists: Hans Joachim Moser.

The case of Hans Joachim Moser

Hans Joachim Moser was born in Berlin on May 25, 1889, into a family with deep musical roots. His father, Andreas Moser, was a violin teacher at the *Berliner Musikhochschule* while his godfather was the great violin virtuoso and nineteenth-century pedagogue Joseph Joachim. After graduating from the *Bismarckgymnasium* in Berlin's Wilmersdorf, he embarked on a course of study in musicology, which would take him to some of Germany's most prestigious universities, including Marburg, Berlin, Leipzig, and finally the University of Rostock, from which he earned his PhD in 1910 with a dissertation entitled "*Die Musikergenossenschaften im deutschen Mittelalter*" (Musical Confederations in the German Middle Ages). In addition to early musical training on the violin from his father, Moser studied with a number of the most prominent figures in the nascent discipline of musicology, including Gustav Jenner, Hugo Riemann, Arnold Schering, Hermann Kretzschmar, and Johannes Wolf. Upon the outbreak of the First World War, he served as a clarinetist in an ensemble attached to a military regiment based in Danzig, eventually achieving the rank of Lieutenant, and became leader of a *Schallmesstrupp*. Immediately following the war, Moser completed his Habilitation in 1919 at the University of Halle under the supervision of Hermann Abert and worked there until 1925 at which time he secured his first major position as Director of the Musicological Seminar at the University of Heidelberg.[39] This would mark the beginning of a long career that spanned the Weimar Republic, Third Reich, and first fourteen years of the Federal Republic of Germany.

Yet as a scholar and champion of the German classics, Moser—like many of his culturally conservative peers—has been taken to task for introducing a nationalism and anti-modernism into his work that some scholars have seen as preparing the ground for the perversions of Nazi musicologists.[40] At one level, this is understandable, for as we will see below, Moser eventually became one the most prestigious musicologists to lend his services to the regime. However, some scholars have detected the early traces of Moser's later excesses in his scholarship during the Weimar period. According to Erik Levi, Moser was a "patent anti-Semite," whose "opinions on the irreconcilable nature of Judaism and Germanness were to be reiterated in [his] three volume *Geschichte der deutschen Musik*, which was published between 1922 and 1924. The equality between music and race, drawn by a scholar of Moser's distinction, was especially important, for it cloaked racism in an aura of musicological respectability."[41] Pamela Potter has similarly singled out Moser as the embodiment of a cultural conservatism, which arose in the postwar period aligned against, among other things, "experimentation, ... technology, the working class, encroaching foreign capitalist interests, and not least among them, the increasingly threatening image of the Jew."[42] To be sure, there is no questioning Moser's unquestioned and enthusiastic participation in state-sponsored musicological projects even before 1940 by which point he was named to the directorship of the *Reichstelle für Musikabteilungen*. In 1936, for example, Moser attempted to compose a suitably "Aryanized" libretto to accompany the Mozart oratorio *Betulia liberate* tainted by its "Jewish associations" with the Book of Judith.[43] It is based, in part, on such evidence that scholars like Levi and Potter have rendered Moser doubly damned, not only due to his perceived affinities for Nazi ideals during the Weimar Republic but also for the way in which those affinities tainted his scholarship and made his later publications natural outgrowths of his earlier musicological activity.

Yet Moser's overall record, particularly during Weimar, suggests a more complex picture and calls into question the extent to which we can approach Moser's scholarship from Weimar to the Third Reich in a linear fashion. For one thing, Moser did not join the Nazi Party until 1936.[44] Following the Nazi seizure of power in 1933, Moser was quickly identified as "politically unreliable" and pensioned off.[45] Second, his writings up to the year 1939 were hardly a model of Nazi scholarship but rather evinced a strong belief in the international influences on German music and—as late as 1938—recognition of Jewish contributions to German musical life. For reasons which will be explained below, Moser seems to have come around to Nazism quite late, a conversion that seems to have been motivated much more by careerism than ideology.

Moser first garnered widespread acclaim following the publication of his three-volume *Geschichte der deutschen Musik* over the years 1922–1924 and it is this work that some scholars have identified as containing early signs of Moser's cultural chauvinism and hostility toward Jews.[46] The offending passage appears in the third volume during which Moser, following a lengthy diatribe against Shimmy, Foxtrot, Ragtime, and other examples of "Grotesk-Nigger-Songs," writes,

> It is frequently said that the blame for the one-sided, unpatriotic (*unvolkhafte*) musico-political trials of the present (which is to say, either snobbishly international or just plain trash) belongs to the Jews. That is undoubtedly to a large extent true ... and is not only a consequence of their economic clout and organized collaboration but also their undeniably extraordinary talent for musical performance.[47]

On its own, this is straightforward enough, but the passage that follows is central to Moser's analysis of music in postwar Germany and seriously challenges the extent to which we can view Moser's diagnosis of the problems facing Germany's postwar musical life as solely, or even primarily, a result of the negative influence of Jewish musicians and composers. It merits inclusion here in its entirety:

> But especially it is above all due to our neglect which all too often is still accompanied by a deeply rooted "peasant mentality" that mistrusts "art as decadence," and "rootless nomads" instead of recognizing the powerful possibilities which art can bring to the idea of the *Volk*. We need to finally understand that there exist, besides military marches and song books, chamber choirs and pianola circles, artistic concerns of the *Volk* which in the long term are more important for the future of our *Volk* than narrow-minded party politics and class interests, short-lived economic advantages and sports entertainment. Occasional showing off on plaques of honorary committees of choirs and music festivals is not enough nor are generous donations every once in a while; there rather needs to be a willingness to self-sacrifice. Only when the nobility as well as the middle class have learned to once again actively join the choral society, the church choir of small and large city alike, the amateur orchestra and serious performance, and to provide their children with appropriate music instruction and therefore consciously raise in their own house a new chamber music culture, and do not regard the choice to become a musician by a talented son to be a family shame—only then will the Jewish question in music resolve itself and take a more healthy direction. Even better, much of our misery in the realm of musical art will be healed.[48]

From this, it is clear that Moser formed a connection between negative Jewish influence and those musical genres—especially jazz and swing—which he clearly detested. But as this larger excerpt illustrates, Moser's anxieties about the "Jewish-driven" proliferation of foreign music paled in comparison to the much larger structural problems plaguing German society for which Germans alone were responsible and whose successful resolution would expunge all of Germany's other perceived ills. In other words, unlike musicologists such as Heinrich Blessinger and Herbert Gerigk for whom the "Jewish question" remained the primary threat and one to which all others must be subordinated, in Moser's hands Jewish influence remained a secondary concern. It is a reminder of the need to speak in the plural of *anti-Semitisms* not only during the Weimar Republic but the Third Reich itself for, as we will see below, Moser's antipathy for foreign, modern "Jewish" music of the present coexisted alongside considerable respect for the Jewish composers of Germany's past.[49]

Some of his early scholarship indicates that Moser found himself in broad agreement with the views of Ruah outlined at the beginning of this chapter and held the best of German music—above all, Beethoven—as belonging to all of humanity and viewed the composer himself as a "citizen of the world" (*Weltbürger*).[50] Such perspectives were strongly rebuked by cultural nationalists like Wilibald Nagel who responded

> his eighteenth-century world gushed about a "world citizenry." But as with so many other resurrected concepts, that by no means suggests that Beethoven is a "citizen of the world" as the term is understood today. He remains a German full of joy in his heritage which he serves will all his gifts and yearns to conquer the world with his works.[51]

Moser's views on the cosmopolitan foundations of German music would be elaborated further in his 1923 *Geschichte der deutschen Musik*, which reveals some important insights surrounding the musicologist's views on the relationship between nationalism and internationalism in art. In this work, Moser underscored the mutual exchange that undergirded the development of Gregorian chant, on the one hand, and Germany's modern musical tradition, on the other.[52] In his analysis of the rise of German Baroque music, Moser claimed it took "the arrival of the (*ausschwingende*) old classical style from Italy (Carissimi, Legrenzi, Steffani, Veracini, Corelli, Albinoni) for the great masters Bach and Händel to be able to develop as they did."[53] Though acknowledging the Italian influence and largely positive regarding its long-term impact on German musical development, Moser himself rather despaired at its short-term effects, for "unfortunately, rather than [the music of Bach and Händel] resulting in an abundance of inner self-cultivation, Germany experienced the most thoroughgoing overexposure to foreignness through Italian art"; a dependence revealed in subsequent German composers' sojourns to Italy.[54] In the final analysis, Moser was ambivalent on the Italian influence on German music, for while it unquestionably perpetuated Germans' continued work in "monuments of fashionable weakness, it also contributed to the urges for the unilateral nature of its own *völkisch* style in the beautifully drawn textural form and lyricism [inherited from] the Italians."[55]

For some, Moser's emphasis on the foreign influences in German music went too far, which is perhaps what prompted the appearance one year later of an essay entitled "On the Particularity of German Musical Gifts" (*Über die Eigentümlichkeit der deutschen Musikbegabung*) in which he endeavored to lay out the "positive special features" of German music.[56] In this work, Moser offered an early hint of the opportunism that clearly emerges in his later professional appointments following the outbreak of the Second World War. In this apologia of sorts, Moser continued to hew closely to the international model, which formed the basis of his earlier monograph, insisting that his task to uncover particular German musical aptitudes was treacherous and that "if one artistically compares the three great speaking regions of Germany, France and Italy with one another, it is important to add that it does not submit to making up a simple clear cut list of qualities or neat oppositions which are mutually exclusive or amount to straightforward divisions, but rather [presents] a rather arbitrary picture," where one could just as easily find "certain commonalties between two against the other" as one could between each individually.[57] In his overall findings—which did indeed resort to vague characterizations and gross generalizations of each musical tradition—Moser pleaded that "one should not see such confrontations as the result of a glossing over of national [styles] and vanity, but rather only as a serious effort towards distinguishing the important essences and natures of three artistically rich peoples."[58]

And yet despite his various references in this and other essays to the interconnectedness of art music and mutual indebtedness nations owed to each other in fostering its growth, Moser did not end with a clarion call to internationalism in music, about which "almost everything (and nearly more than that)" had been said before.[59] With this essay, his goal had simply been to show that "art is the most national outgrowth of the nation" (*Das Völkischste am Volkstum ist die Kunst*).[60] This is certainly not the only instance of Moser's nationalism, the evidence for which one finds scattered throughout the pages of his professional and personal correspondence. It is a nationalism perhaps best reflected in a short piece entitled *Ten Commandments* published in a 1927 edition of the *Arionenzeitung*, which celebrated the transformative power of polyphony and the lied and called on Germans to "ward off the kitsch and trash of the foreign arias and big-city hits."[61] Yet, when we view nationalist pronouncements like these alongside Moser's wider attitudes toward subjects like censorship and the relationship between politics and music, a more complex picture emerges. In an essay that appeared in a 1929 issue of the *Deutsches Volksturm*, for example, Moser professed that despite his self-image as a "quasi-conservative," he deeply believed in the need for a separation between art and politics and regarded spiritual freedom as the most important precondition for a healthy national culture.[62] He frowned upon the appropriation of composers from the German past by singling out the cultivation of Wagner in right-wing political circles with particular scorn. Indeed as we will see in the next chapter, Moser would engage in heated debates with fellow conservatives about the place of Wagner in German society over the course of the 1920s and 1930s.[63]

After 1933, Moser found himself on somewhat shaky ground as Nazi ideologues reexamined not only his academic writings but his pedagogy during Weimar. Among several cultural sins, perhaps the most damning was Moser's collaboration with the Jewish pedagogue Leo Kestenberg (1882–1962), an innovative music reformer who named Moser director of the *Berliner Akademie für Kirchen- und Schulmusik* in 1927. A closer look at the circumstances surrounding this appointment reveals the opportunism, which was to prove so characteristic of Moser during the Nazi period, for just five years before his appointment by Kestenberg, Moser railed against "criminal, pedagogical insanity within the Jewish-communist reform schools which now reduces the teacher to a perfect shoe cleaner found on every street corner."[64] In 1931, matters appeared rather differently. In a piece entitled "The Music Teacher as Social Phenomenon," Moser declared that "the music teacher should always be grateful for the opportunity to rub shoulders with such non-experts as there are whose own acquired technical training is foundational ... in the final analysis, the ultimate goal of the music teacher is for the 'creation of a cultivated lay public' [*Aufbau einer musikalischen Laienbildung*]."[65] Moser's professional involvement with Kestenberg and the school reform movement did nothing to help the musicologist's career following the Nazi seizure of power; among the seven exhibits which formed the core of Hans Ziegler's *Entartete Musik* exhibition (see image 12) in Düsseldorf in 1938, was one devoted to Leo Kestenberg and musical education in Germany before 1933.[66]

In terms of his academic publications, Nazi cultural critics, though often freely acknowledging the learnedness of his scholarship, shunned his work and espousal of claims which fit uncomfortably with Nazi ideology, not least his estimation of the important role played by Jewish composers in the course of Germany's musical past. The brief entry for "Jewish Music" in the 1935 edition of his influential *Musik-Lexikon* matter-of-factly recounts the history of music within Jewish life since Biblical times with no anti-Semitic innuendo whatsoever.[67] In his 1938 *Kleine Deutsche Musikgeschichte* (Short History of German Music), Moser claimed that following their emancipation in the early nineteenth century, Jewish artists had finally been able to make their full contribution to German musical life as embodied by the works of Meyerbeer, Mendelssohn, Offenbach, Joachim, Mahler, and Schoenberg, who "through their different natural styles had contributed in many different ways to German musical development. While Meyerbeer and Offenbach have, above all, influenced French music history, Mendelssohn and Joachim were themselves fully connected to German musical life." As regards Mahler and Schoenberg, the latter of whom figured among the

Image 12 Poster for the 1938 *Entartete Musik* Exhibition. Source: Voix Ettouffées, Wikimedia Commons. Image Retrieved from https://commons.wikimedia.org/wiki/File:Entartete_Musik.png.

most radical modernists of the interwar period, Moser insisted that judgment "be left to a later generation to speak."[68] If his emphasis on the transnational foundations of German music had irked Nazi musicologists, for many this kind of pronouncement—as late as 1938, no less—on the contributions of Jewish composers to German musical life proved even more unforgiveable. A scathing 1936 review of the work by A. Krüll merits inclusion here in its entirety:

> The considerable academic output of the well-known author in his three-volume *History of German Music*, which probably owes in no small measure to the

model [set] by Scherer's *History of German Literature* in terms of its inner structure, was at the same time a liability (*Verpflichtung*) for the future work of the author. Every cultural politician should have expected that Moser would have unconditionally started from the results of race and prevailing worldviews in his *Short History of German Music* since this work essentially represents a shortened version of his earlier *History of German Music*. Unfortunately, that is not the case. As much as we recognize through Moser the defense of the unjustified "confiscation" of Germany's musical masters by the deliberately false statements of foreign "researchers"; as much as we appreciate his deftness and value his clarification of hypotheses made by other scholars. Still, all of this cannot mislead us as regards the errors and cultural-political unreliability of his latest work. Our standpoint is that books which intentionally adopt a wide-ranging framework demand absolute musical-political clarity. But what Moser has to say regarding the musical emancipation of the Jews in his *Short History of German Music*—associated with the names Mendelssohn, Meyerbeer, Offenbach, Joachim, Mahler, Schönberg—is forced upon the reader and completely falls outside the boundaries of our worldview. With his inclusion of the word "German" in the title of the book comes a certain obligation. Here, every attempt to speak out for the representatives of Jewish emancipation of the nineteenth-century based on favorable remarks or personal relationships of German musicians to them must implode; just as it should not be forgotten that there are just as many voices against the decomposition of the Jewish spirit in art from the mouths of the foremost musicians of the nineteenth-century. Whoever writes a "Short History of German Music" must inevitably eliminate the Jews from his explanation.[69]

This was not the first time that Moser's scholarship had come under the scrutiny of the *Westdeutscher Beobachter* for its political unsuitability, nor would it be the last. One year later, another scathing review of the book appeared, this time directly linked with Moser's favorable judgments regarding Mendelssohn's original score for a *Midsummer Night's Dream*:

> The discussion of the Jews in this book reflects a hopeless feeble endeavor which tends towards the negative side of recent book publications in engaging in private music politics. Every cultural politician has the right to expect Moser to accept unconditionally modern racial ideology ... our motto for books destined to be read by a large public can only be absolute musical political reliability.[70]

Finally, the fact that Moser continued to write glowing obituaries for recently deceased Jewish composers such as Max Friedländer (1855–1933) and Arnold Mendelssohn (1852–1934) well after the Nazi seizure of power gave Party ideologues still more ammunition in their efforts to marginalize him.[71]

As these reviews and others make clear, by 1938 Moser had made a number of enemies both within the musicological establishment and without, a fact that goes far toward explaining how, in 1940, he found himself wrongly included in the notorious *Lexikon der Juden in der Musik*, a compilation of names of Jewish musicians, composers, and those otherwise involved in musical affairs published by Alfred Rosenberg's Music Bureau under the direction of the musicologist Herbert Gerigk.[72] Moser's erroneous inclusion owed at least as much to the methods employed by Gerigk as it did to the enemies Moser made during the Weimar period and early years of Nazi rule. In assembling the text, Gerigk relied not only on the cultural-political archive at Rosenberg's Bureau but also on the knowledge of several musicologists with whom he was in close contact, including Karl Blessinger, Erich Schenk, Robert Lach, and others. Rumors surrounding Moser's Jewishness had been in circulation since early 1933 and it is likely that it was through informal discussions with other scholars, rather than by way of the cultural-political archive, that Moser unenviably found himself included in the *Lexikon*.[73] This possibility becomes more convincing when we consider the strained relationship between Moser and Gerigk, the latter of whom had sharply criticized Moser's work in both his personal and public correspondence.[74]

Nevertheless, despite his sustained positive statements about the influence of Jewish composers on German musical life and sometimes contradictory views regarding the national versus international, not to mention the scathing reviews, personal attacks, and continuous infighting with well-positioned Nazi functionaries, it would be wrong to mistake Moser for a victim of the Third Reich. Indeed, an examination of his behavior during the Nazi period—particularly following the outbreak of war in 1939—reveals that he played a central role in legitimating key Nazi foreign and cultural policies. Nowhere is this more in evidence than in his interest and participation in musicological projects under the supervision of the SS, above all as part of Heinrich Himmler's special projects wing *Ahnenerbe*[75]—devoted to researching the cultural and anthropological history of the "Aryan race"—and as a regular contributor to the SS periodical *Germanien*.[76] As for the term *Jewish Music* within the second edition of his *Musik-Lexikon*, gone was the measured, value-neutral summary found in the first edition. Instead, Moser left the original passage unchanged while attaching the following screed onto the end of the entry:

> As everywhere else, so too has Jewry pressed forward in the area of music within Europe and the USA, only with particular vigor; its followers have understood to bring their own publishers, agents and journalists to nearly all the leading posts and thereby sought to impose their taste on the host peoples. We need not

deny that certain among them have achieved distinction through assimilation and talent, particularly as performers [*Reproduzierende*]. Still, if since 1933 they have been pushed out of our cultural life, they have to thank the righteous self-defense of Aryanism against the spiritual as well as economic tyranny which Jewry has imposed upon us.[77]

Conclusion

As is the case with so many binaries, the boundaries separating the "national" from the "international" and its advocates in music were far more porous than scholars have often let on. In addition, in the hands of the hyper-nationalist National Socialists, the virtues of even the most committed nationalist could not save him from a fate demanded by the exigencies of racial purity. Robert Hernried, a culturally conservative composer who defended Germany's musical tradition in stridently nationalist essays over the course of the Weimar Republic as a regular contributor to the conservative *Zeitschrift für Musik*, received the following praise in 1933 on the occasion of his fiftieth birthday and to celebrate his tenure as the oldest serving music theory and composition teacher at the *Akademie für Kirchen- und Schulmusik* in Berlin:

> As a music pedagogue he always fought against the decaying influences of atonalism and jazz; as a composer and in his work in music theory he supported the healthy development of German art music and explored and published unknown details and letters of Wagner, Brahms, Cornelius, Hugo Wolf and Hermann Goetz. His name has thereby won approval across broad circles.[78]

Hernried was a model conservative nationalist—"a reliable man, the picture of youth, German through and through, Protestant and a veteran of the First World War."[79] There was only one problem; in addition to all of these things, Hernried was also a converted Jew as would be defined by the Nuremberg Laws in 1935. Following this revelation, he immediately left Germany, first for Vienna and later the United States.

He was hardly alone. The life of the great Mozart biographer Alfred Einstein reads almost identically with that of his contemporary Hans Joachim Moser. Editor of the *Zeitschrift für Musikwissenschaft* since 1919 and an early music devotee who, like Moser, had written pioneering studies of Schütz and Gluck, Einstein also carried out the first major revision of the Mozart Köchel catalogue in 1936.[80] Einstein himself had maintained a friendly correspondence with Moser since the First World War, when the young Moser reached out in a letter to Einstein from the front to offer praise over the musicologist's work in early music that was proving foundational to Moser's planned *History of German Music*, which appeared during the 1920s.[81] Though the two later came to tensions over Moser's planned *Musiklexikon*, a book that threatened to compete with Hugo Riemann's classic work in the genre whose 1929 eleventh edition was edited by Einstein, both scholars were able to smooth things over in a series of letters in 1932.[82] Whatever Einstein's squabbles with other members of the German musicological establishment, his forced emigration in 1933 did nothing to diminish a cultural conservatism that shone through in his own music survey *Geschichte der Musik*, the English translation of which appeared in 1937. Reflecting upon the place of culture in Beethoven and Schubert's Vienna with his own in US exile, Einstein wrote,

> [There] never was an age when art was more isolated, more completely divorced from life ... or [there] so wide a gulf as between the art of our real artists and that abominable substitute for popular music which is eagerly gulped down by the masses in the musical comedy theaters or absorbed by the aid of the radio and the phonograph.[83]

"International" music was "violent" and filled with "hatred of everything that was conventional in method, expression or feeling."[84] He deemed jazz "orgiastic" and "the most abominable treason against all the music of Western civilization," as well as those classical composers who sought to incorporate it into their music. Stravinsky's music was described as "barbarism, triviality and mechanism," while Schoenberg's compositions, in addition to sharing Stravinsky's barbarism, were characterized by "sheer vulgarity."[85] Contemporary reviewers, while recognizing the learnedness of Einstein's scholarship, duly noted Einstein's overwhelming emphasis on the German masters at the expense of non-German ones.[86]

Yet 1933 marked a fundamental break in the careers of Moser and Einstein, whose scholarly interests and cultural outlooks had been so similar up to that point. For just as a commitment to musical nationalism could not safeguard against persecution by the Nazis after 1933, recognition of Germanness in music as based on its interaction with and interdependency on foreign models did not foreclose on taking advantage of the research opportunities, which opened up within the occupied territories following Nazism's initial military successes. While the Jewish Einstein was never able to secure a professorship in Germany during Weimar and was eventually forced into exile in the United States, Moser quickly recognized that his long-standing interest in and recognition of the mutual exchanges and influences between Germany and its neighboring countries lent itself well to opportunities, which opened up in the wake of Germany's early military conquests in the West in 1940. His early contributions to Nazi organs focused on military music, folk songs, and the like, and in April 1940, following on the heels of the Nazi occupation of Denmark, Moser sent the following letter to the editor of *Germanien* J. O. Plassman: "*Would you rather have in the meantime a more politically topical essay on the Flemish-Dutch-German musical connection? Also one on the musical culture-bridge to Scandinavia would certainly be feasible.*"[87] This interest in the history of German folk music throughout Europe reveals itself in another letter one year later devoted to "musical-cultural Eastern questions" to one of his superiors in which Moser indicated his wish "to pursue the emigration of the German folk song [*Volksliedwanderung*] from inner Germany to upper Hungary and Siebenbürgen."[88] The opportunity to pursue this line of research had for decades proved impossible, according to Moser, due to the fact that this part of Europe had been hitherto dominated by Poles on the one hand and Viennese Jews on the other (he singles out Guido Adler and Eduard Hanslick, in particular). With the German conquest of Poland and Czechoslovakia in 1940, Moser saw the perfect opportunity to uncover the roots of German musical influences and expressed his desire "to introduce a suggestion for the expansion of [research] on the entire German East."[89]

After the war, Moser himself was well aware of his own mixed record up to 1938. Because of his position as a leading musicologist in the *Ahnenerbe*, Moser was quickly brought to the attention of de-Nazification authorities and subsequently blacklisted. He would only be rehabilitated in February 1949—well after other musicologists like Friedrich Blume, Eugen Bieder, Fritz Stein, and Wolfgang Boetticher who had proven no less zealous in their efforts to enlist their scholarship in the service of the regime.[90] His reputation within the musicological community, particularly among the German émigré cohort, had likewise largely been left in ruin. In a December 1948 letter, the American violinist Julius Gold related to Moser the attitude of Curt Sachs, a German-Jewish musicologist who emigrated to the United States in 1933 following his dismissal from the *Akademie für Kirchen- und Schulemusik* on racial grounds: "His letter [to me] was strong with insulting remarks! You are made out to be a terrible ogre and a hateful enemy of Jews, a *Judenhetzer*."[91] In his response, Moser—like so many Germans—viewed himself as a consummate victim whose suffering had been every bit as great as that of his former Jewish colleagues. In addition to having lost a son to the Wehrmacht, Moser recalled the fact that he was pensioned off in 1933 on political grounds as well as the rumors surrounding his Jewishness that circulated up to the outbreak of war. As far as his more dubious record—particularly between the years 1939 and 1945 which, in the letter, go wholly unmentioned—Moser recalled the conductor Wilhelm Fürtwangler's well-known canard: "Whoever was not himself in Germany back then, cannot hope to get a clear picture of how things were."[92]

Still, it is precisely because of the capricious and at times contradictory ways in which Moser's thought developed over the period 1923–1945 that he could feign such victimhood in the first place. First, his view of Germanness in music and its interdependence on foreign models could be mistaken for the attitudes of an unrepentant cosmopolitan and, indeed, as threatening to undermine the very project of uncovering Germanness in music itself. Second, an examination of Moser's outlook on Jewishness illustrates the need to consider his anti-Semitism during Weimar in more nuanced fashion, which sometimes resembled the venomous kind practiced by the Nazis but more often took on a more complex appearance. In Moser's case, we find, on the one hand, a scholar in full agreement with a large cohort of voices detecting "the Jewish menace" behind jazz, modern music, and other foreign-derived idioms but who, on the other hand, maintained the supreme contributions of traditional Jewish composers to German musical life not only over the course of the Weimar Republic but well into the Third Reich itself. Finally, Moser's nationalism was not of a piece with the hyper-nationalist, populist variety practiced by the Nazis but rather looked backward to the imperial Reich as evidenced by his membership, from 1932, in the *Stahlhelm* and *Deutschnationale Volkspartei* (DNVP).[93] This, of course, by no means had the effect of making him a believer in Weimar democracy, nor did it exempt him from holding certain anti-Semitic prejudices. As this chapter has shown, these were attitudes that, though they at times brought Moser into confrontation with leading Nazi cultural authorities, could be reconciled to fit the changing circumstances in which the musicologist found himself following the establishment of the Nazi dictatorship. That dictatorship, moreover, did not envision an autarkic cultural future with works produced solely for Germans, by Germans. Rather, as Benjamin Martin has recently shown, Nazi cultural authorities saw it as their mission not only to preserve German institutions and German art, but also to create a postwar transnational cultural order where a new "European culture" could be forged under German leadership.[94]

In the final analysis, then, Moser less resembles an ideological "old fighter" in the mold of a Himmler or Goebbels than a kind of cultural "free agent" ready to contract his services out to the highest bidder. Like his contemporary Heinrich Müller, who faithfully served the Weimar state in smashing the radical left *and* right long before his better-known role as Gestapo Chief under Hitler, Moser's chameleon-like capacity to serve multiple and often contradictory causes over the course of his career more closely resembles the working methods of an opportunist, not an ideologue.[95] If his unquestioned and enthusiastic participation in Nazi musicological projects cannot, as this chapter has tried to suggest, be said to have stemmed from sincere ideological convictions on Moser's part, how can we explain it? In the end, there is no reason to disbelieve the true motive lurking behind Moser's collaboration with Nazism, the rationale for which Moser himself later provided: "So there I stood in 1935; two times married and, along with my present family, ostracized from all official functions within the 'totalitarian state.'"[96] In the end, for Moser the need to financially support his family coupled with the lure of financial reward and promotion proved, as with so many in the academy, too great to resist.

Notes

1. H. Ruah, "Einiges über 'nationale' und 'internationale' Musik," *Die Tonkunst*, 27 (9) (1915): 327–328.
2. Ibid., 328.
3. Wilibald Nagel, "Kosmopolitische oder nationale Musik?" *Neue Musik Zeitung*, 36 (17) (1915): 197–201.
4. Ibid., 198.
5. Ibid., 197–199.
6. Ibid., 201.
7. Ruah, "Einiges über 'nationale' und 'internationale' Musik," 327–328 (emphasis in the original).
8. Ibid., 328.
9. Donald Tovey, "German Music," in *German Culture: The Contribution of the Germans to Knowledge, Literature, Art and Life* (New York: Scribner's Sons, 1915), 239–240.
10. On these and other rightist political organizations, see Geoff Eley, *Reshaping the German Right: Radical Nationalism and Political Change after Bismarck* (Ann Arbor: University of Michigan Press, 1991).
11. Helmut Walser Smith, *The Continuities of German History: Nation, Religion and Race across the Long Nineteenth Century* (Cambridge: Cambridge University Press, 2002), 4.
12. On German political nationalism, see Rogers Brubaker, *Citizenship and Nationhood in France and Germany* (Cambridge: Harvard University Press, 1992).

13 See, for example, Daniel Laqua, ed., *Internationalism Reconfigured: Transnational Ideas and Movements between the World Wars* (London: IB Tauris, 2011); Carol Fink, *Defending the Rights of Others: The Great Powers, the Jews and International Minority Protection, 1878–1938* (New York: Cambridge University Press, 2004).
14 Philip Hart, *Orpheus in the New World: The Symphony Orchestra as an American Cultural Institution* (New York: Norton, 1973).
15 Jessica Gienow-Hecht, "Trumpeting down the Walls of Jericho: The Politics of Art, Music and Emotion in German-American Relations, 1870–1920," *Journal of Social History*, 36 (3) (2003): 585–613.
16 Hermann Kretzschmar, "Öffentliche Musikpflege in Deutschland," in *Über den Stand der öffentlichen Musikpflege in Deutschland* (Leipzig: Breitkopf & Härtel, 1881), 212. The "political mishap" is an oblique reference to Germany's failed efforts at unification until 1870.
17 Joseph Horowitz, *Classical Music in America: A History of Its Rise and Fall* (New York: Norton, 2005), 267.
18 Edmund Bowles, "Karl Muck and His Compatriots: German Conductors in America during World War I (and How They Coped)," *American Music*, 25 (4) (2007): 405–440.
19 Robert Hernried, "Nationale Musik," *Zeitschrift für Musik*, 88 (17) (1921): 447–448.
20 Ibid., 448 (emphasis in the original).
21 Hugo Riemann, *Kleines Handbuch der Musikgeschichte mit Periodisierung nach Stilprinizipen und Formen* (Leipzig: Druck und Verlag, 1922), 273.
22 Ibid., 273–274.
23 Paul Bekker, "Nationale und Internationale Musik in Deutschland und Anderswo," *Musikblätter des Anbruch*, 6 (5) (1924): 173–177.
24 Ibid., 174–175.
25 Alfred Heuss, "Weltbürgertum und Internationalität in der Tonkunst," *Zeitschrift für Musik*, 89 (12) (1922): 113–115.
26 Ibid., 114.
27 Peter Franklin, "Audiences, Critics and the Depurification of Music: Reflections on a 1920s Controversy," *Journal of the Royal Music Association*, 114 (1) (1989): 80–91 (here 85).
28 For an extended discussion on this aspect of critical reception of Beethoven, see Scott Burnham, *Beethoven Hero* (Princeton: Princeton University Press, 2000).
29 Martin Friedland, "National—Uebernational—International?," *Allgemeine Musik Zeitung*, 49 (1922): 351–355.
30 Ibid., 352 (emphasis in the original).
31 Memo Schachiner, *Politik und Systematik: Wiener Musikwissenschaft im Wandel der Zeiten—Die Ära Guido Adler (1898–1927)* (Vienna: MC Publishing, 2008).
32 Guido Adler, "Internationalism in Music," *The Musical Times*, 11 (2) (1925): 281–300.

33 Pamela Potter, *Most German of the Arts: Musicology and Society from the Weimar Republic to the End of Hitler's Reich* (New Haven: Yale University Press, 1998), 200–234.
34 Alfred Heuss, "Händel und Bach als zwei Seiten deutschen Wesens," *Zeitschrift für Musik*, 101 (5) (1934): 489–494.
35 Ibid., 489–490.
36 See Potter's brief account of Moser's findings in Potter, *Most German of the Arts*, 206–208.
37 Bekker, "Nationale und Internationale Musik in Deutschland und Anderswo," 174.
38 Bernd Sponheuer, "Reconstructing Ideal Types of the 'German' in Music," in *Music and German National Identity*, ed. Celia Applegate and Pamela Potter (Chicago: University of Chicago Press, 2002), 36–58.
39 Hans Joachim Moser, Lebenslauf, Nachlass: 31/K.5.
40 Pamela Potter was among the first to look extensively at Moser's personal papers, housed at the Staatsbibliothek in Berlin, in her book *Most German of the Arts*.
41 Erik Levi, *Music in the Third Reich* (London: Macmillan, 1994), 64, 5.
42 Potter, *Most German of the Arts*, 2.
43 Erik Levi, *Mozart and the Nazis: How the Third Reich Abused a Cultural Icon* (New Haven: Yale University Press, 2011), 84–85.
44 Late- or even non-membership in the Nazi Party does not always serve as a good predictor for individual behavior during the Third Reich. The musicologist Friedrich Blume, for example, never joined the Party yet went to great lengths to ingratiate himself within the Nazi musicological establishment. Still this fact, taken together with other evidence, is an important one to consider when measuring Moser's enthusiasm for Nazi ideology.
45 See Dagmar Droysen-Reber's entry "Hans Joachim Moser," in *Allgemeine Deutsche Biographie* (Bd. 18) (Berlin: Duncker & Humblot, 1997), 191–193.
46 See, for example, Potter, *Most German of the Arts*; Jost Hermand, *Culture in Dark Times: Nazi Fascism, Inner Emigration, and Exile* (New York: Berghahn Books, 2012), 72.
47 Hans Joachim Moser, *Geschichte der deutschen Musik* (Stuttgart: J.G. Cotta'sche, 1926) (vol. 3), 497–502.
48 Ibid., 502.
49 Claudia Koonz, *The Nazi Conscience* (Cambridge: Harvard University Press, 2005).
50 Hans Joachim Moser, "Beethoven und die Zeitstile," *Neue Musik-Zeitung*, 42 (6) (1921): 89–91.
51 Wilibald Nagel, "Der Beethoven-Kult der Zukunft," *Neue Musik-Zeitung*, 42 (6) (1921): 96–99 (here 99).
52 Moser, *Geschichte der deutschen Musik*. Cited in Potter, Most German of the Arts, ff. 27, p. 324.
53 Hans Joachim Moser, *Geschichte der deutschen Musik: vom Auftreten Beethovens bis zur Gegenwart* (drei Bänden) (2nd ed.) (Berlin: J.S. Cotta, 1928, 481).

54 Here, Moser includes the early classicists "Haffe, J.C. Bach, Schwanenberg and classicists Graun, the young Gluck, the young Mozart as well as composers from the Romantic period, such as Mendelssohn and Nicolai." See Ibid., 482.
55 Ibid., 482.
56 Hans Joachim Moser, "Über die Eigentümlichkeit der deutschen Musikbegabung," in *Jahrbuch der Musikbibliothek Peters für 1924*, ed. Rudolf Schwartz (Leipzig: C.F. Peters, 1925), 35–45.
57 Ibid., 37.
58 Ibid., 45.
59 A reference to the musicologist Guido Adler's keynote lecture "Internationalismus in der Tonkunst" given at the 1924 Kongress-Bericht in Basel, the English translation of which appeared one year later in the journal *Musical Times* (see below).
60 Ibid., 45.
61 Hans Joachim Moser, "Zehn Gebote," in *Abhandlungen*. Nachlass 31/285.
62 Hans Joachim Moser, "Zensur und Geistesfreiheit," in *Abhandlungen*, 1929. Nachlass: 31/285.
63 See Hans Rudolf Vaget, "Hitler's Wagner: Musical Discourse as Cultural Space," in *Music and Nazism: Art Under Tyranny, 1933–1945*, ed. Michael Kater (Laaber: Laaber Verlag, 2004), 15–31.
64 Ulrich Günther, "Opportunisten? Zur Biograhie führender Musikpädagogen in Zeiten politischer Umbrüche," in *Musikalische Erfahrung: Wahrnehem, Erkennen, Aneignen*, ed. Hermann J. Kaiser *(Band 13)* (Essen: Verlag die Blaue Eule, 1992), 267–285.
65 Ibid., 276.
66 For a discussion of the debates and figures who loomed large over the exhibition itself, see Albrecht Dümling, "The Target of Racial Purity: The 'Degenerate Music' Exhibition in Düsseldorf, 1938," in *Art, Culture and Media under the Third Reich*, ed. Richard Etlin (Chicago: University of Chicago Press, 2002), 43–72.
67 Hans Joachim Moser, *Musik-Lexikon* (1st Aufl.) (Berlin-Schöneberg, 1935). As we will see below, this would change in the second edition from 1942.
68 Hans Joachim Moser, *Kleine deutsche Musikgeschichte* (Stuttgart: Verlag J.G. Cottasche, 1949), 241–242.
69 A. Krüll, "*Private Musikpolitik in Westdeutscher Beobachter, 1936*," in *Musik im Dritten Reich: Eine Dokumentation*, ed. Josef Wulf (Sigbert Mohn Verlag, 1963), 324. Even more problematic was that this did not mark the first time that Moser had drawn attention to the musicality of Jewish composers. The Jewish-German composer Heinrich Kaminksi (1886–1946), who after the Nuremberg Laws of 1935 found himself categorized as a *Mischling*, first of the first degree (1938) and later the second degree (1941), but who managed to survive the war, had earlier earned Moser's praise in a 1929 article for the *Zeitschrift für Musik*. See Hans Joachim Moser, "Heinrich Kaminski," *Zeitschrift für Musik*, 96 (10) (1929): 601–607.

70 Quoted in Levi, *Music in the Third Reich*, 62–63.
71 Hans Joachim Moser, "Arnold Mendelssohn," *Monatsschrift für Gottesdienst und kirkliche Kunst*, 15 (1933) and "Max Friedlaender," *Gesellschaft für deutsches Altertum*, 16 (1934): Nachlass 31/286.
72 Herbert Gerigk and Theophil Stengel, eds., *Lexikon der Juden in der Musik. Veröffentlichungen des Instituts der NSDAP zur Erforschung der Judenfrage*, no. 2. (Berlin: Hahnefeld, 1940).
73 See, for example, Pretzch's letter to the Reichpressestelle der NSDAP on February 15, 1933, which reads, "Was die Bevorzugung H.J. Moses als Quelle durch Eichenauer anlangt, so bemerke ich noch, dass der Nachweis von Mosers juedischer Abstammung immer schluessiger wird, und zwar nach der Seite der Mutter Mosers hin, die eine geborene Elcho war und im Aussehen als vollkommene Rassejuedin geschildert wird. Ich bin noch dabei, weitere Belege dafuer zu beschaffen. Heil Hitler! Pretzsch" in Josef Wulf, *Musik im Dritten Reich: Eine Dokumentation* (Sigbert Mohn Verlag, 1963), 431, 434.
74 In this, Moser was not alone as several other individuals found themselves wrongfully included in the *Lexikon* both as a result of willful distortion and unintended errors. Because most of Gerigk's files were destroyed in Allied air attacks it is not always easy to determine how individuals made their way into the Lexikon. For more on Moser and the history of the *Lexikon*, see Eva Weissweiler, *Ausgemerzt! Das Lexikon der Juden in der Musik und seine mörderischen Folgen* (Köln: Dittrich-Verlag, 1999), 42, 53, 57.
75 For more on Himmler's efforts in the occult, anthropology and prehistory of the "Aryan" race to whose study Ahnenerbe's special projects division was geared, see Peter Longerich, *Heinrich Himmler: A Life* (New York: Oxford University Press, 2012), 275–279.
76 See Pamela Potter, "Did Himmler Really Like Gregorian Chant? The SS and Musicology," *Modernism/Modernity*, 2 (3) (1995): 45–68 and Potter, *Most German of the Arts*, 135–136, 160–161.
77 Hans Joachim Moser, *Musik-Lexikon* (2nd Aufl) (Berlin: Hesse, 1942).
78 "Personalien," *Die Musik*, 26 (1) (1933): 79–80. Examples of Hernried's strident criticism against modern and foreign music include Robert Hernried, "Internationale Musiktage in Ludwigshafen," *Zeitschrfit für Musik*, 90 (3) (1923): 80–82, "Musikpädagogische Tagung in Frankfurt a.M.," *Zeitschrift für Musik*, 94 (*10*) (1927): 561–563, and "Frontalangriff gegen die Kulturorchester und Theaterplanwirtschaft durch Notverordnung?" *Zeitschrift für Musik*, 98 (10) (1931): 863–866. In 1931, Hernried's fairly regular contributions to the *Zeitschrift* suddenly stopped.
79 Fred Prieberg, *Musik im NS-Staat* (Frankfurt: Fischer Verlag, 1982), 56.
80 Alfred Einstein, *Heinrich Schütz* (Kassel: Bärenreiter, 1928) and Alfred Einstein, *Gluck: Sein Leben, seine Werke* (Basel: Bärenreiter, 1936).

81 Hans Joachim Moser to Alfred Heuss, May 10, 1918, Box 6 Folder 659, Alfred Einstein Papers 1835–1985, Jean Hargrove Music Library, University of California, Berkeley.
82 On this exchange, see Hans Joachim Moser to Alfred Heuss, July 23, 1932, and Alfred Einstein to Hans Joachim Moser, July 26, 1932, Box 6 Folder 659, Alfred Einstein Papers 1835–1985, Jean Hargrove Music Library, University of California, Berkeley.
83 Alfred Einstein, *A Short History of Music* (New York: Knopf, 1937), 244–245.
84 Ibid., 248.
85 Ibid., 250–251.
86 See, for example, E. J. D., "A Short History of Music by Alfred Einstein," *Music & Letters*, 18 (2) (1937): 185–189 and H. G., "A Short History of Music by Alfred Einstein," *The Musical Times*, 78 (1128) (1937): 134.
87 Quoted in Potter, *Most German of the Arts*, 136 (emphasis in the original).
88 Hans Joachim Moser an M. Leiter, "Betr. Musikkulturelle Ostfragen," Berlin, March 21, 1941 (2 pgs.) Nachlass: 31/K.1.
89 Ibid., 2.
90 Blume and Boetticher in particular sought vigorously to establish the importance of race as a factor in music and published a number of articles suggesting how this might be established within the parameters of the accepted methodologies of German musicology, though interestingly in Blume's case, the word "Jude" is not mentioned even a single time. See Friedrich Blume, "Musik und Rasse: Grundfragen einer musikalischen Rassenforschung," *Die Musik*, 30 (11) (1938): 736–748 and Wolfgang Boetticher, "Zur Erkenntnis von Rasse und Volkstum," in *Musik im Volk: Grundfragen der Musikerziehung* (Berlin: W. Stumme, 1939), 217–229.
91 Hans Joachim Moser, "Letter to Curt Sachs," December 25, 1948. Nachlass: 31/K.5, 1–8.
92 Ibid., 2.
93 Hans Joachim Moser, "Anlage zur Eingabe Prof. Moser." Nachlass 31/K.5. In the same file, Moser also claims to have had close contact with several conservative monarchists who took part in the 1944 assassination attempt on Hitler, including Ulrich von Hassell, Friedrich von Rabenau, and Ernst von Harnack.
94 Benjamin Martin, *The Nazi-Fascist New Order for European Culture* (Cambridge: Harvard University Press, 2016).
95 Mark Roseman, *The Villa, The Lake, The Meeting: Wannsee and the Final Solution* (New York: The Penguin Press, 2002), 90.
96 Hans Joachim Moser, "Letter to Curt Sachs," December 25, 1948. Nachlass: 31/K.5, 1–8.

4

Wagner under Weimar

"The great protagonists are those who fight for their ideas and ideals despite the fact that they receive no recognition at the hands of their contemporaries. They are men whose memories will be enshrined in the hearts of the future generations … beside Frederick the Great we have such men as Martin Luther and Richard Wagner." Hitler wrote these words while imprisoned in Landsberg following the failed putsch attempt of 1923. That Hitler would name Wagner alongside Frederick the Great, whose portrait was among the small number of possessions the dictator deemed important enough to bring with him to his bunker in the waning days of the war, says something about the high regard Hitler had for the composer. Hitler's notorious love for Wagner and his music has done much to cement the relationship between the composer and Nazism down to the present day. One historian has described the entire Nazi project as little more than the application of Wagnerian aesthetics to the whole of German social and political life, while for an older generation of scholars, the axis of Germany's "special path" (*Sonderweg*) to National Socialism ran from Luther to Hitler via Wagner.[1] In a telling example, the eminent historian Gordon Craig, reflecting on his course of study at Princeton in the 1930s, recalled an undergraduate class on Wagner as little more than "an exercise in nationalism and Nazi propaganda."[2]

This chapter examines Wagner reception during Weimar and reveals the ways in which our close association of the composer with Nazi ideology was, in some ways, among Nazism's greatest propaganda success stories. To be sure, Bayreuth had its share of fervent Nazi supporters, above all Houston Stewart Chamberlain and Winifred Wagner who, next to Hitler, are chiefly responsible for the connection between Wagner and Nazism. Yet for much of the Weimar Republic, Bayreuth was under the supervision of the composer's son Siegfried Wagner, who tried to steer a middle course between retaining Bayreuth's right-leaning Wagnerians without alienating the considerable number of international supporters upon whom the festival counted for artistic and financial support.

Siegfried, like many artists and musicians of the interwar period, was likewise wary of the intrusion of politics into art, and an examination of conservative responses to Wagner's operas both inside and outside of Bayreuth suggests a need to reexamine the nature of the composer's relationship to German politics during Weimar. If limitations attending to the Wagner-Hitler connection can be found even at Bayreuth, this was even truer of a wider world populated by Wagnerians of every stripe. I argue that Wagnerians in Weimar Germany held a diverse set of political and social views that deviated from Nazi ideology in important ways and that their shared worship of the composer should not distract from their wider ideological commitments, sense of Wagner's place in interwar culture, and his music's proper role in postwar German society.

Before turning to Wagner's reception during Weimar, it is worth briefly revisiting Wagner's relationship to Nazism and the transformation of the sleepy town of Bayreuth, Germany, into a haven for nationalist Wagner worship during the late nineteenth century. The historian does not have to look far in determining how so many have come around to the notion that "Richard Wagner composed the score for the Third Reich."[3] First, the composer's own voluminous writings provide an almost limitless well of material from which scholars have drawn in identifying parallels between the composer's worldview and later Nazi ideals. The composer was, of course, far from the only cultural figure who the Nazis remade in their own image—as one historian has recently shown, Goethe, Nietzsche, Dürer, and countless other German icons were retrofitted with Nazi ideals and sympathies to varying degrees from the middle years of the Weimar Republic to the end of Hitler's Reich.[4] However, the Nazi appropriation of most of these figures depended in large measure upon manipulating the written record and wrenching ideas out of historical context. The ideas of a Nietzsche, for example, whose concepts of the "will to power" and the "superman" might seem to anticipate Nazi ideology in certain respects, owed far more to the obscene oversimplification of the philosopher's ideas by his deeply anti-Semitic sister Elizabeth Förster and the Nazi philosopher Alfred Bäumler than a close reading of *The Will to Power, Thus Spoke Zarathustra* or any of Nietzsche's own writings would merit.[5] Wagner, for his part, was far from lacking in propagandists of his own, and the circle of admirers gathered together at Bayreuth were decisive in shaping our association between Wagner and Nazism. The English-born Houston Stewart Chamberlain relocated to Bayreuth in 1909, nearly a decade following the publication of his influential *Foundations of the Nineteenth-Century*—a book that achieved a cult-like status among Pan Germanists, völkisch thinkers, and other groupings of the German political right. Though he died before the Nazi seizure of power in 1933, Chamberlain also greatly admired Hitler and lent the early Nazi movement crucial legitimacy. Winifred Wagner, who married the composer's son Siegfried in 1915, had a warm, personal relationship with Hitler, and after her husband Siegfried's untimely death in 1930, rumors circulated that she and Hitler intended to marry.[6] Undoubtedly, Hitler's promises to act as Bayreuth's cultural and financial benefactor played a role, as did Winifred's rabid nationalism and anti-Semitism. Yet as we will see below, even among members of the Bayreuth Circle there is more to this story than meets the eye.

Wagner's music itself has also played a role in transforming the composer into the proto-fascist bête noire of the German right. Even in the composer's own lifetime, some listeners detected an intoxicating, seductive quality in Wagner unequalled in the Western tradition. Wagnerians found themselves so overwhelmed by the emotional power of the music so as to be virtually hypnotized, causing many former admirers to abandon their zeal for "the Master."[7] This was at least in part the reason behind Nietzsche's falling out with Wagner, which resulted in the former's well-known 1888 anti-Wagner polemic *Der Fall Wagner*. The critical theorist Theodor Adorno detected an authoritarian impulse in Wagner's music beyond the stage characters Mime and Beckmesser that some commentators have viewed as anti-Semitic allegorical stereotypes that Wagner deliberately injected in the operas *Siegfried* and *Die Meistersinger von Nürnberg*. These pernicious qualities in Wagner's music were not limited to vocal works in which texts could be infused with anti-Semitic and nationalistic content; for some observers, Wagner's instrumental writing itself was capable of holding a dark, sinister power over the listener. As Adorno wrote at the end of the Second World War, "a minute musical analysis of Wagner's works yields insight into the repressive, compulsory, blind and ultimately anti-individual way of his composing in a very concrete and tangible sense. His music itself speaks the language of Fascism, quite apart from plots and bombastic words."[8] Indeed, Wagner's *Gesamtkunstwerk* (total artwork) was predicated upon what Adorno perceived to be Wagner's deeply authoritarian control over not only the composition of his works but the circumstances surrounding their proper performance as well.[9] The whole Bayreuth project, where Wagner assumed artistic control over all aspects of his works, from the theater's architectural plans and acoustics to the performers' costumes and the set designs, could be said to be emblematic of this domineering impulse.

Yet Adorno was writing as the rubble was still smoldering and while the scars of the Second World War were still fresh. Next to the music itself, Wagner's relationship to Nazism has centered on the composer's biography and is itself the subject of a vast and contested literature dating back to the 1930s. For Thomas Mann, if it was important to distinguish between Wagner's political thought and his music, this was even truer for any parallels drawn between the composer and Nazi ideology, and the writer deflected attempts to transform Wagner into a proto-Nazi composer.[10] Adorno, on the other hand, detected in Wagner's music a sinister and irrational allure that readily lent itself—indeed prepared the ground for—nationalist instrumentalization and political mobilization.[11] This insight inspired a large number of subsequent studies that mined Wagner's prose and musical works for further evidence in support of Adorno's claim.[12] There can be no question that unlike many other cultural figures onto whom the Nazis projected their own ideology, a large documentary record attests to Wagner's vehement nationalism and anti-Semitism. There is some debate over the source of the composer's anti-Semitism; some scholars have seen it as a by-product of the composer's attraction to radical anti-capitalist politics in the years leading up to the Revolutions of 1848, while others see Wagner's animus toward Meyerbeer, whose operas enjoyed considerably greater public acclaim, as a decisive factor.[13] Whatever the cause, writing in Swiss exile in 1850 Wagner published his notorious polemic *Das Judenthum in der Musik* (Jewishness in Music) in the *Neue Zeitschrift für Musik* under the pen name Freigedank (or "free thinker"). Wagner, of course, did not invent anti-Semitism, nor was he particularly unique in harboring anti-Semitic prejudices. However, unlike many of his contemporaries who perceived Jews' "otherness" as rooted in religion and viewed assimilation as the key to a harmonious European future, Wagner's *Das Judenthum* is notable for injecting race into contemporary understandings of Jewish difference. In one of the more venomous passages, Wagner writes, "The Jew ... arrests our attention in ordinary life firstly by his exterior appearance. It matters not to which particular European nationality he may belong, the Jew's appearance strikes us as something so unpleasantly incongruous that, involuntarily, we wish to have nothing in common with him."[14] The exclusionary nature of Wagner's anti-Semitism, with its emphasis on Jews' immutable difference from Germans, stood out from garden-variety nineteenth-century anti-Semitism and, it could be argued, in some ways anticipated the biological racism of Nazism.

Wagner chose Bayreuth as his new home following German unification and his years abroad in European exile and established the Bayreuth Festival in 1876. In addition to a new opera house designed exclusively by the Master with his own music dramas in mind, Wagner commissioned the construction of a new villa on the site later named Wahnfried. The composer's association with the reactionary right that began in Wagner's own lifetime grew apace at the turn of the century as a new cast of characters entered the family orbit. The English-born Winifred Wagner was introduced into the world of nationalist politics by her adopted parents who counted Heinrich Class, leader of the Pan-German League, among their closest friends. The town newspaper, the *Bayreuther Blätter* founded in 1878, quickly acquired a reputation for hyper-nationalism and conservatism that would continue to grow over the course of Weimar and into the Third Reich. With contributions regularly appearing by the likes of the racist French writer Arthur de Gobineau, the *Blätter* sought to infuse Wagner's music dramas with extramusical political and social ideals. According to one typical example from 1897, the title character in Wagner's opera Siegfried was described as "the embodiment of the soul of the people and purest representative of the Aryan race."[15] This devoted core grew as passionate Wagnerites streamed into Bayreuth in the composer's last years. Hans von Wolzogen, a fervent German nationalist and disciple of Wagner, was offered the editorship of the *Bayreuther Blätter* by Wagner himself in 1877 and stayed in that post until the paper's final year in 1938. The *Blätter*'s manic obsession with Wagner struck even many contemporaries as bizarre and extreme. As the critic Eduard Hanslick prophesied in 1882, the paper would furnish ample proof of "how strongly the *delirium tremens* of the Wagner intoxication raged amongst us, and what sort of abnormalities of thought and feeling it occasioned in the 'cultured' people of its time."[16] Following Wagner's death in 1883, the composer's wife Cosima assumed control of the Festival and worked tirelessly to preserve the Wagner cult both at home and around the globe. The racist philosopher and writer Houston Stewart Chamberlain arrived in 1909. In addition to an almost unfathomable attachment to the composer, these personalities—collectively referred to as the "Bayreuth Circle"—shared a set of commitments with which the name "Wagner" has remained inextricably linked to this day: devotion to German culture, fierce nationalism, and virulent anti-Semitism.

However, the worship of Wagner's music was not confined to those gathered at Bayreuth at the turn of the century but rather was a truly global phenomenon. The major music centers of America, England, France, and Russia could each plausibly challenge Bayreuth for the mantle of world capital of Wagnerism, though the ideological outlooks and politics of Wagnerians outside Bayreuth often bore little resemblance to those gathered at Haus Wahnfried. Of the 599 staged performances at the Metropolitan Opera in New York City during the period 1884–1891, an astounding 320 were works by Wagner.[17] The strong female characters in Wagner's operas inspired a whole generation of Gilded

Age feminists, such as Mary Garrett and M. Carey, and, as Celia Applegate has shown, Wagner resonated with women around the world who drew inspiration from the composer and his music in both their personal and public lives.[18] In fin de siècle France, Wagner found passionate devotees in Baudelaire, Mallarmé, and the composer and musicologist Vincent D'Indy, whose claim that Wagner's music was the foundation for modern French masters, including Debussy, persisted even after the outbreak of the First World War.[19] James Joyce's library contained scores of *The Flying Dutchman, Die Meistersinger, Siegfried, Das Rheingold*, and other operas, as well as volumes of Wagner's prose writings and correspondence.[20] Marxist thinkers across Europe adapted Wagner's ideas to their own socialist politics, from the Bolshevist Anatoly Lunacharsky to the writer George Bernard Shaw, whose Marxist rereading of the *Ring* he preserved in the 1898 *The Perfect Wagnerite*.[21] Wagner, in short, was compatible with all sorts of politics and social concerns beyond the Bayreuth nationalists we typically associate with him. Yet the year 1900 would see the public craze for Wagner at its peak as the composer's popularity experienced a remarkably rapid decline within a generation, and by the First World War, Wagner's time had passed in the minds of many music lovers. Critics remarked on the collapse in public demand, culminating in 1913 with Emil Ludwig's *Wagner oder die Entzauberten* (Wagner, or the Disenchanted Ones) that proclaimed Wagnerism as little more than an antique historical curiosity from a bygone century.[22] The First World War and the postwar inflation that followed had a shattering impact on Wahnfried's already precarious finances with the result that the Festival was shuttered entirely between 1914 and 1924.

Wagner among the critics

In the wake of the First World War, contemporaries wondered how the new Bayreuth would adapt to a changed world. In the eyes of the Austrian critic Paul Stefan, Wagner had never fully recovered from his falling out with Nietzsche whose devastating *The Case of Wagner* caused the composer's anti-Semitism and nationalism to overshadow his musical works. Stefan had warned the public not to overreact to Nietzsche's message and sought to rehabilitate the composer, particularly among the younger generation before the war, in his 1914 book *Die Feindschaft gegen Wagner* (The Hostility toward Wagner) that went through several reprintings during Weimar. Wilibald Nagel, editor of the *Neue Musik-Zeitung*, wrote a glowing review of the work and urged his readers to pick up a copy.²³ Yet it was far from clear if Bayreuth would lead the way in an imagined postwar Wagner renaissance. While generous state support had shielded many German theaters and public concert halls from the vagaries of a volatile economy, declining concert receipts, and unpredictable taste, as a private organization none of these benefits extended to Bayreuth.²⁴ To make matters worse a copyright law passed by German parliament safeguarding, among other things, Bayreuth's exclusive right to stage the opera *Parsifal* had expired in 1913. Just as opera houses around the world gained greater access to Wagner's works the composer's beloved Wahnfried was forced to endure lean years, prompting some critics to demand both an extension to the copyright period and Wahnfried's rights to a portion of the proceeds for public performances and publisher receipts of Wagner's music in the wider world.²⁵ The music critic Carl Hagemann lamented how much of Bayreuth's future success now seemed dependent upon American and British goodwill in the form of donations and wondered if the "Bayreuth idea" itself—the site's devotion to the music of Wagner alone—could survive at all.²⁶ In an effort to raise much-needed funds for Bayreuth's grand reopening and again put the Festival on a solid financial footing, the composer's son Siegfried Wagner launched an aggressive but ultimately disappointing fund-raising campaign in America that was mocked by the American and German press alike.²⁷ An illustration in *Simplicissimus* (image 13) titled "Bayreuth" with Siegfried depicted front and center poked fun at the irony of just how much the renaissance in Wagner's "true German art" depended on non-Germans with the caption: "Now our old voices sing again; The old German Empire can once again rise in all its glory—so long as paying foreigners show up!"

If Wagnerians outside of Bayreuth hoped to be able to look to the Festival as the staging ground for a Wagner fit for the new century, the much heralded grand reopening did not inspire confidence. From the outset, the 1924 Festival was a complete fiasco. Approaching the Festival theater, attendees were greeted by the old black, white, and red colors of the imperial flag, a less than subtle jab at the fledgling Republic. Following the last scene of *Die Meistersinger von Nürnberg*, the audience broke into a loud, spontaneous rendition of the national anthem, including the jingoistic first stanza much beloved among German nationalists. The homogeneous and boorish character of the audience struck many in attendance who went on to register their disgust in both public pronouncements and private correspondence. While leftist and foreign observers were naturally appalled at such overt displays of nationalism, many monarchists and cultural conservatives were no less disturbed. According to Prince Heinrich Reuss XLV, "We saw Wagner and his work of art desecrated by a

Image 13 "Bayreuth," *Simplicissimus*, 1924. Source: *Simplicissimus, 29* (20), 1924. Image retrieved from http://www.simplicissimus.info/index.php?id=5.

non-artistic demonstration ... they (the anthem singers) are the enemies of the artist Wagner, and they are digging the grave of the Bayreuth idea."[28] Thomas Mann, also in attendance, was similarly dismayed and wondered if Bayreuth had any future at all if such protests were allowed to continue.[29] For their part, conservative music critics evinced deep concern with the marriage of art and politics evident in such episodes at Bayreuth. The musicologist Hans Joachim

Moser acknowledged the emergence of a "national anti-Semitic Wagner" strongly linked to the writings of Chamberlain and Gobineau, whose cause the Nazis had so successfully championed that "one finds today that the National Socialists have taken Wagner up and claimed him for themselves."[30] Others held out hope that the Festival might moderate its tone with the passage of time. Writing in the conservative *Zeitschrift für Musik*, the music critic Albert Wellek admired the extent to which the reopened Festival appeared to live up to the high aesthetic standards established by Cosima prior to the First World War, yet pleaded for a new Bayreuth "disengag(ed) from small self-interest, from desire, from envy, from 'interest'; even a liberation from nationalism itself and all its horrors."[31]

Critics writing in the modernist press attempted to meet the challenge presented by an overtly nationalist Bayreuth head-on. The critic Paul Bekker, who authored a well-received 1924 biography of the composer titled *Richard Wagner: Das Leben in Werke* wrote from Paris that Wagner—like Bach, Beethoven, and Mozart—"was the communal property of both nations" and suggested that any claim to the contrary arose from a misplaced emphasis on Wagner's philosophical and prose writings rather than his music.[32] These protests surrounding the cultural appropriation of Wagner by the political right reached an apotheosis in a 1928 biography of the composer by the Swiss theater critic and essayist Bernhard Diebold.[33] Disturbed by the apathy of liberal and progressive critics who did little to avert efforts by nationalist writers keen to turn Wagner into a harbinger of racist ideology and völkisch nationalism, Diebold wrote:

> Something unbelievable has happened! Since the war, the politically right-leaning educated middle classes have elevated Richard Wagner as its own artistic and cultural god ... confronted with this spiritual-political Wagner phenomenon, the left wing press has evinced more than a little thoughtlessness ... they have relinquished the enormous cultural cachet of this world famous name ... instead of drawing a fundamental distinction between Wahnfried and Wagner's cultural ideas and thereby winning over the vast majority of Wagnerians through these efforts; instead of proclaiming Die Meistersinger a celebration of democracy and construing every performance of this apologia of the people as a political celebration ... (German Democrats) have delivered the whole of Richard Wagner to the nationalists naively and without a fight.[34]

Some Weimar writers, from the musicologist Hugo Leichtentritt and critic Adolf Weissmann to writer Franz Werfel, were so disgusted by the right's appropriation of Wagner that they turned abroad for sources for inspiration and found it in the operas of Verdi, whose refinement and virility served as the perfect "antidote" to Wagner's notorious ponderousness and vanity.[35] These efforts bore fruit, as in the 1931–1932 season Verdi would surpass Wagner for the first time in total public performances across Germany.[36]

These rejoinders were met with a vigorous response from some conservative Wagnerians. Albert Wellek, in a review of Bekker's Wagner biography for the conservative *Zeitschrift für Musik*, accused the critic not only of having "erred" in his assessment of Wagner's influences but of dishonestly writing with a hidden agenda: "one can rightly say that in his core arguments, Bekker has something in mind outside of the topic at hand, namely the justification and confirmation of prevailing musical wisdom and the gratification of a certain public among whom he clearly counts himself."[37] Bekker's well-known support for modern music and regular contributions to leading journals devoted to it was likely not the only driving factor behind Wellek's harsh review. One of Bekker's central theses was that Wagner's music dramas were informed by the composer's political and social experiences, an approach that threatened to raise some uncomfortable truths about the composer. Wagner's well-documented espousal of liberal and socialist ideals during the Revolutions of 1848 and his ambiguous views on Christianity put him at odds with many German conservatives during the composer's own lifetime and well into the twentieth century. However uncontroversial this perspective strikes us today, Bekker's biography ran counter to long-standing conservative perspectives, which viewed musical works as emerging from the force of the composer's will alone. Influenced by the philosophy of Schopenhauer, Wagner's nineteenth-century biographers were consummate exponents of this approach and any suggestion to the contrary rankled Wellek, who fumed at Bekker's suggestion that Wagner "had to become a politician, a revolutionary, a socialist, an atheist—not because these questions as such interested him personally but because his art depended on the answers to them."[38] This was not the first time Bekker found himself embroiled in controversy with the conservative establishment. The year 1920 had witnessed him squaring off with the nationalist and anti-Semitic composer Hans Pfitzner, who seethed at the notion that artists were products of their social and political environment and balked at the suggestion that Beethoven's music was anything other than the product of an autonomous creative genius.[39] By the mid-1920s, conservative critics found a biographer they could call their own in Alfred Lorenz, a vehement nationalist and anti-Semite, whose formal analysis of Wagner's works appeared in 1924 under the title *Das Geheimnis der Form* (The Secret of Form). This study and Lorenz's other prolific work on the composer attracted widespread admiration, and members of the Bayreuth Circle were undoubtedly familiar with

Lorenz's method. Upon his death in 1938, the *Bayreuther Blätter* proclaimed him the "discoverer and revealer" of Wagnerian form.[40]

Yet it would be a mistake to view all conservative Wagnerians as blind adherents to tradition. According to the music critic Josef Wenz, Bayreuth desperately needed to modernize if it hoped to survive into the twentieth century. This would necessitate not only dispensing with a strict adherence to Wagner's wishes surrounding the proper performance of his music dramas but also expanding the repertoire at Bayreuth beyond the works of the Master. Wenz envisioned "a future where not only *Parsifal*, but also the 'Parsifal of the eighteenth century,' Mozart's *The Magic Flute* (is played); namely, everything that is great and worthy in the realm of dramatic music."[41] The Munich critic Paul Marsop went one step further, claiming that while the acoustics of the Bayreuth Festival Theater were the envy of the opera world, instrument design and performance practices had greatly changed in the five decades since it was designed, abandoning his prewar position that Wagner only be performed at Bayreuth.[42] Economic fears loomed over discussions of Wagner performance immediately upon the Festival's reopening and would continue over the course of the next decade. Following the 1929 economic crisis, debate raged in the pages of the *Zeitschrift für Musik* as conservative Wagnerians wondered how music critics might do their part in helping the composer again secure the kind of public demand that existed for his music at the turn of the century. Alfred Heuss highlighted the need for small opera houses to stage productions of the composer outside the confines of Bayreuth, particularly given the economic uncertainties that continued to reverberate in the wake of hyperinflation. Many Wagnerians simply could not afford to make the pilgrimage, and many of the composer's most devoted followers were, in any case, not German, but French, Italian, and English with competent ensembles in their home countries.[43] In reality, while the public mania for the composer never approached the levels seen before the First World War, Wagner was far from underperformed in Weimar Germany from the time of the Festival's reopening to the end of the Republic. A 1930–1931 statistical analysis of opera performances across Germany revealed that two of the five most-performed operas belonged to Wagner (*Tannhäuser* and *Lohengrin*) and that he outpaced Verdi, Puccini, and Mozart as the most performed composer in the entire country for that year.[44]

Other critics, such as Hans Joachim Moser, signaled a need to wholly rethink the relationship between Wagner and Bayreuth. Admittedly, obstinate Wagnerians would likely look on such efforts "as sacrilege … like faithful pilgrims to the Frankish Grail" and refuse any modification to Bayreuth's long-standing mission of preserving Wagner's music alone. Still, Moser argued that such a narrow focus on Bayreuth's function as a shrine to Wagner risked overlooking another goal to which the Master was equally committed: the wider musical edification and education of the German people. "Was not Wagner's idea," he wrote, "above all aimed at the artistic education of the German *Volk*, and to avoid sinking into a pitiful little capital—a 'German Drip at the Rhine'?"[45] To achieve this latter goal, Germans required a steady diet of canonical works beyond the music dramas of Wagner, though to appease the conservative Wagnerians, the Master's works would appear every season alongside those of other proposed classics. Moser offered one such version of how this future Bayreuth might look, seen in table 2 below.

Moser's choice of works was telling. This was a conservative schedule consisting largely of operas by German eighteenth- and nineteenth-century masters that had long since entered the standard repertory and would have held wide appeal among cultural conservatives.[46] In addition, there were limits to how far Moser was willing to push the envelope—the years 1935 and 1938 omitted from his calendar were designated "purely Wagner years" (*reine Wagnerjahre*) where only the Master's works were to be played.[47] Still, Moser's call for reform resonated with other voices within the conservative press. Franz Rühlmann reminded readers that Wagner himself would be horrified at the suggestion that Bayreuth perform his works alone, pointing to comments the composer had made over the course of the 1870s that Bayreuth be devoted to "dramatic works of every sort." With Wagner's own wishes fulfilled, Rühlmann envisaged a future where Bayreuth assumed the status of a truly national theater devoted to the work of all German masters, rather than remain a provincial entity committed to a single composer.[48] For those unable to stomach such a redefinition of Bayreuth's role, Moser suggested at the very least abandoning another custom many conservative Wagnerians viewed as sacrosanct: performing Wagner's music exactly as the composer intended in his own lifetime. Strict adherence to this practice threatened to drive away the world's best conductors and musicians accustomed to bringing their own musical ideas and interpretations to the performance of the Master's operas.[49] For some critics, while these proposals went too far there was clearly a need to rethink how Bayreuth had traditionally operated. While Siegmund Benedict rejected out of hand the notion that Bayreuth play anything except Wagner, he implored its management to seek out "the best of the best" among performers regardless of political or social considerations.[50]

Even members of the Bayreuth circle, whose ties to the Nazi movement grew ever closer through Winifred's warm relationship with Hitler, evinced a certain willingness to abandon its stage conservatism and place art above politics in the

Table 2 Future Bayreuth

1932	1933	1934	1936	1937	1939
Mozart: *The Magic Flute*	Wagner: *Lohengrin*	Mozart: *Don Giovanni*	Wagner: *Tannhäuser*	Handel: *Rodelind*	Wagner: *Rienzi*
Gluck: *Iphegenia in Tauris*	Wagner: *Parsifal*	Beethoven: *Fidelio*	Wagner: *The Flying Dutchman*	Mozart: *The Abduction from the Seraglio*	Wagner: *Die Meistersinger*
Weber: *Der Freischütz*	Wagner: *Der Ring des Nibelungen*	Weber: *Oberon*	Wagner: *Der Ring des Nibelungen*	Weber: *Euryanthe*	Wagner: *Der Ring des Nibelungen*
Wagner: *Die Meistersinger*	————	Wagner: *Tristan*	————	Wagner: *Parsifal*	————
Pfitzner: *Palestrina*	————	Wolf: *Corregidor*	————	Strauss: *Elektra*	————

later years of the Weimar Republic. This was a radical departure from Bayreuth under Cosima, who acquired a reputation for austere conservatism and cult-like fidelity to performing the music dramas according to Wagner's own wishes. As the writer George Bernhard Shaw recalled following his own visit to Bayreuth in 1889, "Where the Master's widow … sits in the wing as the jealous guardian of the traditions of his personal direction, there is already a perceptible numbness—the symptom of paralysis."[51] In his capacity as director, Siegfried injected an initial measure of innovation and experimentation into new productions. Following the 1927 Festival, the critic Werner Kulz wrote that Bayreuth, "whose technical capabilities in the postwar years were among the weakest to any seasoned observer, has undergone fundamental change. Contrary to the claims one frequently hears, the entire, newly reimagined scenery for *Tristan* and the *Ring* shows that Bayreuth has the firm will to bring the latest technical innovations in theatre stage design to bear."[52] Innovations within special effects and lighting drew criticisms from some conservative critics irked by the anachronistic use of electric torches where fire had previously been used and other novelties that deviated from Wagner's formal instructions.[53]

Yet Siegfried pressed forward in his efforts to secure the most talented musicians to lead Bayreuth's productions, whatever the objections raised by nationalist Wagnerians. To lead the 1930 rendition of *Tannhäuser*, he demurred at the candidacies of Furtwängler, Fritz Busch, Clemens Krauss, or some other suitably "German" conductor, opting instead for the Italian Arturo Toscanini. These appointments did not win Siegfried any admirers in certain circles, as Toscanini was not a popular choice among some nationalist Wagnerians who would have preferred a German conductor for the country's "most German" composer. Yet as his other appointments reflected, Siegfried was driven first and foremost by artistic rather than political considerations, and as arguably the most famous conductor in the world at the time, Toscanini was an obvious choice. Faced with this reality, some observers found themselves falling back on a tactic used by Chamberlain in his *Foundations of the Nineteenth-Century*: rendering Toscanini German. Though nationalists like Chamberlain were keen to emphasize the particular genius of German and "Germanic" figures past and present, they could obviously not claim that genius resided in Germans alone. Non-Germans, from Dante and Shakespeare to Michelangelo and Columbus, were admired alongside Goethe and Kant by conservatives and Nazis alike. Indeed, as David Dennis has shown, one of the key cultural tasks that the flagship Nazi organ the *Völkischer Beobachter* set itself upon being taken over by the Nazis in 1920 was to demonstrate the National Socialist outlook of historical icons across the entire Western tradition.[54] Thus, conservative music critics had models from which they could readily draw in Germanizing the Italian conductor. As one conservative critic noted, for example, there was much to admire about Toscanini's chemistry with the German orchestra that he led, without the benefit of a score, as well as any German conductor. In a 1930 review of the preceding summer's festival, Ferdinand Pfohl wrote admiringly that "Toscanini's Tannhäuser performance respected a number of the 'German tempi,' which must be considered the real Wagnernian Tempi that Wagner himself wanted, and which have been faithfully retained in uninterrupted fashion from Wagner's time to the seminal conductors (*Meisterdirigenten*): Hans Richter, Felix Mottle, Karl Muck."[55] The critic Paul Pretzsch likewise praised Toscanini's fidelity to the score and attributed his faithful rendition to the conductor's alleged Nordic ancestral ties.[56]

At the same time, there were limits to Siegfried's iconoclasm. While he introduced electric lighting and some other innovations, productions during his tenure were still seen by many as unimaginative and stale, from the use of dated sets and staging to the performers' dress, which remained little changed from the Wagner's own lifetime.[57] Indeed, as Siegfried himself had commented in 1924, "We intend to have nothing to do with modern excesses, which are in contradiction to the character of the Master's works."[58] In a 1927 letter to his stage assistant Kurt Söhnlein regarding an upcoming production of *Tristan und Isolde*, he noted, "I do not wish to alter the staging arrangements etc. that have been traditional since Munich in 1865. We essentially want to aim for a beautiful, classic staging and rather do not care for a historically informed, crooked one."[59] Recycling old costumes and props had the added benefit of cost savings in a post-hyperinflation Bayreuth that left the Festival with precious few funds to lavish on new set designs.[60] By the end of the Weimar years, however, this ironclad commitment was wearing thin among some observers. The conservative composer Hans Pfitzner, while commending Bayreuth for not engaging in the worst artistic excesses of "leftist theaters," cautioned that some measure of stage modernization was necessary if Wagner was to be as relevant in the twentieth century as he was in the nineteenth.[61] Siegfried would not live to see Pfitzner's vision through; overworked and determined to take on all the responsibilities for the running of the Festival himself, he suffered a massive heart attack and died in August 1930 at the age of 61.

Despite Winifred Wagner's clear admiration for Hitler, several of her initial measures as director following Siegfried's untimely death raised concerns among Nazi cultural authorities about her willingness to toe the Party line. First, she followed her late husband's lead in recruiting the most talented artists available irrespective of political or ideological considerations by naming Heinz Tietjen Bayreuth's new artistic director and retained the Italian-American Toscanini over the German Karl Muck as music director for the 1931 season.[62] Tietjen had cut his teeth in the hypermodernist *Kroll Oper* in Berlin under the Jewish music director Otto Klemperer. His 1929 production of *Der Fliegende Höllander* had required uniformed police to be stationed outside the theater in anticipation of riots from disapproving traditionalist Wagnerians.[63] Though the performance contained no explicit political messaging, detractors were undoubtedly aware of Tietjen's well-known political sympathies with the Sozialdemokratische Partei Deutschlands (SPD), Germany's flagship socialist party, and alert to the ways in which these loyalties might inform his own productions. A critic writing in the conservative *Allgemeine Musikzeitung* disapprovingly wrote that "the clean-shaven Dutchman seemed like a bolshevist agitator, Senta a fanatical and eccentric communist woman, Erik, with his wild, tufted hair and in woolen sweater, a pimp."[64] Max Chop, editor of *Signale für die musikalischen Welt*, thundered at members of the audience "who looked on with sadistic pleasure at the martyrdom that was being inflicted on German art by a group of degenerates."[65] Nazi cultural authorities would not forget the outrage. At the 1938 *Entartete Musik* exhibition in Düsseldorf, Tietjen's Kroll production of *The Flying Dutchman* occupied center stage and Kroll's conductor Otto Klemperer indicted as just another case of "Jews against Wagner" (image 14).

In addition to Tietjen, Bayreuth's new set designer, Emil Preetorius, was likewise less than desirable from a National Socialist perspective. A member of the *Verein zur Abwehr des Antisemitismus* (Union to Combat Anti-Semitism), Preetorius spoke out against the regime's anti-Semitism over the course of Weimar and into the Third Reich, drawing the ire of Party ideologues and a scathing denunciation in the pages of the *Völkischer Beobachter*.[66] When Thomas Mann failed to respond to Preetorius's 1942 invitation to author an essay shunning the Nazis appropriation of Wagner, the set designer decided to undertake the work himself.[67] Neither Tietjen nor Preetorius would join the Party. On the stage, Bayreuth's continued innovations generated backlash among certain traditionalists who, following a 1933 production of *Parsifal*, issued a written petition to Winifred requesting that the Festival management "not produce the Festival music drama *Parsifal* in any other form than its original set design of 1882."[68] For these conservative Wagnerians, the iconoclastic changes on the stage and the political unreliability of Bayreuth's new managers off of it were too much and they made a direct appeal to Hitler for intervention to preserve the

Image 14 "Jews against Wagner," *Entartete Musik Exhibition Catalog*, 1938. Source: Hans Severus Ziegler, "Juden gegen Wagner," *Entartete Musik: Eine Abrechnung*, 1938. Image retrieved from https://archive.org/details/EntarteteMusik_758.

"old Bayreuth."[69] In 1933, Goebbels himself launched a press campaign against Tietjen, and the Party "philosopher" Alfred Rosenberg personally sent Winifred a letter protesting Tietjen's candidacy.[70] Goebbels objections were especially disingenuous, as Winifred's motivations were a page out of the Propaganda Minister's own book. Like Winifred, Goebbels could overlook certain qualities that were problematic from an ideological standpoint if the regime stood to gain in favor and prestige. In September 1933, as he mulled over whom to install at the head of the individual chambers of the newly formed *Reichskulturkammer* (Reich Chamber of Culture) Goebbels desired not only Richard Strauss, Germany's most famous living composer, but also the modernist author Stefan George and famed Jewish director Fritz Lang (of *Metropolis, Dr. Mabuse the Gambler* and *M-A City Seeks a Murderer* fame, among others) to oversee the literature and film chambers.[71]

Despite these protestations, Winifred remained unmoved. In addition to his undoubted talents as a director, Tietjen's dual appointment as general director of the prestigious Berlin Staatsoper gave Wahnfried access to a stable of world-class singers and musicians upon which it could draw for the foreseeable future. These artistic considerations were soon joined by personal ones as Tietjen and Winifred entered into a romantic correspondence. In the late Weimar years 1930–1933, Winifred thus continued Siegfried's legacy of placing the Festival's interests above all else and could do so thanks to the personal protection of Hitler. Neither Siegfried's efforts at depoliticizing Bayreuth nor Winifred's iconoclastic appointments, however, should be taken as evidence of either's resistance against the regime. Indeed, as Hans Rudolf Vaget has argued, a nonpolitical Wagner was in some ways more effective and of greater use to Nazism than a crassly politicized version.[72] As we shall see, however, any lingering ambiguity in Bayreuth's formal allegiance to National Socialism would be torn away once the Nazis were firmly in power.

Bayreuth under Nazism

For all her unwillingness to succumb to Party pressure demanding the removal of some of her artistic appointments, Winifred Wagner presided over a fundamental transformation of the Bayreuth Festival after 1933 as covert support for Hitler and the Nazis gave way to open enthusiasm and solidarity with the new regime. Following the enactment of the Enabling Law in March 1933, which allowed Hitler to bypass the Reichstag indefinitely and effectively rule by decree, Winifred wrote in her diary, "We are certainly living through elemental times, and the Führer and his work stand before us like an incomprehensible miracle that we can only admire with gratitude. What a joy it was when we were able to hoist our flag in front of Wahnfried at last."[73] For their part, the Nazis were keen to champion Wagner as their own cultural hero in public displays throughout the Reich, such as the "Day of Potsdam" during which the Prussian State Opera put on a special performance of *Die Meistersinger*. While Winifred's support for the new regime was clearly rooted in ideology, there were financial reasons to be hopeful about the Festival's future under the banner of the swastika. While the Festival had endured lean years for much of Weimar, in Hitler Bayreuth had found an admirer keen to alleviate these problems. Eager to stage entirely new productions of *Parsifal* and *Siegfried* to mark the semi-centennial of Wagner's death in 1933, Winifred called on the regime to subsidize part of the total cost of 300,000 marks and was granted a special dispensation in the form of 50,000 marks by the Bavarian Council of Ministers. Hans Schemm, the Bavarian Education Minister, pledged to buy advance tickets totaling another 50,000 marks. Hitler, who had not publicly appeared at the Festival since 1925, stayed a full week so as to hear the Ring cycle in its entirety. This patronage by the regime continued following the outbreak of war as organizations like *Kraft durch Freude* bought up large numbers of advance tickets, giving the Festival unprecedented financial security and stability. Hitler also granted the Festival a certain measure of autonomy and room to operate despite continued protests from Goebbels, Rosenberg, and other party functionaries' attacks against various aspects of the Festival, from the Festival's ongoing reliance on Jewish musicians to the continued employment of Preetorius and Tietjen as Festival managers. In exchange, Hitler and the Nazis gained the cultural prestige that came with an endorsement by one of the most famous music halls in the world.

But this clearly came at a cost as the formal marriage between Winfred's Bayreuth and Hitler's Germany pushed away many of the true devotees of Wagner's music who no longer felt welcome and wanted nothing more to do with the Festival. Wagnerians had long been bound together through their love of the composer and his music but otherwise had little in common. The loss of German Jewish and Social Democratic Wagnerians uneasy with Bayreuth's embrace of the nationalist right was in evidence from the moment of the Festival's 1924 reopening. What began as a trickle of diminished support during Weimar turned into a flood after 1933 as the threat posed by Nazism became ever more apparent. These listeners would turn elsewhere to hear the public performance of Wagner's music, to say nothing of Wagnerians residing abroad in France, England, or the United States. While Nazi support did allow Bayreuth to fill the seats, those sitting in them could not be said to share their former occupants' devotion to Wagner and his music. For the 1939 Festival the organization *Kraft durch Freude* allocated one hundred tickets to Italian workers on leave from Cremona whose only comment after attending a performance of *The Flying Dutchman* was that they were not accustomed to sitting for so long.[74] At Bayreuth's War Festivals that commenced after 1940, exhausted soldiers were subjected to lectures on Wagner and made to endure operas like *Parsifal* and *Die Meistersinger*, which typically ran four to five hours in length. Those that did not show up drunk and subsequently fall asleep during the performance fled to the countryside to escape having to attend.[75] Such apathy—and in some cases, outright hostility—extended beyond ordinary theatergoers as the Nazi leadership itself was far from unanimous in its enthusiasm for the composer.

While the Propaganda Minister Goebbels and Reinhard Heydrich, head of the Reich Security Main Office, appear to have shared Hitler's fondness for the composer, the architect Albert Speer admitted finding Verdi "more impressive" than Wagner.[76] Other Nazi leaders left behind a mixed record in their musings on the composer. In his *The Myth of the Twentieth Century*, the party philosopher Alfred Rosenberg hailed Wagnerian characters like Siegfried and Hans Sachs as embodiments of the "Nordic soul" yet suggested that Wagner's striving toward the *Gesamstkunstwerk* (total artwork) had ultimately been one of failure and ridiculed the composer's suggestion that speech and sound deserved to be placed on an equal footing.[77]

Put simply, the cultural traditionalism of Nazism as embodied by Wagner was no foregone conclusion, nor did it possess the kind of uniform consensus that historians have often subsequently given to it. In the almost civil-warlike atmosphere and turf wars within the Party, which accelerated in the late 1920s and culminated with the 1934 Röhm Putsch, the Party's left and right wings fought to leave their stamp on various jurisdictions and offices on both the state and Party side of the regime. In cultural matters, this inter-Party infighting pitted Alfred Rosenberg, editor of the *Völkischer Beobachter* and founder of the *Kampfbund für Deutsche Kultur* (Fighting League for German Culture) against Joseph Goebbels whose considerable power flowed from his dual position as Gauleiter of Berlin and, later in March 1933, as Reich Minister of Public Enlightenment and Propaganda. Bayreuth itself was a staging ground for such battles. This Rosenberg-Goebbels rivalry was further complicated by the machinations of Hermann Goering, a native of Bavaria who sought to undermine both and forcefully intervened on more than one occasion to shield Tietjen and Preetorius from other Party officials.

While Bayreuth was assured a captive audience during Nazi rule the same could not be said of the rest of the Reich. It is striking to note that the total number of Wagner performances throughout the rest of Germany actually saw a gradual *decline* every year over the course of the Third Reich, from 14.8 percent of the total in 1933–1934 to only 7.5 percent by 1942–1943.[78] As Joan Evans has pointed out, the notion that contemporary music suddenly vanished from the stage in 1933 to be replaced with Wagner and Bruckner is a seriously misleading one; Hindemith and Weill continued to be popular with German audiences, to say nothing of the music of the foreigners Bartok and Stravinsky.[79] We will never know what Wagner would have made of Nazi ideology or the Holocaust, but it is safe to assume that he would have been appalled by what Bayreuth had become under National Socialism. The Festival Theater, designed by Wagner himself as a space for the composer's most devout followers to listen to his music as he intended it, was reduced to a propaganda tool by a regime that valued Wagner only insofar as he could be made to serve its larger political and social policy ends.

Notes

1. Hans Rudolf Vaget, "Wagnerian Self-Fashioning: The Case of Adolf Hitler," *New German Critique*, *101* (2007): 95–114.
2. Gordon Craig, *The Germans* (New York: Meridian Books, 1983), 8.
3. The phrase is Celia Applegate's from *The Necessity of Music*, 275.
4. David Dennis, *Inhumanities: Nazi Interpretations of Western Culture* (New York: Cambridge University Press, 2012).
5. Richard Evans, *The Coming of the Third Reich* (New York: Penguin Press, 2003), 39.
6. Jonathan Carr, *The Wagner Clan: The Saga of Germany's Most Illustrious and Infamous Family* (New York: Grove Press, 2007), 189.
7. It is not by accident that this moniker has become attached to Wagner and not, say, Beethoven, Mozart, or Bach, and says something about the almost religious terms in which Wagnerians view the composer and his music.
8. Theodor Adorno, "What National Socialism Has Done to the Arts," in *Essays on Music* (Berkeley, University of California Press, 2002), 373–390 (here 375).
9. For a stimulating discussion of various writers' and intellectuals' musical encounters with Wagner's Bayreuth, see Juliet Koss, *Modernism after Wagner* (Minneapolis: University of Minnesota Press, 2010), 245–273.
10. This view, articulated in a 1933 lecture, is now preserved in Thomas Mann, *Pro and Contra Wagner* (Chicago: University of Chicago Press, 1986).
11. Theodor Adorno, *In Search of Wagner* (New York: Verso, 2009).
12. On the anti-Semitism of Wagner's operas, see Marc Weiner, *Richard Wagner and the Anti-Semitic Imagination* (Lincoln: University of Nebraska Press, 1995) and Barry Millington, "Nuremberg Trial: Is There Anti-Semitism in Die Meistersinger?" *Cambridge Opera Journal 3* (3) (1991): 247–260. For a polemical account of how Wagner's ideology anticipated and mirrored Hitler's own, see Joachim Köhler, *Wagners Hitler: Der Prophet und sein Vollstrecker* (München: Blessing, 1999).
13. On the 1848 context, see Paul Lawrence Rose, *Wagner: Race and Revolution* (New Haven: Yale University Press, 1996). Wagner's often-tortured relationship to Meyerbeer is detailed in Jacob Katz, *The Darker Side of Genius: Richard Wagner's Anti-Semitism* (Hanover: Brandeis University Press, 1986).
14. Edwin Evans, trans., *Richard Wagner: Judaism in Music* (London: William Reeves, 1910), 9.

15 Harold Graewell, "Germania oder Siegfried?" *Bayreuther Blätter*, 4 (1897): 106–111.
16 Thomas Grey, "Hanslick contra Wagner," in *Richard Wagner and His World*, ed. Thomas Grey (Princeton: Princeton University Press, 2009), 411.
17 Joseph Horowitz, *Classical Music in America: A History of Its Rise and Fall* (New York: Norton, 2005), 141.
18 Celia Applegate, *The Necessity of Music: Variations on a German Theme* (Toronto: University of Toronto Press, 2017), 238–259.
19 See Jane Fulcher, *The Composer as Intellectual: Music and Ideology in France, 1914–1940* (New Haven: Yale University Press, 2005), 28–32, 134–135.
20 Timothy Martin, *Joyce and Wagner: A Study of Influence* (Cambridge: Cambridge University Press, 1991).
21 On Wagner reception in these and other locales, see David C. Large and William Weber, eds., *Wagnerism in European Culture and Politics* (Ithaca, NY: Cornell University Press, 1984).
22 Emil Ludwig, *Wagner oder die Entzauberten* (Berlin: Felix Lehmann Verlag, 1913).
23 Wilibald Nagel, "Die Feindschaft gegen Wagner," *Neue-Musik Zeitung*, 40 (5) (1919): 56–59, 71–74.
24 This state of affairs prompted at least one critic to call for state support and public subsidy of the Festival. See Paul Marsop, "Bayreuther Festspiele 1924," *Die Musik*, 16 (1924): 910–911.
25 These proposals and others are cited in "Wahnfried," *Neue Musik-Zeitung*, 44 (13) (1923): 209–210.
26 Carl Hagemann, "Bayreuth am Grenzweg," *Die Musik*, 15 (4) (1923): 241–245.
27 Siegfried's behavior during the US trip was a disaster as the director made little effort to conceal the anti-Semitism and chauvinistic nationalism for which Bayreuth was so well known. Prearranged meetings with the notoriously anti-Semitic Henry Ford ostracized many potential benefactors, and newspapers published reports about an underlying motive behind Siegfried's trip—to fundraise and drum up American support for Hitler's nascent NSDAP. A reporter from the liberal *Berliner Tageblatt* could scarcely conceal his shock upon seeing Siegfried set off for a fund-raising banquet in New York only to harangue the audience with politically charged attacks against the Weimar government and insult eminent Jewish musicians, such as the conductor Bruno Walter. See Oliver Hilmes, *Cosimas Kinder: Triumph und Tragödie der Wagner-Dynastie* (München: Siedler Verlag, 2009), 196–197. Far from meeting the hoped-for $200,000 fund-raising goal, a disappointed Siegfried and Winifred returned to Germany with a meager $9,552.
28 Brigitte Hamann, *Winifred Wagner: A Life at the Heart of Hitler's Bayreuth* (New York: Harcourt, 2006), 101.
29 Ibid., 102.

30 Hans Joachim Moser, "Richard Wagners Bedeutung für unsere Zeit," in *Abhandlungen*, (1929). Nachlass: 31/285.
31 Albert Wellek, "Bayreuth," *Zeitschrift für Musik*, 92 (9) (1925), 506–508.
32 Paul Bekker, "Wagner und Die Gegenwart," *Die Musik*, 23 (1) (1930): 1–14.
33 Bernhard Diebold, *Der Fall Wagner* (Frankfurt: Frankfurter Societäts-Druckerei GmbH, 1928).
34 Quoted in Sven Oliver Müller, *Richard Wagner und die Deutschen: Eine Geschichte von Hass und Hingabe* (München: C.H. Beck, 2013), 110.
35 On Verdi reception during Weimar, see Gundula Kreuzer, *Verdi and the Germans: From Unification to the Third Reich* (Cambridge: Cambridge University Press, 2010), 138–189 (here 145–146).
36 Ibid., 161.
37 Albert Wellek, "Paul Bekkers 'Wagner: Das Leben im Werke'," *Zeitschrift für Musik*, 93 (1) (1926): 9–12.
38 Paul Bekker, *Richard Wagner: His Life in His Work* (New York: W.W. Norton & Co., 1931), 223.
39 Peter Franklin, "Audiences, Critics and the Depurification of Music: Reflections on a 1920's Controversy," *Journal of the Royal Music Association*, 114 (1) (1989): 80–91. Bekker had written a 1912 biography of Beethoven that attempted a similar contextualization and historicization that he later brought to bear on the 1931 Wagner biography.
40 For a discussion of Lorenz's life and work, see Stephen McClatchie, *Analyzing Wagner's Operas: Alfred Lorenz and German Nationalist Ideology* (Rochester: University of Rochester Press, 1998), (here 1).
41 Josef Wenz, "Bayreuth," *Zeitschrift für Musik*, 89 (1922): 208–210.
42 Paul Marsop, "Bayreuth, Die Zeitenwende und Das Reich," *Die Musik*, 17 (1) (1924): 1–13. Marsop's earlier insistence on Bayreuth at the only venue suitable for Wagner's music met with resistance from American critics, among others, who defended the Met's performances as equal to any German production. See, for example, *The New Music Review and Church Review*, 4 (43) (1904): 278–279.
43 Alfred Heuss and Ernst Latzko, "Zwiegespräch: Wie Denken Sie Über Richard Wagner," *Zeitschrift für Musik*, 97 (8) (1930): 620–627.
44 Wilhelm Altmann, "Opernstatistik August 1930 bis Juli 1931," *Zeitschrift für Musik*, 98 (11) (1931): 948–968. As we saw earlier, however, Verdi would overtake him the following year.
45 Hans Joachim Moser, "Fortsetzung Bayreuths?" *Zeitschrift für Musik*, 98 (7) (1931): 560–561.
46 The one exception here, of course, is the English Handel, though during the Weimar German critics waged a campaign to reclaim him for Germany. See Pamela Potter, "The Politicization of Handel and His Oratorios in the Weimar Republic, the

Third Reich, and the Early Years of the German Democratic Republic," *The Musical Quarterly*, 85 (2) (2001): 311–341.

47 Moser, "Fortsetzung Bayreuths?" 562. Moser's essay launched a debate within the conservative press with critics like Paul Pretzsch attacking Moser's credentials and disposition toward tradition while Gustave Bosse, who would become Director of Artistic Affairs of the Nazi leisure organization *Kraft durch Freude*, rushing to the musicologist's defense. See Gustav Bosse, "Fortsetzung Bayreuths?" *Zeitschrift für Musik*, 98 (1931): 736, and Moser's response to Pretzsch in Hans Joachim Moser, "Nachwort zur Aussprache über Bayreuth," *Zeitschrift für Musik*, 99 (7) (1932): 579.

48 Franz Rühlmann, "Wagnertheater—Nationaltheater—Originaltheater in Bayreuth?" *Zeitschrift für Musik*, 98 (12) (1931): 1040–1048.

49 Moser, "Fortsetzung Bayreuths?" 560–562.

50 Siegmund Benedict, "Bayreuther Gedanken," *Neue Musik-Zeitung*, 45 (12) (1924): 300–303.

51 Quoted in Koss, *Modernism after Wagner*, 249.

52 Werner Kulz, "Bayreuth 1927," *Zeitschrift für Musik*, 94 (9) (1927): 500–501.

53 For one example, see Joseph v. Engel, "Nachträge zu den Bayreuther Festspielen 1927," *Zeitschrift für Musik*, 94 (12): 691–693.

54 Dennis, *Inhumanities*.

55 Ferdinand Pfohl, "Die Bayreuther Festspiele 1930," *Die Musik*, 22 (12) (1930): 884–890 (here 885).

56 Frederic Spotts, *Bayreuth: A History of the Wagner Festival* (New Haven: Yale University Press, 1994), 153.

57 See Ibid., 147–158.

58 Patrick Carnegy, *Wagner and the Art of the Theatre* (New Haven: Yale University Press, 2006), 157.

59 Kurt Söhnlein, *Erinnerungen an Siegfried Wagner und Bayreuth* (Bayreuth: ISWG, 1980), 94.

60 Spotts, *Bayreuth*, 148.

61 Geoffrey Skelton, *Wagner at Bayreuth: Experiment and Tradition* (New York: George Braziller, 1965), 107–108.

62 It should be pointed out, however, that Winifred's decision to reappoint Fürtwangler helped quell the backlash.

63 Carnegy, *Wagner and the Art of the Theatre*, 256.

64 Quoted in Ibid., 260.

65 Quoted in Peter Heyworth, *Otto Klemperer: His Life and Times, 1885–1993* (Vol. 1) (New York: Cambridge University Press, 1983), 282.

66 Carnegy, *Wagner and the Art of the Theatre*, 272.

67 Emil Preetorius, *Wagner: Bild und Vision* (Godesberg: Küpper, 1949).

68 Barry Millington, *The Sorcerer of Bayreuth: Richard Wagner, His Work and His World* (New York: Oxford University Press, 2012), 282.

69 Wolfgang Wagner, *Acts: The Autobiography of Wolfgang Wagner* (London: Weidenfeld & Nicolson, 1994), 23.
70 Haman, *Winifred Wagner*, 155–156.
71 Jonathan Petropoulos, *Art as Politics in the Third Reich* (Chapel Hill: University of North Carolina Press, 1996), 24.
72 Hans Rudolf Vaget, "The Political Ramifications of Hitler's Cult of Wagner," in *Zum Gedenken an Peter Borowsky* (Hamburg: Hamburg University Press, 2003), 103–127.
73 Hamann, *Winifred Wagner*, 186. The use of the pronoun "our" is telling.
74 Hamann, *Winifred Wagner*, 309.
75 Frederic Spotts, *Hitler and the Power of Aesthetics* (New York: Overlook Press, 2003), 261.
76 It is possible that Heydrich's fondness owed, at least in part, to Heydrich's father Bruno, a modestly gifted composer and opera singer who greatly admired Wagner. See Robert Gerwarth, *Hitler's Hangman: The Life of Heydrich* (New Haven: Yale University Press, 2011), 14–24. Speer's thoughts on Wagner can be found in Albert Speer, *Inside the Third Reich* (New York: MacMillan, 1970), 9.
77 Alfred Rosenberg, *The Myth of the Twentieth Century* (New York: Noontide, 1982), 94–100.
78 Kreuzer, *Verdi and the Germans*, 203.
79 Joan Evans, "Stravinsky's Music in Nazi Germany," *Journal of the American Musicological Society*, 56 (3) (2003): 525–594. On Weill and Hindemith in Nazi Germany, see Michael Kater, *Composers of the Nazi Era: Eight Portraits* (New York: Oxford University Press, 2002).

5

Judging Performance, Performing Judgments: Race and Performance in Weimar Germany

In the summer of 1930, the pianist John Flaffith concertized throughout Europe and astounded audiences with his vivid interpretations of a varied repertoire, ranging from Debussy and Stravinsky to Bach and Mozart. In Poland, the *Kurjer Polski* raved: "Yesterday John Flaffith played before a wild audience. What this great artist understands and brings [to the music] can only be appreciated still more by the expert. The present author, who has heard the great masters of the piano play and can be regarded as the quintessential critic has only this to say: John Flaffith was better than them all." In Budapest the *Magyarorszag* reported, "It brings us great pleasure to report on the enormous success [enjoyed] by John Flaffith, who played the most difficult pieces with great technique and the most intimate feeling for the piano." But, as the article went on to say, what most astonished concertgoers "is that Mister Flaffith is a Negro! [One] infused with the soul of Beethoven and Liszt. In short: a phenomenon who should serve as a model for the white piano player."[1]

Alas, Flaffith's success did not last. Just prior to an engagement before a packed house in Germany, Flaffith was confronted by a crazed fellow artist who shouted, "I want us white artists to be free of the black menace!" before pulling out a revolver and shooting Flaffith in the shoulder. As stagehands scurried to get medical attention, Flaffith's agent was heard to cry out, "No water, no water!" It was not long before the sentiment behind this curious aversion was revealed, for no sooner had one stagehand put a wet washcloth on Flaffith's forehead than loud cries were heard throughout the hall: "Flaffith is no Negro, he is white!" Months later, Flaffith found himself fully recovered but unable to secure even a single engagement. Eventually, he revealed to a German reporter the inspiration behind his successful, if short-lived, ruse:

> It was not my idea, but rather that of my wife ... After we had married I played in a bar in New York, which went rather badly. But I lost the position because my playing was too serious. Anny, who always gave me encouragement, said that I should try being a piano virtuoso. It came to nothing. A negro film, which we saw together during this time, suddenly gave Anny the idea that I could try doing things as a Negro artist. The last of our savings brought us across the ocean. In the beginning I tried to concertize in several cities as a white pianist, but had no success. But if I appeared as a Negro, I found myself enthusiastically welcomed; in short: I was soon a true great known the world over.[2]

Appearing as a satirical grotesque in a 1930 issue of the *Zeitschrift für Musik*, the story is pure fiction and no other traces of Flaffith turn up in contemporary sources. But its underlying claim—that musical performance has never been purely about the music itself but rather has found itself bound up in larger questions surrounding what is performed, when, and by whom—is a concern, which loomed large in the minds of music critics of the interwar period. While musical performance and its relationship to contemporary radio, film, aesthetic debates, and aspects of Weimar culture has attracted scholarly interest, historians and musicologists alike have stayed remarkably silent on the issue of race and performance to see what it can tell us about Weimar nationalism and anti-Semitism.[3] As Christopher Small has argued,

> The part played by the performers in the perception of [musical works] has often not come into consideration; when performance is discussed at all, it is spoken of as if it were nothing more than a presentation ... of the work that is being performed. It is rare to find the act of musical performance thought of as possessing, much less creating, meanings in its own right.[4]

If the function of race within the performance of classical instrumental music has until recently largely been ignored, its place within other musical traditions has been better documented by ethno-musicologists. From the centrality of "blackness" in jazz to the importance of "Jewishness" in performing Klezmer music, reconceptualizing musical performance as central to the construction of ethnic identity, negotiation of power, and assertion of agency has been well recognized.[5] In this chapter, I examine the place of the performer in interwar Germany, a figure onto whom Weimar critics projected their greatest hopes and fears, ambitions and anxieties as they took measure of the place of traditional culture in the modern world. What I am interested in here, in other words, is unpacking the notion, as the pianist Claudio Arrau put it, "that only a German can play Beethoven ... only a Viennese can feel Schubert."[6] Critical views toward the performer can indeed tell us much about the dispositions of those who articulate them. How were the connections between national identity and performance understood, articulated, and ultimately deployed by Weimar critics and musicologists? What can an examination of music through the lens of performance tell us about the underlying currents of nationalism and anti-Semitism so characteristic of the interwar period? Finally, to what extent can these views on performance be said to have anticipated, mirrored, or diverged from those under National Socialism? As we have seen elsewhere in this book, this chapter will show that the views of cultural conservatives toward race and performance exhibited a diversity that once again underscore important ruptures in conservative thinking between Weimar and the Third Reich.

National identity and modern musical performance

"Is there any such thing as a typical German form of playing? Every German musician knows it, and still it is difficult to describe and explain in words."[7] Although figures like Hermann Zilcher debated such questions with fellow critics in the musical press during Weimar, it would be a mistake to claim they originated with them. The late imperial Reich gave rise to initial forays into these and other mysteries in the form of Rudolf Louis's highly influential *Die Deutsche Musik der Gegenwart* (Contemporary German Music), which seized on "the ethnic qualities of the man" in seeking to understand the artistic acumen of the conductor Hans von Bülow.[8] Feruccio Busoni, mentor to hundreds of pianists over the course of his distinguished career, similarly recalled an incident involving his Dutch-born student Egon Petri's border-crossing into Germany in 1907:

> He was carrying Beethoven's sonatas in his suitcase, which were pulled out and inspected in the customs office. "What is that?" asks the officer. "They are scores—Beethoven's sonatas." "Ah, those are Beethoven's sonatas," replies the officer as he leafs through them. "To understand them is the most difficult thing of all," he says, handing back the volume. "And," he adds, taking Egon for an Englishman, "a foreigner is incapable of it; for that you have to be German.[9]

Even critics who were themselves skeptical of the connection between race and performance had to admit that the issue was not easily solvable. During the First World War, the musicologist Alfred Einstein maintained a regular correspondence with Paul Bekker, who remained in the dark about musical happenings in Germany as a soldier stationed on the Western Front. In a January 1917 letter to Bekker, Einstein described some of the fierce attacks being directed at the conductor Bruno Walter whose Jewishness precluded artistic insight into the works of Beethoven, Wagner, and Bruckner in the minds of a circle of Munich critics.[10] Although not sharing the anti-Semitic views of those writers, Einstein wrote, "It is their right (to criticize Walter's interpretations) and as a Jew myself cannot decisively say what role race plays in the interpretation of an artwork—only that the question is not so readily settled."[11]

For some, birthright was often held responsible for the cultural insights that it conferred onto performers of German music. Although, as we saw earlier, conceptions of musical nationalism were often malleable in the hands of some critics, when it came to explaining the interpretive insights performers could reach with particular performers some critics pointed toward national origin. While Bruno Walter had his share of critics, the conductor's supporters understood his stirring renditions of Beethoven and Wagner as owing to his Germanness, reminding readers that "the man was born in Berlin … and he belongs to us."[12] For those performers who failed the birthright test, a proper upbringing in the musical culture often sufficed, as it did, for example, with the Chilean pianist Arrau. Reminiscing on his days playing in 1920s Berlin, Arrau observed, "If someone would say, 'You know, he is from South America,' he was told, 'Oh yes, but his *upbringing* was in Berlin.'"[13]

A further way of judging performance credentials was through the imagining of "national schools" of performance. Critics, musicologists, and performers invented and immersed themselves within pedagogical traditions that connected by direct lineage the modern-day performer with the intentions of its long-dead creator. The most illustrious of these schools in twentieth-century Europe was undoubtedly the Leschetizky School, centered on the famous Viennese pedagogue of the same name and renowned for producing interpreters of Beethoven. Leschetizky could claim authority as a student of Carl Czerny (1771–1857) who, in turn, inherited the stamp of authentic interpretation by virtue of his lessons with Beethoven himself. Through such narratives, performers were often imagined as bringing the true intentions of the composer to light, though not all performers entirely agreed with such an assessment. Even those who would clearly benefit from such a genealogy, such as the pianist Arthur Schnabel who was himself a former student of Leschetizsky celebrated for his Beethoven, remarked in his memoirs: "There is no Leschetizky method. It is a mere legend—an absolute fallacy."[14] Commenting more generally on the notion of national schools, Schnabel was entirely dismissive: "I lived for thirty years in Germany and even so I would not be able to say what the 'German technique' is. For in Germany all kinds of piano techniques were taught—flat or round fingers, stretched out or drawn in, elbows fixed or waving, glued to the hips or far out … Which one was the 'German technique?'"[15]

This fixation on national schools was itself a relatively new phenomenon during Weimar and contrasted with nineteenth-century conceptions of performance. In the so-called Romantic Age piano playing was characterized as much by its preference for extemporization as its fidelity to the printed score: a performer's improvisatory powers was often viewed as a yardstick for measuring their overall artistic capabilities.[16] One wonders if the consolidation of the Western canon beginning around 1800—and the subsequent sacralization of composers, which accompanied it—ushered in a shift in performance practice, whereby complete fidelity to the composer's intentions came to assume an overriding importance.[17] Whatever the origins of this new *Werktreue* ideal, by the time of Beethoven's death in 1827, increasingly little room was left for ingenuity on the part of the performer. Rather, his or her new function as mediator between the deceased composer and his living audience reduced the performer to a new role as the vessel through which the sacred notes of the composer could be transmitted. This was surely driving logic behind Berlioz's conception of Liszt as "the pianist of the future" following a June 1836 recital: "not a note was left out, not one added … no inflection was effaced, no change of tempo permitted."[18] In Berlioz's experience, such an approach clearly deviated from prevailing practice.

Testimonies by twentieth-century performers reveal the extent of this shift from earlier room for maneuver in performance to the musical score's new position of authority. After the First World War, the radicalism of Liszt's fidelity to the score was seen as de rigueur among performers of serious music. According to German pianist Walter Gieseking, writing in 1942:

> A sensible, artistically valid and truthful interpretation is inextricably linked with the concept of the work in its true form (*Werktreue*). Every artwork of any significance is endowed with definite expressive content by its creator which the interpreter must communicate and bring to life. *The interpreter must force himself to generate with intensive feeling not the personal feelings or the ephemeral mood of the player, but rather the expressive content which the composer has rendered in artistic form.* That alone can, as far as is possible, be identified with the composer. This identity, realized in its highest degree in the resultant interpretation, is, as I see it, the ideal.[19]

By the interwar period, national "schools" and "traditions" emerged in place of individual teachers and methods. What was formerly the Edwin Fischer method, for example, came to be known as the "German school," while disciples of Vladimir Sofronitsky were labeled as exponents of a "Russian school."[20] It could be argued that this move from what could be considered a more fluid to a more fixed arrangement had the effect of opening up rather than closing off the secrets of the musical score to outsider groups: national identity might have figured more (not less) prominently in the previous age when multiple renditions were competing for legitimacy. Many critics, however, reached the opposite conclusion, as the case of Otto Schmitt reveals. Schmitt claimed the "German singer" remained "the only one capable of embodying the primordial German (*urgermanischen*) character of *Der Ring des Nibelungen* and the other music dramas because they are wholly German in thought and feeling!"[21] While the greatness of German music resided in its universal meaning, it was ultimately only through the acumen of German artists that such meaning could be derived.

The importance of having German performers was paramount in the case of vocal music in particular as Schmitt's comments on the Italian tenor Enrico Caruso revealed. For Schmitt, it was "characteristic that the greatest Italian singer, Caruso, has never sung Lohengrin or Tannhäuser, let alone Sigmund or Siegfried, in his guest performances in Germany—that is because, before all else, they must be sung in the German language!" The importance of Germans performing German music was in some cases even more important abroad where it lay vulnerable not only to "inauthentic" renditions by foreign artists but also to performance in other vernaculars:

> German performers provide the occasion for a cultural mission of the highest rank not only in Germany, where they understand it must be so, but also in the neutral and even in the enemy countries! What tremendous successes German performers have already exhibited in this area since the war! Spain and Italy have readily experienced German art performed by Germans in their greatest cities and France, our most irreconcilable adversary, must again open its doors, after many years of opposition, to the art of Wagner within its capital city of Paris ... [either way, they will be] forced open by the elemental need for art (*Kunstbedürfnis*) among its own people!

In the final analysis, Schmitt concluded, "It appears that the German conductor, the German singer, the German musician already faces an enormous, and at the same time encouraging, task abroad—to increase his artistic performances to the highest plane!"[22]

While choral and operatic works raised pressing questions about authentic performance among conservative Weimar critics, symphonic music, too, raised its own set of problems voiced by Alfred Heuss in a 1930 review of Beethoven's Third Symphony conducted under Italian-American maestro Arturo Toscanini. While conceding that "after reading parts of some of the really excessive critics, one must unabashedly reach the opinion, that the *Eroica* has, for really the first time, been revealed in its true form," Heuss identified what he called "cracks [which] appeared right in the foundation."[23] He observed how "one notices the Italian in Toscanini insofar as he has no real feeling for polyphony. He does not think to allow the middle voices to really sing, for example in the wonderful measures in the strings of the funeral march immediately before the return of the theme in F minor." Heuss perceived this insensitivity as rooted in an inability on the part of Italian performers to realize German music in the appropriate manner, an inability not ascribed to German conductors: "How marvelous are such places under the direction of Furtwängler! ... It reminds me of the great singer Battistini, the onetime singer of German Lieder. [Both cases] can only lead to the tragic conclusion that the innermost part of the German character is thoroughly lost on the Italians." Despite this, the German public "still places the Italian conductors above all German ones in the performing of German works," a fact that Heuss viewed as "connected to the general feeling of inferiority of Germans today." Situating his critique in the traumatic post–First World War years, Heuss evinced grave concern that Germans might ever regain their nationalist footing: "This feeling is nothing other than the expression that one feels ... as part of the devastating effects of the postwar period. We are, in a word, musically becoming, if we have not already become, an international province. One searches in vain for a Germany ready to be musical, at least in our great cities."[24] German nationality did not always confer a straightforwardly privileged status on Weimar's leading maestros, as German-Jewish conductors like Otto Klemperer learned. The critic Walter Jacobs, comparing two 1923 performances of Bruckner's Eighth Symphony, likened Klemperer's interpretation to a Mahlerian "clarity of scoring" while the non-Jewish Hermann Abendroth was credited with achieving "more of a full, Wagnerian sonority." The subtle linking of Klemperer with his famous Jewish predecessor and Abendroth with the German Wagner illustrated that German-Jewish musicians could not quite escape being cast in a German-Jewish tradition that was at once a part and yet at a remove from German musical life.[25]

Others ascribed the crisis of performance to the German concertgoing public and its susceptibility to the pernicious influence of Americanization.[26] That catchall term—metonym for the many demons of the interwar period from capitalism and modern media to mass culture—held particular sway over Weimar's new middle class and especially over its youth.[27] According to critic Roderich Regidür, the developing tastes of the German youth for "foreign, American Negro music or things like that" led to "our [Germany's] good serious German musicians sit[ting] at home and liv[ing] in poverty." In Regidür's view, the influx of foreign musicians was directly tied to the lifting of oppressive censorship laws, which were a legacy of imperial Germany, an opinion that betrayed Regidür's authoritarian leanings: "Before the war, many German musicians engaged the entire world with their art. [Now] they are hindered or completely barred from practicing their art in most hostile states. Only Germany would permit these foreign national musicians to perform Jazz and other noise unimpeded."[28] Regidür was merely one of many culturally conservative critics who derided jazz for its foreignness and decadence during the Weimar Republic. But not all castigated it to the same extent, though they often seized upon perceived connections between ethnic-racial identity and authentic performance. Cultural progressives like Frank Warschauer hailed jazz as "the most entertaining and vital phenomenon in contemporary music … not only in America but everywhere."[29] Not only did African-Americans possess "an extraordinarily original sense of rhythm anchored deep in their nature," but they also had—a profound sense of melody that they brought to bear on musical performance. While Warschauer certainly deplored social segregation, which prevented blacks and white from playing together, this separation, it seems, also had its benefits: with racial purity came authenticity. For the European interested in experiencing authentic (American) jazz, it was not enough to seek out the nearest ensemble at hand; rather, Warschauer argued that "to appreciate [jazz] one must listen to a Negro orchestra."[30]

Nationalism, universalism, and the conservative press

While there is ample evidence of a cultural hostility toward all things non-German in the pages of the interwar conservative press, not all traditionalists hewed to the views of an Alfred Heuss or Otto Schmitt. A close examination of contemporary sources reveals that while some critics held German music to be uniquely universal, those who possessed the cultural insights necessary to perform it were not found in Germany alone. In his coverage of the same 1921 German tour by Caruso so derided by his fellow conservative critics, Georges Armin wrote in the conservative *Allgemeine Musik-Zeitung*, "Although a foreigner, [Caruso] knew that he had won over the hearts of the Germans through his rare synthesis [*Vereinigung*] of finished tone and genuine feeling, of unparalleled technique and dramatic power to shape [*Gestaltungskraft*]."[31]

With his profound, *universal* musicality, Caruso was living proof for Armin of the inadequacy of the concept of national schools of performance style, which he labeled as "preposterous" and added that "there is no German, American or Italian school ... rather the art of singing is, like all art, purely absolute." Invoking one of the central maxims of nineteenth-century aesthetic theory, it was in the beauty of Caruso's performances that Armin glimpsed the eternal:

> So long as the eternal human heart remains as it is now, so will artistic revelations of the voice continue to remain on the basis of the same great and deep secret, namely that of beauty. This is a quality that every receptive disposition immediately feels and celebrates, and which every genuine singer seeks to come closer to through his tone.[32]

Of course, the great trick of this rhetoric of "absolutes" and "eternals" was to somehow retain—and even endorse—German national identity. Hermann Zilcher, for example, claimed that Germans were best suited not only for Bach, Schumann, and Brahms but also for performances of works by composers from other nations. In a 1932 essay for the *Zeitschrift für Musik*, he wrote, "Many souls reside in the breast of the German; this is at once both his greatest strength and weakness. He yearns after the rarely heard ... and exotic." While acknowledging some performing traits as characteristic of all musicians irrespective of nationality—including "fidelity to the notes, and a general awareness (*lebendiges Empfinden*) for the character of the music or stylistic structure"—the success of German renditions of foreigners' music was for Zilcher bound up with native performance habits such as "a certain cleanness in rhythm and melody; [a] strong need for clarity in architectural construction and (in spite of his temperament) a certain restrained silence."[33] These were German traits, but they were also universal.

One of the keys to the unmatched profundity of German interpretations of German music, Zilcher claimed, was found in performers' deep cultural immersion into and familiarity with their own musical tradition. It was especially important for performers to focus not simply on works within the narrow confines of the repertory of their particular instrument or of a certain period but on *all* German music:

> It is not enough that the pianist of Bach only knows the piano works or that the German singer only knows the songs of Schubert, Schumann, and Brahms. Rather, [they must] learn to not only play the two part inventions of Bach, but also love [his] Passions and many rich Cantatas. In the case of the German singer, she finds that she sings Brahms Lieder with adequate expression if she also has studied the orchestral works and chamber music of Brahms.[34]

Others echoed Zilcher in their assessment of Germans' ability to excel in the performance of music from other nations. Sigmund Pilsung, for example, documented the case of Walter Gieseking, describing how the pianist's successful renditions of French impressionistic music owed both to his German identity as well as his immersion in French music culture:

> Up through the present day, it is the nature of impressionistic sound [as opposed to] *substance* that causes it to remain foreign to Germans. The German esteems thematically sound music as the true spice ... Walter Gieseking, a German through and through, (*Kerndeutscher*) breathed the French air in his youth. One must have experienced living under the French sky, to grasp the appropriate mood with such tender feeling. How easily corrupted is Impressionism's own style that it [could only] exist at all through cross-breeding with German 'feeling!'[35]

In France, some critics could display similar ethnocentric attitudes. In the case of Gieseking, pianist Arthur Rubinstein, remembered that while some French critics resented that the German Gieseking should be so inextricably linked with French composers such as Debussy and Ravel, "the bitter pill that a German should deserve this honor was swallowed more easily thanks to the fact that his mother was French."[36]

For those less concerned with cementing Gieseking's relationship to French music by dint of his maternal lineage, the fact that he had "breathed the French air" in his youth went furthest to explain his aptitude for performing the music of the French masters. Herbert Gigler, for example, saw the relationship between music and environment as self-evident. Drawing parallels with architectural differences of concert halls and opera houses in the capitals of Europe, he wrote how

> a piano will sound better, a violin address itself more lightly, an oboe or a clarinet sound in other tone colorations from one territory to the other ... [and while] a good portion of these variations in style and architecture, harmony and melody come down to racial differences ... even in the racial question, we find that climate accounts for an important part of the difference.

Chopin and Liszt, who immigrated to Paris from "eastern cultural backwaters" provided the strongest evidence for this fact. Prior to finding success in the French capital, the Polish Chopin had languished in Warsaw while the Hungarian Liszt toiled in Sopron and Bratislava.[37] In this line of argument, while national origin was an important factor in shaping the profundity of artists' musical creations, climate was an important factor in stimulating and enhancing the muse. Yet here again German artists often proved an exceptional case. Confronted with the examples of the Germans Handel and Haydn, who produced some of their best compositions while living abroad in England, Gigler demurred that London had left these composers "entirely unaffected" and that their masterworks were produced not because but in spite of their unmusical surroundings.[38]

Of course, most critics could not simply ignore the contributions of outsiders to German musical life in major cities like Berlin and Hamburg but deployed newfound strategies for explaining the musical insights of select foreigners. In the 1920s, the pianist Claudio Arrau (mentioned in the introduction) made a splash on the European concert scene, achieving success with audiences and critics alike. The pianist's South American origins, however, were not lost on German critics: familiar devices were deployed to explain how a foreigner could arrive at such incisive interpretations of German music. According to a 1926 review from the *Allgemeine Musik-Zeitung*:

> There is here absolutely no trace of hothouse cultivation. Healthily and naturally, musically practical and straightforward, as one expects from a child, but at the same time with all the infallible signs of an extraordinary talent, this good-looking boy played his Mozart, Weber, Schubert, and Mendelssohn ... It appears to me that this fresh, Germanically impregnated boy must become a distinguished artist.[39]

Despite reviews like this, most references to race in the Weimar musical press remained subtle and, as Pamela Potter has shown, race found itself on precarious footing and was dismissed by most serious scholars and musicologists in the early 1920s as a "scientifically unsound" means by which to measure musical profundity.[40] The musicologist Robert Lach, for example, ridiculed efforts to link race with performance, scale systems, formal constructions, and other aspects of musical thought as little more than the work of untrained dilettantes and charlatans, claiming that "currently comparative musicology is not yet equipped to demonstrate racial elements and other criteria in human musical creation."[41] Yet as the case of Rudolf Maria Breithaupt shows, not all were so dismissive.

Race and performance

In Weimar music circles, Rudolf Maria Breithaupt (1873–1945), a piano teacher at the *Stern'schen Konservatorium*, was widely recognized as one of Germany's foremost authorities on pianism. His 1907 *Die Natürliche Klaviertechnik* (The Natural Piano Technique) made a quick sensation and remains today one of the definitive reference works on modern piano arm-weight technique. However, in 1922, his writings on performing artists took a turn away from the role played by proper technical training and education toward matters concerning race. In Breithaupt's words: "Talent as it applies to instrumental music is in the first place a racial question; that is, of things having more to do with the blood, heredity and aptitude than with teaching organization, education and the atmosphere and culture." Skill in performance, Breithaupt went on, was not derived from technique but "from the blood and wellsprings of energy of race and from [other] inherited instincts." In contrast to the "nurture" arguments of critics like Zilcher, Breithaupt claimed that while certain "qualities of character" such as "energy, steadfastness, stamina, affection, and warmth of feeling ... could probably be refined and deepened, they must first be present from birth."[42]

However, unlike his fellow conservatives Heuss and Schmitt Breithaupt did not agree with the sentiment that Germans were inherently superior players of German music or that of any other national tradition. Given the knowledge that Breithaupt, like Heuss, was a member of the Nazi Kampfbund für Deutsche Kultur, assuming the role of liaison between the organization and German conservatives in 1932, his views on race and performance in the early years of the Weimar Republic might come as a surprise.[43] Writing a decade before this appointment, Breithaupt observed that "two races exhibit a peculiar aptitude and adaptation to the instrumental arts, especially piano and violin music: the *Semitic* and the *Slavic.*" Breithaupt's ideal racialized performer was a combination of both: "The best breeding ground for playing talent, both amongst ourselves as well as other völkisch tribes, consists in the cross-breeding and mixing of both races, like the ancient Germans, Hungarians, Romanians, etc."[44] Summarily dismissive of "pure cultures" (*Reinkulturen*) as "more suspicious," Breithaupt viewed the racial hybrid as predisposed to fresher, more authentic renditions. For this reason, it was not the ethnically homogeneous Germany but the multinational territories of the former Austro-Hungarian Empire that figured as the ideal geographical setting for producing talented performers: "the greatest percentage of Austrian talent is mixed blood, combining Hungarian, Bohemian, Polish, Croat-Slovene, and Roman-Italian elements with or without Jewish ingredients." In particular, Austria proved well disposed toward producing Breithaupt's idealized hybrids: "Russian father with Polish-Jewish mother, pure Polish father with Russian-Jewish mother, or Russian Jew with pure polish or German mother. To these we might add the many mixtures of Jewish blood with Hungarian, Croatian, Slovenian, Czech, etc., as well as the mixture of Jewish and Slavic hybrids with German blood."[45] If Austria was the breeding ground par excellence for producing talented artists, racially homogenous England was a place bereft of any musical talent whatsoever: "English stock appears, since the fall of a period of blossoming under Elizabeth, to be completely without [any sign of] the muse and grace." For Breithaupt, the more general absence of a sufficiently highbrow culture in England was due "to an irresistible fondness for soccer and boxing as well as water sports which, from the outset, stamped out artistic activity in the area of the musically-inspired arts."[46]

In his analysis of performance, Breithaupt proved the consummate *bricoleur* in the sheer range of arguments he marshaled to support his overarching claim. In one striking passage, he dabbled in phrenology: "The frontal lobe is more developed than the sensitive area of the brain. A desire for imitation and sense of reality lead to a more complete technique." Elsewhere, Breithaupt drew upon older climatological arguments dating from the early modern period.

> The cheerfulness, the love of singing and playing as well as the greater personal freedom and autonomy of the Austrian tribes does not allow for imitation. That is a tribal merit, like climatic influences. One thinks of the sun in Italy and its influence on the human voice, which comes more naturally to the hotter southern climes than the colder and stricter northern ones.[47]

However, no matter how important Slavic and Semitic racial lineage was for Breithaupt, a proper musical interpretation still required the performer to possess certain German cultural attributes: "whether mixed or unmixed, race itself, like the Bohemian or Slavic strains, together delivers more and more of the really first rate material for talented pianists and [performers of] violin and cello music, especially if it [race] is wedded to German discipline and thoroughness, German views and cultural taste."[48] Rather than back up his claims with abstractions such as the "nature" and "character" of "German music-making" or "Jewish methods of performance," Breithaupt instead attempted a more "empirical" line of argument: "Which [race] contains a higher percentage [of performers], especially among virtuosi, than the Semitic race?"[49] Pure Jews or hybrids, according to Breithaupt, dominated the ranks of some of the illustrious musicians of the nineteenth century and beyond.

Breithaupt was not alone in his views, nor were they unique to the Weimar period. As we saw above, if Arthur Schnabel resisted efforts to inject race or ethnicity into discussions of musical performance, the same cannot be said of his mentor—the Polish pedagogue Theodor Leschetizky—who would famously ask his students if they were of Jewish and Slavic descent and "rub his hands with glee" upon hearing them answer in the affirmative.[50] Some of these laudatory perspectives continued into the Weimar years. In a 1926 essay published in the conservative *Signale für die musikalische Welt*, critic Karl Westermeyer lamented the rise of anti-Semitic rhetoric both in the street and in music journalism. Unlike Heuss, in whose eyes Jewish influence remained foreign and unhealthy, Westermeyer held that Jews were a wholly positive influence on German musical culture. Mendelssohn, for example, was as much a part of the German canon as Mozart and Haydn, while Mahler continued to be performed in front of sold-out audiences. And Westermeyer also celebrated Jewish performers: "We have to thank the Jews, who [have bestowed upon us] a long succession of competent, even eminent musicians ... [a fact which] only malice can deny!!"[51] The violinist and pedagogue Carl Flesch made a similar claim in a 1931 book titled *The Problem of Sound in Violin Playing* (*Das Klangproblem im Geigenspiel*), positing that the roots of modern Jewish virtuosity originated in the Jewish "ghetto fiddler."[52] Similarly, in his 1926 *Jewishness in Music* musicologist Heinrich Berl described musical virtuosity as quintessentially Jewish. Adopting the same title as Richard Wagner's notorious 1869 tract of the same name, Berl stood Wagner's argument about Jews as mere cultural imitators and imposters on its head and aimed to defend the virtues of the Jewish virtuoso. In response to the long-standing stereotype, which claimed that Jewish success in the musical reproduction of German and other musical traditions masked their own inability for true cultural creativity, Berl claimed that "the virtuoso brings music to life again and again; he releases it from its abstraction into life ... He is not simply the dazzler, but rather *the creator of music.*"[53] There was, it seemed, much to admire about Jewish contributions to Germany's renowned musical culture over the past century.

At the same time, it would be wrong to regard these critics' views as wholly philo-Semitic for underneath the superficial praise often lurked a certain anti-Semitic logic. As Annkatrin Dahm has shown, aside from praise for Jews as performers, the rest of Berl's book is full of vulgar anti-Semitism, from denouncing the "oriental-Asian" character of Jewish composers' music to describing Jews' cultural foreignness as stemming from a "false-morphosis" [*Pseudomorphose*] into German society.[54] During Weimar, vehement anti-Semites such as publisher Theodor Fritsch attributed the widespread European acclaim of Jewish performers in musical and mainstream print as little more than proof of Jewish control of the press.[55] Flesch's thesis surrounding Jews' innate virtuosity triggered a critical response in the conservative *Allgemeine Musik-Zeitung* from the German violinist Gustav Havemann, who wrote that Flesch's claim "offended him as a German" and insisted "this is a tone that our race rejects, as it is too soft and sensuous."[56] As for Breithaupt, who had extolled the "Semitic race" as exceptionally talented when it came to performance, Jews had to attain excellence in performance through "other kinds of ambition and vanity achieved through a thousand years of a business mercantile instinct [which] yielded money and fame."[57] In his view, success gained through centuries of achievement in finance and money-making ventures somehow translated, over time, into even greater success within the European concert hall. Moreover, however great Jews might appear in their capacities as performers, there could be little question as to which was the most innovative race in Breithaupt's view:

> When one casts a glance at the history of *creative* music, the exact opposite is true. Here, in any case, the Jews are in the minority, even though they have forever dominated the lighter kinds of art like operetta and the market for so-called popular music (*Gebrauchsmusik*). Talents, the likes of Halévy, Mendelssohn and Meyerbeer, in any case, remain exceptions to the rule.[58]

Breithaupt's essay sparked vigorous debates in the Weimar musical press. Scarcely two months following its publication, Richard Sternfeld published a review of "Spieltalent und Rasse" in the pages of the *Allgemeine Musik-Zeitung* acknowledging that no matter how "nice and lucid" the essay was, "things still do not mesh as easily as Breithaupt thinks." Along with Breithaupt's habit of ascribing Jewishness based solely on Jewish-sounding last names, Sternfeld called into question both the alleged Jewishness of those performers cited as well as the "pure" Slavishness of the composers Liszt and Chopin. Sternfeld pointed out that Liszt's parents were of central European (Austrian and German) extraction, while Liszt himself, "blond haired and blue eyed," was born in the German-speaking frontier town of Raiding and received his formal schooling in German schools. As for Chopin, his father was French and spoke no other language. Sternfeld pointed toward factors outside of race as the best means for understanding those gifted not only in music but also in the arts in general:

> I believe that such an investigation [into race and playing talent] must employ other means ... Should [we] only consider the descent of artists, poets and musicians and take scarcely any account of [the role of] the environment, the fatherland one is born into, language in particular, education and other mysteriously congenial strengths which are never allowed to be brought into certain explanations?[59]

Even among critics who found themselves in agreement with Breithaupt's central argument, a closer examination of their claims reveals important ruptures in race thinking between Weimar and the Third Reich within musical discourse.

Writing in a late 1923 edition of the *Allgemeine Musik-Zeitung*, Gustav Ernest claimed that although many of the performers cited by Breithaupt may have been born Jewish or assimilated through conversion, many had shed their Jewishness to fully become part of the German *Volk*. With delicious irony, Ernest cited Houston Stewart Chamberlain, whose *Foundations of the Nineteenth Century* became a standard text of the anti-Semitic right during Weimar and well into the Third Reich. According to Ernest, Chamberlain was "a consummate artist" (*Tausendkünstler*) who, "although classified as such, was certainly no Englishman." Through his immersion into and affinity with German culture, Chamberlain had "in no time at all produced irrevocable proof" of his German nature. Chamberlain was not the only convert to the German *Volk*. Quite a few of the so-called Jewish artists cited by Breithaupt could, in Ernest's view, also be considered wholly German, even those whose parents admittedly derived from "Semitic" stock. Anton Rubinstein, for example, though born to Jewish parents was "certainly no Jew."[60]

Such a designation, according to Ernest, was never claimed by Rubinstein himself; rather, it stemmed from both his early biographer Alexander McArthur as well as the *Grove History of Music*. Rubinstein's adoption of German spiritual and cultural values allowed the composer to successfully cast off his Jewishness despite his racial ancestry, a notion that bears a striking resemblance to Chamberlain's own views on "spiritual anti-Judaism." Whispers of "spiritual Jewishness" increased markedly during Weimar and, as Steven Aschheim has shown, loomed large in the anti-Semitic imaginary of a German society threated by "Judaization."[61] Yet its rootedness in behavioral rather than racial difference clearly distinguishes it from Nazi anti-Semitism. It was above all Jewish "attitudes" and "materialist values"—both of which, in Ernest's view, Rubinstein had managed to shake off—which threatened German society. The proper solution resided not in purging Germany of its Jewish elements in Nazi-like fashion but in actively combatting the cultivation of these values among Jews and non-Jews. The successful removal of the behavioral transcended the racial: "a wholly humanized Jew," as Chamberlain himself once explained it, "is no longer a Jew."[62]

Attitudes surrounding the virtues of racial mixing were not confined merely to the performance of art music but also to its composition as well. Influential critic and editor of the *Börsen Zeitung*, the moderate Adolph Weissman, noted, "It is race which colors modernity. But racial mixtures now appear to open up new possibilities [in composition]." Weissman separated contemporary music into "Western" and "Eastern" domains characterized by "sonority" and "instinct for folk-psyche," respectively. Stravinsky, exemplar of the "Western" domain, represented the fulfillment of a long-standing collaboration "between the French and Russian mind," each of which languished for different reasons: "the French folk-spirit was not potent enough of itself to create a new music," while Russian music expressed nothing more than "barbaric folk-feeling."[63] Yet in combining them, "Stravinsky paved the way for that music which we recognize as a synthesis of … the highest refinement, which finds its supreme expression in *Le Sacre du Printemps*." Similarly, Schoenberg, whom Weissman associated with the "Eastern domain," revolutionized compositional technique through a groundbreaking approach that "rests on Jewish racial feeling fused with the characteristic impulse of German music to form a new sonorous tissue."[64] To be sure, modern music, according to Weissman, had to resist the temptation of sustaining difference for its own sake. Still, he concluded, "In music, blood and not the mind is the ultimate determinant."[65]

Conclusion

How are we to make sense of this striking picture in which we find laudatory views of Jewish performance coexisting alongside stock-and-trade anti-Semitic prejudices, often in the same text? In an influential study, Detlev Peukert has argued that scholars must view Weimar on its own terms, as a period in German history whose fourteen-year existence "constitutes an era in its own right."[66] In the case of Weimar Jewry, the historian must perform a careful balancing act that neither normalizes German-Jewish relations to the point of depicting them as wholly harmonious nor views Weimar anti-Semitism solely through the lens of Auschwitz. Reflecting upon this latter point, historian Enzo Traverso has famously claimed that Auschwitz "invented" anti-Semitism for the way in which it has tended to impose a uniform and murderous strain of anti-Semitic prejudice onto a set of attitudes, which, prior to Nazism, are better described as "discordant, heterogeneous, and in many cases decidedly archaic."[67] In many ways, German critics' judgments on racialized performance embody this discord, alternating as they do from the behavioral to the racial, from philo- to anti-Semitism, and from inclusivity to exclusivity. They are, in a sense, quintessentially Weimar.

There was no contradiction for Weimar critics between, on the one hand, lauding Jews as consummate musicians who contributed in profound ways to the performance of the German classics while assailing them as compositionally uncreative, on the other.[68] And although some dismissed race altogether as an unsuitable lens through which to establish a basis for determining musical talent, Breithaupt singled out racial mixing—particularly between Jews and Slavs—as the means for achieving the best possible results. Such arresting juxtapositions can also be found beyond music criticism. In his study of consumer culture during the 1920s, Gideon Reuveni has shown that German crusaders against literary *Schmutz und Schund* (pulp and trash) typically exempted German Jewry from blame on account of their role as "producers" of works with high cultural worth rather than "consumers" vulnerable to the lure of base pulp literature. At the same time, this "producer" role furnished the greatest evidence of a "Jewish controlled press" that so captivated the minds of Weimar's anti-Semitic right.[69]

Another way to make sense of these positive judgments of Jewish musical performance lies in recognizing the repertoire at which Jewish musicians excelled in the minds of most critics: the German canon from Bach to Brahms. The "Jewishness" of many modernist composers and the backlash that it occasioned during the Weimar years has tended to attract the bulk of historians' attention.[70] Yet we would do well to remember the no less pronounced traditionalism of Jews in the arts as musicologists, performers, and pedagogues that reached back to the beginnings of the nineteenth century.[71] Musical observers could marginalize Mendelssohn, Meyerbeer, Mahler, and countless other Jewish-German composers— whether on aesthetic or anti-Semitic grounds—and in so doing marginalize Jews' creative legacies to German music. But Jews' contributions to tradition as performers, educators, and teachers were unmistakable. As Breithaupt himself was well aware, even a partial listing of the great nineteenth- and early twentieth-century Jewish musicians—many of whose interpretations and approaches to music-making deeply shaped the German repertoire—is nothing short of astonishing.[72]

Importantly, views about the virtues of racial mixing did not end with Hitler's rise to the chancellorship. Nazi ideologues were dogged throughout the 1930s by the suggestion that Beethoven was of mixed German and Flemish ancestry and that this had somehow contributed to his status as a "universal" composer.[73] In 1934 Fridolin Solleder, one of Hitler's First World War comrades, wrote an article claiming that the Renaissance artist Albrecht Dürer was of mixed racial stock and that racial mixing rather than purity produced creators of genius.[74] At the same time, many voices were emerging, which challenged such views. None were more forceful than Richard Eichenauer's 1932 *Musik und Rasse* (Music and Race), a book that attacked many of those same performers hailed by his predecessors.[75] After 1933, politics intruded into cultural debates in unprecedented ways as Nazi propagandists sought to refashion the nation's cultural patrimony after its own image and music was no exception. Thus many of the voices that contributed to the diverse views toward race and performance that characterized Weimar fell silent. By 1943, Germany's three leading conservative journals were consolidated into one appropriately called *Musik im Krieg*.[76]

Since 1945, discussions about race, ethnicity, and performance have tended to assume a cosmopolitan disposition, at least on the surface. The pianist Walter Gieseking offered a representative view in a piece entitled "Why I Play Debussy" from 1948:

> It has often been asked—often with astonishment—why exactly it is that an interpreter [meaning Gieseking himself] of German descent should have become so greatly associated with [Debussy's quintessentially] French music. The most simple and obvious answer to this question must be: music knows no boundaries. It is supra-national; a language understood by all peoples.[77]

Behind closed doors, however, Gieseking possibly remained conflicted on this question, as the recollection of one of his students, Marian Filar, reveals. Having sought out Gieseking as a mentor after the Second World War, Filar remembered: "Mr. Gieseking opened one of his pianos for me, so I sat down and played Bach, then Mozart. Mr. Gieseking didn't comment. Then he said to me, 'Since you're Polish, why don't you play some Chopin?'"[78] Gieseking's newfound cosmopolitanism did not exactly cohere with his behavior and pronouncements during, and immediately following, the Third Reich. In interviews with an allied intelligence officer in September 1945, he claimed to have been a "believer in Hitler's New Order" and that Hitler "was a very gifted person, a clever politician and [had] achieved many things for his country."[79] Although he never joined the Party, Gieseking enjoyed a privileged status among officially approved classical musicians and performed throughout Nazi-occupied Europe during the war.

While a cosmopolitan view of performance has loomed largest in most musical circles in the wake of the Holocaust, the ethno-racialist view has not entirely disappeared from view. Rather, we have inherited the historical residue of attitudes from Weimar's past. A recent Deutsche Grammophon review of Georges Cziffra's recording of Liszt's *Hungarian Rhapsodies* S.244, for example, hailed the pianist as the "ideal exponent of this music," not only because of his "superb technique" but also because of his "Hungarian birthright."[80] In a 2005 *60 Minutes* interview with virtuoso pianist Lang Lang, correspondent Bob Simon commented, "Rachmaninoff was this tortured Russian. And here you are ... this very young Chinese man, who seems to be full of life and full of optimism, and full of happiness. How can you relate to this music?"[81] Given all that has and continues to be made of music as a "universal language," we would do well to remember, as Ronald Radano and Philip Bohlman have suggested, "that a specter lurks in the house of music and it goes by the name of race."[82] Such essentialist attitudes may not be as overt as they once were and the characters may have changed, but they serve as a reminder of the myriad ways in which musical performance has often had so much to say about culture and society and so little to do with the music itself.

Notes

1. Josef Robert Harrer, "Ein Neger spielt Klavier," *Zeitschrift für Musik*, 97 (9) (1930): 735.
2. Ibid., 737.
3. Bryan Gilliam, ed., *Music and Performance during the Weimar Republic*, (Cambridge: Cambridge University Press, 1994).
4. Christopher Small, *Musicking: The Meanings of Performing and Listening* (Middletown: Wesleyan University Press, 1998), 4.
5. See, for example, Joel Rudinow, "Race, Ethnicity, Expressive Authenticity: Can White People Sing the Blues?" *The Journal of Aesthetics and Art Criticism*, 52 (1) (1994): 127–137 and Magdalena Waligórska, "A Goy Fiddler on the Roof," *Polish Sociological Review*, 4 (2005): 367–382.
6. Joseph Horowitz, *Conversations with Arrau* (New York: Alfred Knopf, 1982), 120.
7. Hermann Zilcher, "Deutsches Musizieren," *ZfM*, 99 (1932): 1061.
8. Rudolf Louis, *Die Deutsche Musik der Gegenwart* (München: Georg Müller, 1912), 303.
9. Quoted in Albrecht Riethmüller, "Is That Not Something for Simplicissimus?! The Belief in Musical Superiority," *Music and German National Identity*: 293.
10. Walter's harsh attacks on music critics in an October 1916 essay titled "Art and Public Opinion" in which the conductor accused critics of unfairly influencing the public and refusing to give certain works a fair hearing. See Erik Ryding and Rebecca Pechefsky, *Bruno Walter: A World Elsewhere* (New Haven: Yale University Press, 2001), 126–127.
11. Alfred Einstein to Paul Bekker, January 18, 1917, Box 4 Folder 37, Paul Bekker Papers MSS 50, Yale Music Library, Yale University.
12. Joachim Beck, "Bruno Walter," in *Berliner Musikjahrbuch* (Berlin: Julius Kinkhardt, 1926), 71.
13. Horowitz, *Conversations with Arrau*, 121 [emphasis in the original].
14. Arthur Schnabel, *My Life and Music* (New York: St. Martin's Press, 1964), 125.
15. Ibid., 195.

16 Kenneth Hamilton, *After the Golden Age: Romantic Pianism and Modern Performance* (New York: Oxford University Press, 2008), 22.
17 Lydia Goehr, *The Imaginary Museum of Musical Works: An Essay in the Philosophy of Music* (New York: Oxford University Press, 2007).
18 Ibid., 233. Of course, Liszt was also renowned as a virtuoso of unprecedented vision and skill and, as Goehr points out, while Liszt pioneered an approach to performance rooted in absolute fidelity to the printed score, he engaged widely in a virtuoso performances intended to show off his technique and improvisatory powers.
19 Walter Gieseking, *So Wurde Ich Pianist* (Wiesbaden: FA Brockhaus, 1963), 97 (emphasis mine).
20 Sofia Lourenço, "Tendencies of Piano Interpretation in the Twentieth Century: Concept and Different Types of Piano Interpretation Schools." Paper presented at the International Symposium on Performance Science" (Portugal: 2007).
21 Otto Schmitt, "Der deutche ausübende Künstler nach dem Kriege," *Zeitschrift für Musik*, 88 (1921): 329–331.
22 Ibid., 330.
23 Alfred Heuss, "Toscanini in Deutschland," *Zeitschrift für Musik*, 97 (1930): 552–554.
24 Ibid., 554.
25 Quoted in Karen Painter, *Symphonic Aspirations: German Music and Politics, 1900–1945* (Cambridge: Harvard University Press, 2007), 179.
26 Colin Storer, *A Short History of the Weimar Republic* (London: I.B. Tauris, 2013), 142.
27 See, for example, Eric Weitz, *Weimar Germany: Promise and Tragedy* (Princeton: Princeton University Press, 2007), 251–296.
28 Roderich Regidür, "Das Deutsche Publikum und die ausländischen Musiker," *Zeitschrift für Musik*, 94 (1927): 357.
29 Frank Warschauer, "Jazz, Zu Whitemans Berliner Konzerten," *Vossische Zeitung*, (June 19, 1926). I have used the translation in Anton Kaes, et al., eds., *The Weimar Republic Sourcebook* (Berkeley: University of California Press, 1994), 571–572.
30 Ibid., 571.
31 George Armin, "Caruso, der Sänger," *Allgemeine Musik-Zeitung*, 48 (1921): 584.
32 Ibid., 584.
33 Zilcher, "Deutsches Musizieren," 1061.
34 Ibid., 1062.
35 Siegmund Pislung, "Der Stil der impressionistischen Musik," *Die Musik*, 15 (1) (1922): 48.
36 Arthur Rubinstein, *My Many Years* (New York: Alfred Knopf, 1980), 195. That Gieseking's mother was French appears to have had more to do with wishful thinking than reality. Both his father and mother were German, the latter of whom hailed from Hannover. Gieseking set the record straight in his autobiography: "That

I was born in 1895 in Lyon, France, I suppose is well known although all of my ancestors were German." Gieseking, *So Wurde ich Pianist*, 119.
37 Herbert Johannes Gigler, "Musik und Klima," *Die Musik*, 15 (7) (1923): 516–518.
38 Ibid., 520.
39 Quoted in Joseph Horowitz, *Conversations with Arrau*, 44. There is no evidence to support the claim that Arrau was, in fact, "Germanically impregnated." Rather, he belonged to an old, prominent family of Southern Chile. His distant European forbears were, moreover, Scottish and Spanish, not German.
40 Pamela Potter, "The Concept of Race in German Musical Discourse," in *Western Music and Race*, ed. Julie Brown (New York: Cambridge University Press, 2007), 49.
41 Ibid., 57–58.
42 Rudolf Maria Breithaupt, "Spieltalent und Rasse," *Die Musik*, 15 (1) (1922): 37.
43 Michael Kater, "The Revenge of the Fathers: The Demise of Modern Music at the End of the Weimar Republic," *German Studies Review*, 15 (2) (1992): 305.
44 Breithaupt, "Spieltalent und Rasse," 37–38.
45 Ibid., 37–38.
46 Ibid., 41.
47 Ibid., 39.
48 Ibid., 39.
49 Ibid., 43.
50 Harold Schonberg, *The Great Pianists* (New York: Simon & Schuster, 1963), 280. In addition to these two questions, he would also inquire if they were a musical prodigy.
51 Karl Westermeyer, "Die musikalische Streitfragen," *Signale für die Musikalische Welt*, 84 (40) (1926): 1405–1411.
52 Michael Haas, *Forbidden Music: The Jewish Composers Banned by the Nazis* (New Haven: Yale University Press, 2013), 209.
53 Heinrich Berl, *Das Judenthum in der Musik* (Stuttgart: Deutsche-Verlags Anstalt, 1926), 183–189 (emphasis in the original).
54 Annkatrin Dahm, *Der Topos der Juden: Studien zur Geschichte des Antisemitismus im Deutschsprachigen Musikschrifttum* (Göttingen: Vandenhoeck & Ruprecht, 2007), 277–278.
55 Sander Gilman, "Are Jews Musical? Historical Notes on the Question of Jewish Musical Modernism," in *Jewish Musical Modernism: Old and New*, ed. Phillip Bohlman (Chicago: University of Chicago Press, 2009), vii–xvi.
56 Haas, *Forbidden Music*, 209.
57 Breithaupt, "Spieltalent und Rasse," 37.
58 Ibid., 43.
59 Richard Sternfeld, "Spieltalent und Rasse: Eine Entgegnung an Rud. Maria Breithaupt," *Allgemeine Musik-Zeitung*, 49 (1922): 920.
60 Gustav Ernest, "Noch einige Worte zum Thema 'Spieltalent und Rasse,'" *Allgemeine Musik-Zeitung*, 50 (1923): 4.

61 Steven E. Aschheim, "The Jew Within: The Myth of 'Judaization' in Germany," in *Culture and Catastrophe: German and Jewish Confrontations with National Socialism and Other Crises*, ed. Steven E. Aschheim and Robert W. Jensen (New York: New York University Press, 1996), 45–68.
62 Ibid., 58.
63 Adolph Weissmann, "Konzert," *Die Musik*, 15 (4) (1923): 305–306.
64 Ibid., 305–306.
65 Adolph Weissmann, "Race and Modernity," *The League of Composers Review*, 1 (3) (1923): 3–6.
66 Detlev Peukert, *The Weimar Republic: The Crisis of Classical Modernity* (London: Penguin Press, 1991), xii.
67 Enzo Traverso, *The Origins of Nazi Violence* (New York: The New Press, 2003), 6.
68 Breithaupt, "Spieltalent und Rasse," 43–44.
69 Gideon Reveuni, *Reading Germany: Literature and Consumer Culture in Germany before 1933* (New York: Berghahn Books, 2006), 251–252.
70 See, for example, Peter Gay, *Weimar Culture: The Outsider as Insider* (W.W. Norton & Company, 1968). Walter Laqueur, *Weimar: A Cultural History* (New York: Perigree Books, 1974).
71 On the role of music, and culture more generally, as a vehicle for Jewish assimilation into German social and civic life, see Deborah Hertz, *How Jews Became Germans: The History of Conversion and Assimilation in Berlin* (New Haven: Yale University Press, 2009), 124–164.
72 See Breithaupt, "Spieltalent und Rasse," 43. Breithaupt's listing of notable Jewish musicians included Henri und Jacques Herz, Henir Rosellen, Josef Ascher, Wilhelm Goldner, Sigismund Thalberg, Ignaz Moscheles, Felix Mendlessohn, Jakob Blumenthal, Felix Blumenthal, Karl Tausig, Anton and Nikolaus Rubinstein, Alexander Dreyschock, Julius Epstein, Theodor Leschetizky, Arthur Friedheim, Mortiz Moszkowski, Xaver Scharwenka, Raphael Joseffy, Emil Sauer, Moritz Rosenthal, Alfred Grünfeld, Alfred Reisenauer, Ferruccio Busoni, Frederic Lamond, Leopold Godowsky, Vianna da Motta, Mark Hambourg, Ossip Gabrilowtisch, Karl Friedberg, Ignaz Friedman, Gottfried Galston, Arthur Schnabel, Paul Goldschmidt, Leonid Kreutzer, Joseph Lhevinne, Severin Eisenberger, Bruno Eisner, Ignaz Tiegermann, and Alexander Borowski.
73 David Dennis, *Beethoven in German Politics, 1870–1989* (New Haven: Yale University Press, 1996), 73–74.
74 Quoted in Thomas Weber, *Hitler's First War: Adolf Hitler, the Men of the List Regiment, and the First World War* (New York: Oxford University Press, 2010), 316.
75 Richard Eichenauer, *Musik und Rasse* (München: J.F. Lehmanns Verlag, 1937), 303.
76 Fabian Lovisa, *Musikkritik im Nationalsozialismus: Die Rolle deutschsprachiger Musikzeitschriften* (Laaber: Laaber Verlag, 1993).
77 Gieseking, *So Wurde ich Pianist*, 118.

78 Marian Filar, *From Buchenwald to Carnegie Hall* (Jackson: University Press of Mississippi, 2002), 142.
79 David Monod, *Settling Scores: German Music, Denazification and the Americans, 1945–1953* (Chapel Hill: University of North Carolina Press, 2005), 156.
80 Georges Cziffra, Liszt: 10 Hungarian Rhapsodies. EMI Classics (liner notes), 2001.
81 Bob Simon, "Lang Lang: Piano Prodigy" 2005. http://www.cbsnews.com/stories/2005/01/07/60minutes/main665508.shtml?CMP=ILC-SearchStories.
82 Ronald Radano and Philip Bohlman, eds., *Music and the Racial Imagination* (Chicago: University of Chicago Press, 2000).

Epilogue: Rethinking Tradition

While recognizing the strong bases upon which the association between cultural conservatism on one hand and the forces of political reaction on the other has often rested, this book has tried to expand our understanding by examining several instances in which such straightforward associations have been all too prone to break down. Yet an important question remains: if, as I have tried to suggest, the limitations attaching to the "conservative syndrome" are so great, why does it persist? In what follows, I would like to suggest that the association between German conservative culture and Nazism stems from three major sources: the perceived cultural orientation of Nazism, the impact of the First World War on international attitudes toward German culture, and the influence of the émigré generation of scholars on the writing of Weimar history.

First, for many years historians viewed Nazism as wholly anti-modernist and committed in principle to supplanting a German culture sickened by modernity with a healthy traditional one. Although recent scholarship has challenged the extent to which we can view Nazism as fundamentally anti-modernist, few would question its traditionalism within the realm of high culture. As Hitler himself declared in a 1928 Munich speech, "We need not create any new art; if we cannot achieve anything great then let us concentrate on what is already there, which is immortal."[1] This cultural outlook was reinforced through the repeated public denigration of modernist art as "degenerate," and "Bolshevist" over the course of the Weimar and Nazi periods as well as through the staging of large spectacles, such as the notorious *Entartete Musik/Kunst* exhibitions of 1937–1938.[2] Perhaps because Nazism has largely been seen as staunchly traditional, tradition's defenders during Weimar—some of whom, of course, shared the Nazis antipathy toward Jews and modernist art—have often been seen as the incubators of those cultural ideals and hostilities, which later hatched with such terrific force under the Third Reich. In this case, as with so many other aspects of German history, a clear picture of Weimar culture has been occluded by the vast shadow Nazism and the Holocaust has cast over Germany since unification. Nazism, whose rise to prominence is linked in fundamental ways to the crisis of the Weimar state and society, has understandably pushed historians to highlight cultural crises as well, embodied above all in the cultural modernity of Weimar. After 1945, many Germans were keen to advertise their admiration for cultural modernism in an effort to signal their antipathy for Nazism. As the musicologist Alfred Einstein remarked in a 1948 letter to the composer Hans Gál, "In today's so-called Fourth Reich, everyone is enthusiastically embracing anything that between 1933 and 1945 would have counted as 'Cultural Bolshevism' as an effective means of justifying their sudden change of heart."[3] In this sense, Nazism could in some ways be said to have created "Weimar culture" as we have conventionally understood it.

Second, the First World War had a shattering impact not only on German social, economic, and political life but also on the wider public perception of German culture and its relationship to the nation. It would be hard to exaggerate the unrivaled regard with which the international community held German music on the eve of the First World War. Its status as the most profound cultural creation of the Germans—or, indeed, all nations—was without parallel. German conductors held many of the leading posts among America's greatest orchestras, including Boston where the German nationalist Karl Muck served at the pleasure of the Kaiser. The ranks of the world's leading orchestras, too, swelled with German musicians—of the hundred musicians in the Boston Philharmonic before 1914, nearly one-third held German or Austrian citizenship while in Chicago, the German language itself was the lingua franca of orchestra rehearsals in the decades leading up to the First World War.[4] In surveying concert programming across over the period 1890–1915, it has been estimated that more than 60 percent of all repertoire performed in the United States stemmed from Austro-German composers.[5]

The Great War did much to upend this state of affairs. German *Kultur* went from benign and noble cultural export to nefarious, chauvinistic ideology in the service of German imperial aggression and saber rattling on the world stage. Following the US entry into the war in 1917, the Committee on Public Information led by George Creel launched a fierce propaganda campaign to help Americans make sense of why they were fighting in the first place. Allied propagandists evinced real concern with how, exactly, to demonize the new enemy, given the immense German influence on the development of American cultural institutions, from museums and universities to all aspects of classical music culture. Unable to ignore the high regard in which Americans held German culture, propagandists decided on a strategy that depicted "good" and "bad" Germany as two sides of the same coin. Seen in this light, the civilizing impulses of German musicians and artists were not the noble pursuits the casual observer might take them for but rather a cynical facade that masked Germans' underlying goals of conquest and enslavement. Upon the US entry in 1917 Wagner productions ceased at the Metropolitan Opera while Beethoven was dropped by the Pittsburgh Symphony.[6] In Boston, Karl Muck was arrested amid whispers that he was acting as a covert spy for the German government.

Allied propaganda endlessly mocked German claims to cultural superiority in the face of the fervent militarism they displayed during the war. Anti-German propaganda appeared regularly in popular US media, such as *Century Magazine* that commissioned a remarkable series of illustrations by the noted anti-German Dutch cartoonist Louis Raemaekers, while for its part the US government featured German *Kultur* in an iconic 1917 enlistment poster.

Image 15 "Destroy This Mad Brute", US Government poster, ca. 1917. Source: Library of Congress, Prints & Photographs Division, WWI Postersj. Image retrieved from https://www.loc.gov/pictures/item/2010652057.

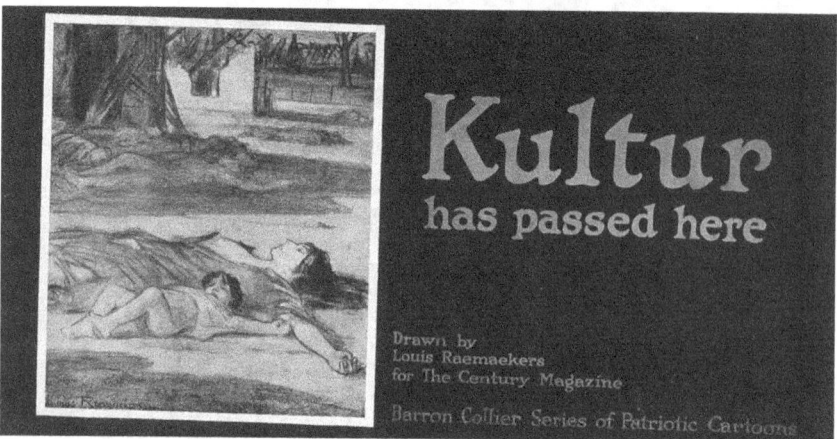

Image 16 Raemaekers's War Cartoons, *Century Magazine*, 1916. Source: Library of Congress, Prints & Photographs Division, WWI Posters. Image retrieved from https://lccn.loc.gov/17031662.

As image 15 illustrates, Germany's legacy of cultural chauvinism, represented on the bloodied club by the word *Kultur* is depicted as of a piece with the German penchant for militarism (the word is faintly scrawled on the ape's helmet), which, having already laid waste to European civilization in the background, posed the greatest threat to American freedom and liberty. Yet as the remarkable series of pieces done for *Century Magazine* as part of the Barron Collier Series of Patriotic Cartoons illustrates (see image 16), American propagandists had already seized on the pernicious relationship between German militarism and *Kultur* before America's formal entry into the war in April 1917. The postcard depicting soldiers hospitalized from a gas attack was apparently inspired by a French report documenting the Germans use of poison gas. According to two French doctors,

> We were able to observe at Calais a relatively important number of soldiers who had been subjected to the action of irritant gases (bromine chlorin vapors) employed by the Germans at Langemark. A certain number of soldiers are not able to flee from the gaseous cloud; they lie vomiting blood. Others, utterly collapsed, drag themselves to the rear; they vomit and spit blood.[7]

Raemaekers's war cartoons appeared together in April 1917 in a special oversize volume limited to just over 1,000 copies with a foreword provided by Theodore Roosevelt.[8]

The American government did not stop there, however. In November 1917, seven months after the official US declaration of war against Germany, the Committee on Public Information published a pamphlet entitled *Conquest and Kultur: Aims of the Germans in Their Own Words*. The pamphlet purported to show a Germany eager for war, where deep-seated cultural chauvinism could be found from the Kaiser down to the ordinary Bürger and everywhere in between. The academy, long viewed as a viper's nest of reaction and nationalism, was singled out as a site of particular infection, as a quotation from the great legal historian Otto von Gierke (1841–1921) showed: "The more it [German Kultur] remains faithful to itself, the better will it be able to enlighten the understanding of foreign races absorbed or incorporated into the Empire, and to make them see that *only from German Kultur can they derive those treasures which they need for the fertilizing of their own particular life*."[9] In another example, propagandists cited a 1915 sermon from a German pastor, who claimed, "*The German nation leads in the domains of Kultur, science, intelligence, morality, art, and religion; in the entire domain of the inner life* … thus this war is a war of envy and jealousy of Germany's leadership. It is a fight of hounds against a noble quarry."[10] German warmongering and *Kultur*, so it appeared from the Allied perspective, appeared not simply curiously compatible with each other but a positively noxious driving force behind German aggression, which, if left unchecked, threatened to spread its tentacles over the entire West.

This was not just an American view but one shared by the French and British who likewise were fond of using the Germans' own words against them. The year 1915 saw the appearance in London of *Germany's War Mania: The Teutonic Point of View as Officially Stated by Her Leaders*, a compilation of alarming quotations and utterances by high-placed government officials, military leaders, and intellectuals, from the military theorist Clausewitz and historian Treitschke to the Emperor Wilhelm II himself. Despite its title, the book claimed that the German hunger for war and conquest was not limited to a small clique of warmongers in the government but a desire widely shared among the German people. Unlike the more tolerant and cosmopolitan British, Americans, French, and Russians, "to the modern German … moral qualities, mental achievement, and spiritual insight serve no useful purpose in the life of a State, unless they can be used to bolster up the doctrine of blood and iron, and the monstrous theory that human society rests on a foundation of force."[11]

It must be said, however, that this depiction of a bellicose Germany waging war in defense of *Kultur* was not merely a consequence of Allied propaganda. Many Germans themselves viewed the conflict in precisely these terms. Military officials assigned the series of forts and defensive positions along the French frontier the code name 'Siegfried' after the Wagnerian hero, a designation that was quickly taken up by the Allies and used for the duration of the war. Leading artists, writers, intellectuals, and other members of Germany's *Bildungsbürgertum* conceived of the war in a series of binaries: *Kultur* vs. *Zivilisation* (culture vs. civilization), *Helden* vs. *Händler* (heroes vs. traders), *Gemeinschaft* vs. *Gesellschaft* (community vs. society). Such German virtues and the vices to which they were opposed found their earliest and most wide-ranging expression in Thomas Mann with the publication of his *Betrachtungen eines Unpolitischen* (Reflections of a Nonpolitical Man), published in 1918. Although he would later emerge as a fierce critic of the Nazi regime in American exile and single out German cultural chauvinism as a factor in the descent toward Nazism, all of this lay in the future. An examination of Mann's attitudes during the first war reveals a nationalist figure committed to the rightness of the German cause in defense of *Kultur*. As Mann put it in the prologue of this jingoistic work, "The political spirit [is] an alien and impossible spirit in Germany … German tradition is culture, soul, freedom, art and *not* civilization, society, voting rights, and literature."[12] Although Mann did not himself invent the *Kultur-Zivilsation* binary—it was first popularized in the twentieth century by Oswald Spengler in his widely popular *Decline of the West* and transmitted, via Mann, to the sociologist Norbert Elias in the latter's seminal *The Civilizing Process*—he gave it a new lease on life as a tool that helped Germans make sense of the catastrophe unfolding before their eyes.

Efforts on the part of fellow intellectuals located within "enemy nations" (*Feindnationen*) to openly renounce the war and German aggression all too often fell on deaf ears. The French essayist and music scholar Romain Rolland's plea to German intellectuals to condemn German barbarism in Belgium in August 1914, for example, was all but ignored. In October 1914, a collection of Germany's foremost artists and academics—including such luminaries as Max Liebermann, Fritz Haber, Max Klinger, Max Planck, and Wilhelm Roentgen—issued the so-called Manifesto of Ninety-three Artists and Scholars, which defiantly declared, "Believe that we shall fight this war to the end *as a cultured people to whom the legacy of a Goethe, Beethoven, and Kant, are just as sacred as hearth and land.*"[13] Less than one year later, many of these same figures were to throw their weight behind the infamous *Intellektuelleneingabe*, a petition calling for the German annexation of territories in east and west, which was ultimately signed by 1,347 professors, artists, and writers.[14] These were men who principally viewed the war not as a political or social conflict but one on which the nation's own cultural survival depended. The year 1914 saw the emergence of a veritable cottage industry of books and pamphlets that looked at the looming conflict through the prism of *Krieg und Kultur* (war and culture) written by leading scholars, from the academic Otto von Gierke to the religious scholar Rudolf Smend.[15] Writing shortly after the outbreak of the war, the noted cultural historian Karl Lamprecht spoke for many when he wrote, "Faced with five invaders ... We can only hope that we will reach a point where the German Empire as a whole [in Europe] attains a position akin to the one Prussia held within the Reich itself and that from this leading position our *Kultur* is able to remain whole and not allowed to be destroyed by foreign elements."[16]

Within musical culture more specifically, many German artists and critics similarly proved eager to rally to the national cause. German composers were recast along nationalist lines as performances of native composers surged across the country while those of foreign artists declined. Even in Germany's cosmopolitan cities, the outbreak of war prompted a turn away from foreign music toward Bach, Beethoven, Brahms, and other German masters. In the winter of 1915 alone, one critic estimated that is was possible to hear Beethoven at least three times a day performed by one of Berlin's many ensembles, even though the overall number of concerts performed across Germany in 1915 was fully 50 percent lower than before the war.[17] Frankfurt was no different. Before the war, nineteen out of the thirty-five composers played by the municipal orchestra were German and sixteen foreign; in 1914, twenty-two out of thirty-one were German.[18] Earlier emphases on the universalist appeal of Beethoven among supporters of the SPD and other leftist political parties fell away, while following the German victory at the Battle of Tannenberg, military and civilian singing clubs joined together in Berlin's Potsdamer Platz to sing sacred music of Johann Sebastian Bach.[19] Cultural conservatives were far from alone in their fervent support for the war effort; in a letter to Alma Mahler in 1914, Arnold Schoenberg enthused, "Now comes the reckoning ... now we will throw these mediocre kitschmongers into slavery, and teach them to venerate the German spirit and to worship the German God."[20]

Finally, the early histories of Weimar so often written by those whom it failed were ones of abject failure, and here, a final important factor—the influence of the émigré generation of Weimar historians, led by Fritz Stern, Peter Gay, Walter Laqueur, and Theodor Adorno on the writing of Weimar history—deserves mention.[21] They differed widely in their approach to German history—Stern's early work evinced a preoccupation with a German *Sonderweg*, while Gay's and Laqueur's studies have established themselves as classics in the historiography of Weimar culture.[22] Yet in all three works, terms such as *crisis, catastrophe*, and *collapse* occurred early and often; for them, Weimar functioned as a mere prelude to Nazism. This, of course, they attributed to real pathologies which characterized Weimar—rising anti-Semitism, political violence, economic crises, and cultural anxieties, among others—but owed at least as much to the fact that Weimar failed all three of them on a deeply personal level. Stern and Gay were more fortunate, both having gotten out of Germany in 1938 and 1939, respectively, their immediate families intact. As for Laqueur, while he escaped in 1938 first to Palestine and the UK before settling in the United States in 1956, his parents were not so lucky—they were murdered in 1942, according to Yad Vashem, "somewhere in the East."[23] Faced with these realities, how could these historians' assessments of Weimar, the historical backdrop of their own shattered youth, have been expected to be anything other than one of failure?

This retrospective orientation toward Weimar was one of which members of the émigré generation were themselves later all too aware. Even postwar figures such as the philosopher Helmuth Plessner, who stood to benefit from his association with the modern, progressive Weimar of historical memory, had to acknowledge the selective and politically self-serving nature of this image and how far it diverged from the lived experience of most Germans who had inhabited that world. This Weimar, refracted through the prism of the Nazi catastrophe, was as much a figment of postwar imagination as historical reality, one that Plessner himself described as "the legend of the Twenties."[24] Plessner was far from alone. As the historian Walter Laqueur, whose *Weimar: A Cultural History* deeply shaped historical understanding of the period, put it in his memoirs:

> What we now call "Weimar culture" was really only part of the scene and for most of the time not even the dominant trend. During those years one hardly ever used the term "Weimar" ... only in the 1960s and 1970s did the term "Weimar" gain wide currency. There had been no Cultural Revolution, only gradual change in some fields. What we referred to as Weimar Culture really only pertained to Berlin and a few of the other big cities.[25]

Yet in his own work, Laqueur often wrote with a particular kind of culture in mind, namely Weimar modernism. There are obvious reasons why this should have been the case—Weimar, after all had been the cultural laboratory of figures like Brecht and Berg, not Beethoven and Bach, and while the latter continued to find a continued and widespread if sometimes unacknowledged interest among the German public, they did not represent the new *Zeitgeist* or register the striking dynamism that was so characteristic of Weimar for contemporaries and beyond. Still, such an emphasis has had the knock-on effect of reinforcing an all-pervasive sense of crisis and conflict between the forces of modernity and those of tradition.

Fritz Stern, whose memoir documents his own family's troubled experiences under Weimar, illustrates this tendency all too clearly. "'Weimar' conjures up two contrasting visions: a time of cultural brilliance, of triumphant modernism in all the arts ... and the reality of a modern democracy in agony. The two visions were visibly and invisibly linked: the political enemies of Weimar waged culture wars against alleged 'degenerate' or decadent art."[26] This picture of a heroic "good" Weimar culture pitted against a debased "bad" Weimar politics has yielded up a grim picture indeed, giving 1933 something of an air of inevitability about it. As Peter Gay said with regard to his own classic *Weimar Culture*, "I can defend my reading of the republic's short history as accurate, but an unmistakable air of mourning hangs over it." The picture of Weimar in his vivid retelling—one in which political suicides and murders, economic crisis, and cultural despair not only dominate but in some cases drive the narrative—was, Gay later had to admit, often "not the cool prose of a distant observer."[27] Reading through *Weimar Culture*, one detects the influence of Gay's advisor and fellow exile Hajo

Holborn, who adopted a similarly bleak and pessimistic register in his own survey of the period.[28]

Finally, perhaps no émigré historian wrote as extensively on music than Theodor Adorno. In addition to incisive studies of individual composers, from Beethoven and Wagner (1952) to Mahler (1960) and Berg (1968), his essays on music run to several hundred pages.[29] Yet Adorno was among the first to judge composers' complicity with the Nazi regime based on a superficial assessment of their musical style. This led him, for example, to rate the nationalist-conservative Arnold Schoenberg "socially clairvoyant" and wrongly assume that Winfried Zillig left Germany following the Nazi "seizure of power" based solely on those composers' modernist musical language.[30] Zillig, in fact, remained in Germany through the war and, in addition to writing the music for the Nazi propaganda film *Posen*, was attached to Goebbels Reich Music Chamber in his capacity as principal music director of the Reichsgautheater in occupied Poznan from 1940 onward.[31] Schoenberg, for his part, remained an unapologetic conservative monarchist even in American exile. Adorno must also be credited with cementing the association between Nazism and Wagner detailed earlier in this book. Reflecting in 1963 on the place of Wagner in postwar German society he wrote, "The form of nationalism that he embodied, especially in his work, exploded into National Socialism, which could draw on him, via Chamberlain and Rosenberg, for its rationalization … As the National Socialist potential continues to smolder within the German reality, now as then, so it is still present in Wagner."[32]

This is not to diminish the historical contributions of this generation as a whole. As a recent edited volume makes clear, they profoundly influenced some of the twentieth century's major historical events, from the First World War to the Holocaust to the Cold War. Their superb sweeping surveys were the general public's first introduction to the world of Weimar, though they also made incisive interventions on specialized debates in German history, from the 1980s *Historikerstreit* (Historians' Debate) to the so-called Fritz Fischer Controversy.[33] In sum, the émigré historians are still well worth reading but at least as much for what they tell us about a generation's efforts to come to grips with the trauma of displacement and exile as for the penetrating historical insights they offer into Weimar.

It has been nearly three decades since Celia Applegate wrote in a groundbreaking piece: "The identification of the nation with its music may have had unfortunate consequences for the political culture of Germany—late critics like Nietzsche and Mann certainly thought so—but firmer conclusions on that subject will have to await further research."[34] This book does not pretend to be the final word on musical culture in Germany during Weimar. It is indeed remarkable how underdeveloped the historiography on German music criticism in the first half of the twentieth century is, especially compared to that for the previous century. One fruitful line of future inquiry might be to do for the left-wing musical press what this study has done for the cultural right; that is, reexamine the no less pronounced connections between cultural modernism and leftist politics under Weimar in an effort to complicate our conventional understanding of their associations. More research is needed on the lives of countless critics whose activities both within and outside of concert life remain shrouded in mystery to measure more clearly where their aesthetic preferences resided and how, if at all, these carried over into their political and social activities. It would likewise be profitable to reexamine traditional culture in other historical settings—that of interwar France, for example—where a historiographical "doom and gloom" orthodoxy has tended to cast it in a similarly reactionary and unfavorable light.[35]

What this book has shown is that any attempt to delineate the cultural battle lines which formed over the course of the Republic must emphatically *not* proceed from a neat bifurcation, which pits culturally conservative political reactionaries on one side and modernist political progressives on the other. Recent work on the relationship between modernity and the rise of Nazism offers a cautionary tale for the historian seeking to establish similarly straightforward relationships between traditional culture and the German past.[36] The fate of the symphony concert under Weimar can indeed tell us much about the culture of the Weimar Republic—one that was no mere rehearsal for fascism.

Notes

1 Quoted in Frederic Spotts, *Hitler and the Power of Aesthetics* (New York: Overlook Press, 2004), 271.

2 David Dennis, *Inhumanities: Nazi Interpretations of Western Culture* (New York: Cambridge University Press, 2012). Amaury Du Closel, *Erstrickte Stimmen: "Entartete Musik" im Dritten Reich* (Köln: Böhlau Verlag, 2010).

3 Michael Haas, *Forbidden Music: The Jewish Composers Banned by the Nazis* (New Haven: Yale University Press, 2013), 274.

4 Joseph Horowitz, *Classical Music in America: A History of Its Rise and Fall* (New York: Norton, 2005), 83.

5 Jessica Gienow-Hecht, *Sound Diplomacy: Music and Emotions in Transatlantic Relations, 1850–1920* (Chicago: University of Chicago Press, 2009), 143.

6 Alex Ross, *The Rest Is Noise: Listening to the Twentieth Century* (New York: Picador, 2007), 101.

7   This account from Ministère des Affaires Etrangerès, *Les Violations des Lois de la Guerre par l'Alleemagne* (Paris: Berger-Levrault, 1915).
8   J. Murray Allison, ed., *The Century Edition Deluxe of Raemaekers' War Cartoons* (2 vols) (New York: Century Co., 1917).
9   Wallace Notestein and Elmer Stoll, eds., *Conquest and Kultur: Aims of the Germans in Their Own Words* (Washington: Committee on Public Information, 1917), 13 (emphasis in the original).
10 Ibid., 15 (emphasis in the original).
11 *Germany's War Mania: The Teutonic Point of View as Officially Stated by Her Leaders* (London: Ballyntine Books, 1915), 18.
12 Thomas Mann, *Reflections of a Nonpolitical Man* (New York: Ungar, 1987), 17 (emphasis in the original).
13 Bernhard vom Brocke, "'Scholarship and Militarism': The Appeal of 93 to the Civilized World" 4 October 1914 http://germanhistorydocs.ghi-dc.org/sub_document.cfm?document_id=938.
14 Peter Jelavich, "German Culture in the Great War," in *European Culture in the Great War: The Arts, Entertainment and Propaganda, 1914–1918*, ed. Aviel Roshwald and Richard Stites (New York: Cambridge University Press, 1999), 32–57.
15 Otto von Gierke, *Krieg und Kultur: Rede am 18. Sept. 1914* (Heymann 1914). Rudolf Smend, *Krieg und Kultur* (Tübingen: Kloeres, 1915).
16 Karl Lamprecht, *Krieg und Kultur: Drei vaterländische Vorträge* (Leipzig: S. Hirzel, 1914), 59–60.
17 See David Dennis, *Beethoven in German Politics, 1870–1989* (New Haven: Yale University Press, 1996), 67 and "Eine Statistik des deutschen Musiklebens," *Frankfurter Nachrichten*, September 28, 1916.
18 Cited in Hansjakob Ziemer, "Listening on the Home Front: Music and the Production of Social Meaning in German Concert Halls during World War I," in *Sounds of Modern History: Auditory Culture in 19th and 20th Century Europe*, ed. Daniel Morat (New York: Berghan Books, 2014), 210.
19 Dennis, *Beethoven in German Politics*, 78.
20 Ross, *The Rest Is Noise*, 72.
21 This is particularly reflected in the scholarship of émigré historians. For an excellent discussion of the other ways in which this generation shaped the historiography on Weimar, see Eric Weitz, "Weimar Germany and its Histories," *Central European History*, 43 (4) (2010): 581–591.
22 See Fritz Stern, *The Politics of Cultural Despair: A Study in the Rise of the Germanic Ideology* (Berkeley: University of California Press, 1961). Peter Gay, *Weimar Culture: The Outsider as Insider* (New York: Norton, 1968). Walter Laqueur, *Weimar: A Cultural History* (New York: G.P. Putnam's Sons, 1974).
23 Laqueur's parents' (Else and Fritz Laqueur) records are retrievable through Yad Vashem's online database at http://www.yadvashem.org/.

24 The quote and a superb review essay on new approaches to Weimar history are from Jochen Hung, "'Bad Politics and 'Good' Culture: New Approaches to the History of the Weimar Republic," *Central European History*, 49 (2016): 441–453.
25 Walter Laqueur, *Best of Times, Worst of Times: Memoirs of a Political Education* (Lebanon: Brandeis University Press, 2009), 35–36.
26 Fritz Stern, *Five Germanys I Have Known* (New York: Farrar, Straus & Giroux, 2007), 71.
27 Peter Gay, *My German Question: Growing up in Nazi Berlin* (New Haven: Yale University Press, 1999), 200–201.
28 Hajo Holborn, *A History of Modern Germany, 1840–1945* (New York: Alfred A. Knopf, 1969), 533–710.
29 These biographical sketches were all published in Adorno's lifetime, except for the Beethoven study. They are now available in English translation as Theodor Adorno, *Beethoven: The Philosophy of Music: Fragments and Texts* (Cambridge: Polity, 1993). Theodor Adorno, *In Search of Wagner* (New York: Verso, 2009). Theodor Adorno, *Mahler: A Musical Physiognomy* (Cambridge: MIT Press, 1993). Theodor Adorno, *Alban Berg: Master of the Smallest Link* (New York: Cambridge University Press, 1991).
30 Pamela Potter, "What Is 'Nazi Music'?" *The Musical Quarterly*, 88 (3) (2005): 428–455.
31 Lorenz Jäger, *Adorno: A Political Biography* (New Haven: Yale University Press, 2004), 85.
32 Theodor Adorno, "Wagner's Relevance for Today," in *Essays on Music*, ed. Theodor Adorno and Richard Leppert (Berkeley: University of California Press, 2002), 584–602 (here, 585).
33 Andreas Daum, Hartmut Lehmann and James Sheehan, eds., *The Second Generation: Émigrés from Nazi Germany as Historians* (New York: Berghahn Books), 2016.
34 Celia Applegate, "What Is German Music? Reflections on the Role of Art in the Creation of the Nation," *German Studies Review*, 15 (1992): 21–32 (here 31).
35 Eugen Weber, *The Hollow Years: France in the 1930s* (New York: W.W. Norton & Company, 1994). For a somewhat more nuanced revisionist account that focuses on musical trends, see Jane Fulcher, *The Composer as Intellectual: Music and Ideology in France, 1914–1940* (New York: Oxford University Press, 2005).
36 While advocates of a German *Sonderweg* attributed a net deficit in modernization to the rise of Nazism, newer approaches have stressed profound aspects of "modernity" that underlay Nazi policy. For a stimulating discussion on the problem, see Mark Roseman, "National Socialism and the End of Modernity," *The American Historical Review*, 116 (3) (2011): 688–701.

Select Bibliography

Archives and Special Libraries

Bekker, Paul. Papers. Gilmore Music Library, Yale University, USA.
Bibliothek des Musikwissenschaftlichen Seminar—Freie Universität, Zeitschriftenabteilung. Berlin, Germany.
Cook Music Library, Indiana University, Bloomington, USA.
Edward Jones Research Center, National World War I Memorial and Museum, USA.
Einstein, Alfred. Papers. Music Library, University of California, Berkeley, USA.
Gorton Music and Dance Library, University of Kansas, USA.
Moser, Hans Joachim. Papers. Staatsbibliothek zu Berlin—Preußischer Kulturbesitz Musikabteilung mit Mendelssohn-Archiv. Berlin, Germany.
Zeitschriftarchiv, Institut für Musikwissenschaft und Medienwissenschaft— Humboldt Universität, Berlin, Germany.

Primary Sources

Newspapers

Allgemeine Musik-Zeitung
Bayreuther Blatter
Berliner Musikjahrbuch
Der Auftakt
Der Merker
Die Musik
Die Tonkunst
The League of Composers Review
Melos
Modern Music
Music & Letters
Musikblätter des Anbruch
Neue Musik Zeitung
Proceedings of the Musical Association
Signale für die Musikalische Welt
Simplicissimus

Sonderabdruck aus den Preussischen Jahrbuchern
Vossische Zeitung`
Zeitschrift fur Musik
Zeitschrift fur Musikwissenschaft

Monographs

Adorno, Theodor. *Essays on Music*. Berkeley: University of California Press, 2002.
Adorno, Theodor. *In Search of Wagner*. New York: Verso, 2009.
Allison, J. Murray (ed.). *The Century Edition Deluxe of Raemaekers' War Cartoons* (2 vols.). New York: Century Co., 1917.
Babbitt, Milton. *Words about Music: The Madison Lectures*. Madison: University of Wisconsin Press, 1987.
Bekker, Paul. *Richard Wagner: His Life in His Work*. New York: W.W. Norton & Co., 1931.
Benjamin, Walter. *The Work of Art in the Age of Its Technological Reproducibility and Other Writings on Media*. Cambridge: Harvard University Press, 2008.
Berl, Heinrich. *Das Judenthum in der Musik*. Stuttgart: Deutsche Verlags-Anstalt, 1926.
Blessinger, Karl. *Die Musikalische Probleme der Gegenwart und ihre Lösung*. Stuttgart: Benno Filser Verlag, 1920.
Brecht, Arnold. *The Political Education of Arnold Brecht: An Autobiography 1884–1970*. Princeton: Princeton University Press, 1970.
Chamberlain, Houston Stewart. *Die Grundlagen des XIX. Jahrhunderts* (2 vols.). Munich: Bruckmann, 1899.
Diebold, Bernhard. *Der Fall Wagner*. Frankfurt am Main: Frankfurter Societäts-Druckerei GmbH, 1928.
Dimendberg, Edward, et al., eds. *The Weimar Republic Sourcebook*. Berkeley: University of California Press, 1994.
Dussel, Konrad & Edgar Lersch, eds. *Quellen zur Programmgeschichte des deutschen Hörfunks und Fernsehens*. Göttingen: Muster-Schmidt Verlag, 1999.
Eichenauer, Richard. *Musik und Rasse*. München: J.F. Lehmanns Verlag, 1937.
Einstein, Alfred. *Gluck: Sein Leben, seine Werke*. Basel: Bärenreiter, 1936.
Einstein, Alfred. *Heinrich Schütz*. Kassel: Bärenreiter, 1928.
Einstein, Alfred. *A Short History of Music*. New York: Knopf, 1937.
Filar, Marian. *From Buchenwald to Carnegie Hall*. Jackson: University Press of Mississippi, 2002.
Furtwängler, Wilhelm. *Briefe*. Wiesbaden: F.A. Brockhaus, 1964.
Furtwängler, Wilhelm. *Notebooks, 1924–1954*. London: Quartet Books, 1989.
Gay, Peter. *My German Question: Growing up in Nazi Berlin*. New Haven: Yale University Press, 1999.
Geck, Martin. *Die Weiderentdeckung der Matthäuspassion im 19. Jahrhundert: Die zeitgenössischen Dokumente und ihre ideengeschichtliche Deutung*. Regensburg: Bosse, 1967.

Gerigk, Herbert & Theophil Stengel, eds. *Lexikon der Juden in der Musik*. Veröffentlichungen des Instituts der NSDAP zur Erforschung der Judenfrage, no. 2. Berlin: Hahnefeld, 1940.

Gierke, Otto von. *Krieg und Kultur: Rede am 18. Sept. 1914*. Berlin: Heymann, 1914.

Gieseking, Walter. *So Wurde Ich Pianist*. Berlin: F.A. Brockhaus, 1975.

Goebbels, Joseph. *Die Tagebücher von Joseph Goebbels* (Band 1/II). München: K.G. Saur Verlag, 2005.

Heinitz, Wilhelm. *Strukturprobleme in Primitiver Musik*. Hamburg: Friederichsen, de Gruyter & Co., 1931.

Hoffmann, E. T. A. *Sämtliche Werke*. Frankfurt: Deutscher Klassiker Verlag, 2003.

Horowitz, Joseph. *Conversations with Arrau*. New York: Knopf, 1982.

Kestenberg, Leo. *Jahrbuch der deutschen Musikorganisationen 1931*. Berlin: Max Hesse, 1931.

Klemperer, Victor. *I Will Bear Witness: A Diary of the Nazi Years, 1933–1945* (2 vols.). New York: Random House, 1999.

Kretzschmar, Hermann. *Über den Stand der öffentlichen Musikpflege in Deutschland*. Leipzig: Breitkopf & Härtel, 1881.

Kunze, Stefan, ed. *Ludwig van Beethoven Die Werke im Spiegel seiner Zeit: Gesammelte Konzertberichte und Rezensionien bis 1830*. Laaber: Laaber-Verlag, 1987.

Lamprecht, Karl. *Krieg und Kultur: Drei vaterländische Vorträge*. Leipzig: S. Hirzel, 1914.

Laqueur, Walter. *Best of Times, Worst of Times: Memoirs of a Political Education*. Lebanon: Brandeis University Press, 2009.

Louis, Rudolf. *Die deutsche Musik der Gegenwart*. München: Georg Müller, 1912.

Ludwig, Emil. *Wagner oder die Entzauberten*. Berlin: Felix Lehmann Verlag, 1913.

Mann, Thomas. *Reflections of a Nonpolitical Man*. New York: Ungar, 1987.

Moser, Hans Joachim. *Geschichte der Deutschen Musik Vom Auftreten Beethovens bis zur Gegenwart* (vols. 1–3). Berlin: Cotta, 1923.

Moser, Hans Joachim. *Kleine deutsche Musikgeschichte*. Stuttgart: Verlag J.G. Cottasche, 1949.

Moser, Hans Joachim. *Musik-Lexikon*. Berlin-Schöneberg: Hesse, 1935.

Niemann, Walter. *Mein Leben fürs Klavier: Rückblicke und Ausblicke*. Düsseldorf: Staccato Verlag, 2008.

Nietzsche, Friedrich. *Basic Writings of Nietzsche*. New York: The Modern Library, 2000.

Nordau, Max. *Degeneration*. New York: Appleton, 1895.

Notestein, Wallace & Elmer Stoll, eds. *Conquest and Kultur: Aims of the Germans in Their Own Words*. Washington: Committee on Public Information, 1917.

Ostwald, Hans. *Sittengeschichte der Inflation: Ein Kulturdokument aus den Jahren des Marksturzes*. Berlin: Neufeld & Henius Verlag, 1931.

Pretzsch, Paul. *Die Kunst Siegfried Wagners: Ein Führer durch seine Werke*. Leipzig: Breitkopf und Härtel, 1919.

Riemann, Hugo. *Kleines Handbuch der Musikgeschichte mit Periodisierung nach Stilprinizipen und Formen*. Leipzig: Druck und Verlag, 1922.

Rosenberg, Alfred. *The Myth of the Twentieth Century*. New York: Noontide, 1982.
Rubinstein, Arthur. *My Many Years*. New York: Knopf, 1980.
Schnabel, Arthur. *My Life and Music*. New York: St. Martin's Press 1963.
Schwartz, Rudolf, ed. *Jahrbuch der Musikbibliothek Peters für 1924*. Leipzig: C.F. Peters, 1925.
Smend, Rudolf. *Krieg und Kultur*. Tübingen: Kloeres, 1915.
Söhnlein, Kurt. *Erinnerungen an Siegfried Wagner und Bayreuth*. Bayreuth: ISWG, 1980.
Speer, Albert. *Inside the Third Reich*. New York: MacMillan, 1970.
Spengler, Oswald. *Der Untergangs des Abendlandes: Umrisse einer Morphologie der Weltgeschichte, I: Gestalt und Wirlichkeit*. Vienna: Verlag Braumüller, 1918.
Stackelberg, Roderick & Sally A. Winkle. *The Nazi Germany Sourcebook: An Anthology of Texts*. New York: Routledge, 2002.
Stein, Leonard, ed. *Style and Idea: Selected Writings of Arnold Schoenberg*. Berkeley: University of California Press, 1984.
Stern, Fritz. *Five Germanys I Have Known*. New York: Farrar, Straus & Giroux, 2007.
Stuckenschmidt, H. H. *Zum Hören geboren: Ein Leben mit der Musik unserer Zeit*. München: Kassel, 1982.
Tovey, Donald. *German Culture: The Contribution of the Germans to Knowledge, Literature, Art and Life*. New York: Scribner's Sons, 1915.
Wackernagel, Peter. *Wilhelm Furtwängler: Die Programme der Konzerte mit dem Berliner Philharmonischen Orchester, 1922-1954*. Wiesbaden: F. A. Brockhaus, 1965.
Wagner, Richard (trans. Edwin Evans). *Judaism in Music*. London: William Reeves, 1910.
Wagner, Richard (trans. W. Ashton Ellis). *Judaism in Music and Other Writings*. Lincoln: University of Nebraska Press, 1995.
Wulf, Josef. *Musik im Dritten Reich: Eine Dokumentation*. Gütersloh: Sigbert Mohn Verlag, 1963.
Ziegler, Hans Severus. *Entartete Musik: eine Abrechnung*. Völkischer Verlag: Dusseldorf, 1938.
Zweig, Stefan. *The World of Yesterday*. New York: Viking Press, 1943.

Secondary Sources

Allen, Ann Taylor. *Satire and Society in Wilhelmine Germany: Kladderdatsch & Simplicisssimus, 1890-1914*. Lexington: The University Press of Kentucky, 1984.
Alter, George. *The German Question and Europe: A History*. New York: Oxford University Press, 2000.
Applegate, Celia. *Bach in Berlin: Nation and Culture in Mendelssohn's Revival of the St. Matthew Passion*. Ithaca: Cornell University Press, 2005.
Applegate, Celia, "How German Is It? Nationalism and the Idea of Serious Music in the Early Nineteenth Century," *19th Century Music*, 21 (3) (1998): 274-296.

Applegate, Celia, "The Internationalism of Nationalism: Adolf Bernhard Marx and German Music in the Mid-Nineteenth-Century," *Journal of Modern European History*, 5 (2007): 139–158.

Applegate, Celia, *The Necessity of Music: Variations on a German Theme*. Toronto: University of Toronto Press, 2017.

Applegate, Celia, "Saving Music: Enduring Experiences of Culture," *History and Memory*, 17 (2005): 217–237.

Applegate, Celia, "What Is German Music? Reflections on the Role of Art in the Creation of the Nation," *German Studies Review*, 15 (1992): 21–32.

Applegate, Celia & Pamela Potter, eds. *Music and German National Identity*. Chicago: University of Chicago Press, 2002.

Aschheim, Steven. *Culture and Catastrophe: German and Jewish Confrontations with National Socialism and Other Crises*. New York: New York University Press, 1996.

Attfield, Nicholas. *Challenging the Modern: Conservative Revolution in German Music, 1918-1933*. Cambridge: Cambridge University Press, 2017.

Birdsall, Carolyn. *Nazi Soundscapes: Sound, Technology and Urban Space in Germany, 1933-1945*. Amsterdam: Amsterdam University Press, 2012.

Blackbourn, David & Geoff Eley. *The Peculiarities of German History: Bourgeois Politics and Society in Nineteenth-Century Germany*. New York: Oxford University Press, 1984.

Bohlman, Philip, ed. *Jewish Musical Modernism: Old and New*. Chicago: University of Chicago Press, 2009.

Bollenbeck, Georg, "German Kultur, the Bildungsbürgertum and Its Susceptibility to National Socialism," *The German Quarterly*, 73 (1) (2000): 67–83.

Botstein, Leon, "Listening through Reading: Musical Literacy and the Concert Audience," *19th-Century Music*, 16 (2) (1992): 129–145.

Bowles, Edmund, "Karl Muck and His Compatriots: German Conductors in America during World War I (and How They Coped)," *American Music*, 25 (4) (2007): 405–440.

Brenner, Michael. *The Renaissance of Jewish Culture in Weimar Germany*. New Haven: Yale University Press, 1996.

Brinkmann, Reinhold & Christoph Wolff, eds. *Driven into Paradise: The Musical Migration from Nazi Germany to the United States*. Berkeley: University of California Press, 1999.

Brown, Julie, ed. *Western Music and Race*, New York: Cambridge University Press, 2007.

Brubaker, Rogers. *Citizenship and Nationhood in France and Germany*. London: Harvard University Press, 1992.

Burnham, Scott. *Beethoven Hero*. Princeton: Princeton University Press, 2000.

Canetti, Elias. *Masse und Macht*. Frankfurt: Fischer Verlag, 1960.

Canning, Kathleen, Kerstin Barndt & Kristin McGuire, eds. *Weimar Public/Weimar Subjects: Rethinking the Political Culture of Germany in the 1920s*. New York: Berghahn Books, 2010.

Carnegy, Patrick. *Wagner and the Art of the Theatre*. New Haven: Yale University Press, 2006.

Carr, Jonathan. *The Wagner Clan: The Saga of Germany's Most Illustrious and Infamous Family*. New York: Grove Press, 2007.

Cebulla, Florian. *Rundfunk und ländliche Gesellschaft, 1924–1945*. Göttingen: Vandenhoeck & Ruprecht, 2004.

Cherney, Brian. "The Bekker-Pfitzner Controversy (1919–1920): Its Significance for German Music Criticism during the Weimar Republic (1919–1932)." PhD Dissertation, University of Toronto, 1973.

Craig, Gordon. *The Germans*. New York, Meridian Books, 1983.

Cuomo, Glenn R., ed. *National Socialist Cultural Policy*. New York: St. Martin's Press, 1995.

Currid, Brian. *A National Acoustics: Music and Mass Publicity in Weimar and Nazi Germany*. Minneapolis: University of Minnesota Press, 2006.

Dahm, Annkatrin. *Der Topos der Juden: Studien zur Geschichte des Antisemitismus im deutschspragigen Musikschriftum*. Göttingen: Vandenhoeck & Rupprecht, 2007.

Dainotto, Robert. *Europe (in Theory)*. Durham: Duke University Press, 2006.

Dennis, David. *Beethoven in German Politics: 1870–1989*. New Haven: Yale University Press, 1996.

Dennis, David. *Inhumanities: Nazi Interpretations of Western Culture*. New York: Cambridge University Press, 2012.

Dowe, Dieter, "The Workingmen's Choral Movement in Germany before the First World War," *Journal of Contemporary History*, 13 (2) (1978): 269–296.

Dussel, Konrad. *Deutsche Rundfunkgeschichte: Eine Einführung*. Konstanz: UVK Medien, 1999.

Eley, Geoff. *Reshaping the German Right: Radical Nationalism and Political Change after Bismarck*. Ann Arbor: University of Michigan Press, 1991.

Etlin, Richard, ed. *Art, Culture and Media under the Third Reich*. Chicago: University of Chicago Press, 2002.

Evans, Richard. *The Coming of the Third Reich*. New York: Penguin Press, 2003.

Evans, Joan. "Stravinsky's Music in Nazi Germany," *Journal of the American Musicological Society*, 56 (3) (2003): 525–594.

Feldman, Gerald, "Der Historiker und die deutsche Inflation," in *Vom Weltkrieg zur Weltwirtschaftskrise: Studien zur deutschen Wirtschafts- und Sozialgeschichte 1914–1932*. Göttingen: Vandenhoeck & Ruprecht, 1984.

Feldman, Gerald. *The Great Disorder: Politics, Economics, and Society in the German Inflation, 1914–1924*. New York: Oxford University Press, 1993.

Feldman, Gerald, Carl-Ludwig Holtfrerich, Gerhard Ritter & Peter-Christian Witt, eds. *Konsequenzen der Inflation*. Berlin: Colloquium Verlag, 1989.

Fink, Carole. *Defending the Rights of Others: The Great Powers, the Jews and International Minority Protection, 1878–1938*. New York: Cambridge University Press, 2004.

Franklin, Peter. "Audiences, Critics and the Depurification of Music: Reflections on a 1920s Controversy," *Journal of the Royal Music Association*, 114 (1) (1989): 80–91.
Führer, Karl Christian, "German Cultural Life and the Crisis of National Identity during the Depression, 1929–1933," *German Studies Review*, 24 (3) (2001): 461–486.
Führer, Karl Christian, "A Medium of Modernity? Broadcasting in Weimar Germany, 1923–1932," *The Journal of Modern History*, 69 (4) (1997): 722–753.
Fulcher, Jane. *The Composer as Intellectual: Music and Ideology in France, 1914–1940*. New York: Oxford University Press, 2005.
Füllmer, Mortiz & Rüdiger Graf, eds. *Die 'Krise' der Weimarer Republik: Zur Kritik eines Deutungsmusters*. Frankfurt: Campus Verlag, 2008.
Gauss, Stefan. *Nadel, Rille, Trichter: Kulturgeschichte des Phonographen und des Grammophons in Deutschland, 1900–1940*. Köln: Böhlau Verlag, 2009.
Gay, Peter. *Weimar Culture: The Outsider as Insider*. New York: Norton, 1968.
Gerwarth, Robert. *Hitler's Hangman: The Life of Heydrich*. New Haven: Yale University Press, 2011.
Geyer, Martin. *Verkehrte Welt: Revolution, Inflation, und Moderne: München, 1914–1924*. Göttingen: Vandenhoeck & Ruprecht, 1998.
Gienow-Hecht, Jessica. *Sound Diplomacy: Music and Emotions in Transatlantic Relations, 1850–1920*. Chicago: University of Chicago Press, 2009.
Gienow-Hecht, Jessica, "Trumpeting down the Walls of Jericho: The Politics of Art, Music and Emotion in German-American Relations, 1870–1920," *Journal of Social History*, 36 (3) (2003): 585–613.
Gilbert, Shirli. *Music and the Holocaust: Confronting Life in the Nazi Ghettos and Camps*. New York: Oxford University Press, 2007.
Gillerman, Sharon. *Germans into Jews: Remaking the Jewish Social Body in the Weimar Republic*. Stanford: Stanford University Press, 2009.
Gilliam, Bryan, ed. *Music and Performance during the Weimar Republic*. New York: Cambridge University Press, 1994.
Goehr, Lydia. *The Imaginary Museum of Musical Works: An Essay in the Philosophy of Music*. New York: Oxford University Press, 2007.
Gooley, Dana, "Hanslick and the Institution of Criticism," *The Journal of Musicology*, 28 (3) (2011): 289–324.
Gramit, David. *Cultivating Music: The Aspirations, Interests and Limits of German Musical Culture, 1770–1848*. Berkeley: University of California Press, 2002.
Grey, Thomas, ed. *Richard Wagner and His World*. Princeton: Princeton University Press, 2009.
Gross, David. *The Past in Ruins: Tradition and the Critique of Modernity*. Amherst: The University of Massachusetts Press, 1992.
Günther, Ulrich, "Opportunisten? Zur Biograhie führender Musikpädagogen in Zeiten politischer Umbrüche," *Musikpädagogische Forschung*, 13 (1992): 267–285.
Gutsman, W. L. *Workers' Culture in Germany: Between Tradition and Commitment*. New York: Berg, 1990.

Haas, Michael. *Forbidden Music: The Jewish Composers Banned by the Nazis.* New Haven: Yale University Press, 2013.

Hailey, Christopher. *Franz Schreker, 1878–1934: A Cultural Biography.* New York: Cambridge University Press, 1993.

Hamann, Brigitte. *Winifred Wagner: A Life at the Heart of Hitler's Bayreuth.* New York: Harcourt, 2005.

Hamilton, Kenneth. *After the Golden Age: Romantic Pianism and Modern Performance.* New York: Oxford University Press, 2008.

Hammermeister, Kai. *The German Aesthetic Tradition.* New York: Cambridge University Press, 2002.

Hart, Philip. *Orpheus in the New World: The Symphony Orchestra as an American Cultural Institution.* New York: Norton, 1973.

Heidenreich, Bernd & Sönke, Neitzel, eds. *Medien im Nationalsozialismus.* Paderborn: Ferdinand Schöningh, 2010.

Heister, Hanns-Werner, ed. *"Entartete Musik" 1938—Weimar und die Ambivalenz.* Saarbrücken: PFAU-Verlag, 2001.

Herf, Jeffrey. *Reactionary Modernism: Technology, Culture and Politics in Weimar and the Third Reich.* Cambridge: Cambridge University Press, 1984.

Hertz, Deborah. *How Jews Became Germans: The History of Conversion and Assimilation in Berlin.* New Haven: Yale University Press, 2009.

Heyworth, Peter. *Otto Klemperer: His Life and Times, 1885–1933.* New York: Cambridge University Press, 1983.

Hilmes, Oliver. *Cosimas Kinder: Triumph und Tragödie der Wagner-Dynastie.* München: Siedler Verlag, 2009.

Hilmes, Oliver. *Cosima Wagner: The Lady of Bayreuth.* New Haven: Yale University Press, 2011.

Hilmes, Oliver. *Der Streit ums "Deutsche": Alfred Heuss und die Zeitschrift für Musik.* Hamburg: Bockel Verlag, 2003.

Holborn, Hajo. *A History of Modern Germany, 1840–1945.* New York: Alfred A. Knopf, 1969.

Holden, Raymond. *The Virtuoso Conductors: The Central European Tradition from Wagner to Karajan.* New Haven: Yale University Press, 2005.

Horowitz, Joseph. *Classical Music in America: A History of its Rise and Fall.* New York: Norton, 2005.

Hung, Jochen. "'Bad' Politics and 'Good' Culture: New Approaches to the History of the Weimar Republic," *Central European History*, 49 (2016): 441–453.

John, Eckhard. *Musik-Bolschewismus: Die Politisierung der Musik in Deutschland, 1918–1938.* Stuttgart: Verlag J.B. Metzler, 1994.

Kaiser, Hermann J., ed. *Musikalische Erfahrung: Wahrnehm, Erkennen, Aneignen.* Essen: Die Blaue Eule, 1992.

Kater, Michael. *Different Drummers: Jazz in the Culture of Nazi Germany.* New York: Oxford University Press, 1992.

Kater, Michael. *Composers of the Nazi Era: Eight Portraits*. New York: Oxford University Press, 2002.

Kater, Michael, "The Revenge of the Fathers: The Demise of Modern Music at the End of the Weimar Republic," *German Studies Review*, 15 (2) (1992): 295–315.

Kater, Michael & Albrecht Riethmüller, eds. *Music and Nazism: Art under Tyranny, 1933–1945*. Laaber: Laaber-Verlag, 2003.

Katz, Jacob. *The Darker Side of Genius: Richard Wagner's Anti-Semitism*. Hanover: Brandeis University Press, 1986.

Kershaw, Ian. *Hitler: 1889–1936, Hubris*. New York: Norton, 1998.

Kershaw, Ian. *The "Hitler Myth": Image and Reality in the Third Reich*. New York: Oxford University Press, 1987.

Köhler, Joachim. *Wagners Hitler: Der Prophet und sein Vollstrecker*. München: Blessing, 1999.

Koss, Juliet. *Modernism after Wagner*. Minneapolis: University of Minnesota Press, 2010.

Kreuzer, Gundula. *Verdi and the Germans: From Unification to the Third Reich*. Cambridge: Cambridge University Press, 2010.

Kurlander, Eric. *Living with Hitler: Liberal Democrats in the Third Reich*. New Haven: Yale University Press, 2009.

Lacey, Kate. *Feminine Frequencies: Gender, German Radio, and the Public Sphere, 1923–1945*. Ann Arbor: University of Michigan Press, 1996.

Laqueur, Walter. *Weimar: A Cultural History*. New York: Perigree Books, 1974.

Large, David C. & William Weber, eds. *Wagnerism in European Culture and Politics*. Ithaca: Cornell University Press, 1984.

Leonhard, Joachim-Felix. *Programmgeschichte des Hörfunks in der Weimarer Republik* (2 Bände). München: Deutscher Taschenbuch Verlag, 1997.

Lepenies, Wolf. *The Seduction of Culture in Modern German History*. Princeton: Princeton University Press, 2006.

Lerg, Winifred. *Rundfunkpolitik in der Weimarer Republik*. München: Deutscher Taschenbuch Verlag, 1980.

Levi, Erik. *Mozart and the Nazis: How the Third Reich Abused a Cultural Icon*. New Haven: Yale University Press, 2011.

Levi, Erik. *Music in the Third Reich*. London: MacMillan, 1994.

Linn, Michael von der, "'Durch und durch entartete': Musical Modernism and the German Critics (1900–1936)," *Current Musicology*, 65 (1998): 7–34.

Longerich, Peter. *Heinrich Himmler: A Life*. New York: Oxford University Press, 2012.

Lovisa, Fabian. *Musikkritik im Nationalsozialismus: Die Rolle Deutschsprachiger Musikzeitschriften, 1920–1945*. Laaber: Laaber Verlag, 1993.

Martin, Benjamin. *The Nazi-Fascist New Order for European Culture*. Cambridge: Harvard University Press, 2016.

Mazower, Mark. *Hitler's Empire: Nazi Rule in Occupied Europe*. New York: Penguin, 2009.

McClatchie, Stephen. *Analyzing Wagner's Operas: Alfred Lorenz and German Nationalist Ideology*. Rochester: University of Rochester Press, 1998.

McElligott, Anthony, ed. *Weimar Germany*, New York: Oxford University Press, 2009.

McMillan, Margaret. *Paris 1919: Six Months that Changed the World*. New York: Random House, 2003.

Meyer, Michael. *The Politics of Music in the Third Reich*. New York: Peter Lang, 1993.

Millington, Barry. *The Sorcerer of Bayreuth: Richard Wagner, His Work and His World*. New York: Oxford University Press, 2012.

Mommsen, Hans. *The Rise and Fall of Weimar Democracy*. Chapel Hill: University of North Carolina Press, 1998.

Monod, David. *German Music, Denazification and the Americans, 1945–1953*. Chapel Hill: University of North Carolina Press, 2005.

Morrow, Mary Sue. *German Music Criticism in the Late Eighteenth Century*. Cambridge: Cambridge University Press, 1997.

Morat, Daniel, ed. *Sounds of Modern History: Auditory Culture in 19th and 20th Century Europe*. New York: Berghan Books, 2014.

Mosse, George. *The Crisis of German Ideology: Intellectual Origins of the Third Reich*. New York: H. Fertig, 1964.

Müller, Sven Oliver. *Richard Wagner und Die Deutschen: Eine Geschichte von Hass und HIngabe*. München: C. H. Beck, 2013.

Neill, Sarah Elaine. "The Modernist Kaleidoscope: Schoenberg's Reception History in America, Germany and Austria 1908–1924." PhD Dissertation, Duke University, 2014.

Nettl, Bruno. *Heartland Excursions: Musicological Reflections on Schools of Music*. Chicago: University of Illinois Press, 1995.

Nicosia, Frank & Jonathan Huener, eds. *The Arts in Nazi Germany*. New York: Berghahn Books, 2006.

Otto, Viktor, "'Der Kampf gegen Wagner ist in Wahrheit ein Kulturkampf.' Die Wagner-Rezeption in der Wochenschrift 'Die Schaubühne'/'Die Weltbühne, [1905–1933],'" *Archiv für Musikwissenschaft*, 56 (1) (1999): 9–28.

Painter, Karen. *Symphonic Aspirations: Music and German Politics, 1900–1945*. Cambridge: Harvard University Press, 2008.

Paxton, Robert O. *The Anatomy of Fascism*. New York: Vintage Books, 2005.

Pederson, Sanna, "A.B. Marx, Berlin Concert Life, and German National Identity," *19th-century Music*, 18 (2) (1994): 87–107.

Petropoulos, Jonathan. *Art as Politics in the Third Reich*. Chapel Hill: University of North Carolina Press, 1996.

Peukert, Detlev. *Inside Nazi Germany: Conformity, Opposition and Racism in Everyday Life*. New Haven: Yale University Press, 1987.

Peukert, Detlev. *The Weimar Republic: The Crisis of Classical Modernity*. London: Penguin Press, 1991.

Potter, Pamela. *Art of Suppression: Confronting the Nazi Past in Histories of the Visual and Performing Arts*. Berkeley: University of California Press, 2016.

Potter, Pamela, "Did Himmler Really Like Gregorian Chant? The SS and Musicology," *Modernism/Modernity, 2* (3) (1995): 45–68.

Potter, Pamela. *Most German of the Arts: Musicology and Society from the Weimar Republic to the End of Hitler's Reich.* New Haven: Yale University Press, 1998.

Potter, Pamela, "The Politicization of Handel and His Oratorios in the Weimar Republic, the Third Reich, and the Early Years of the German Democratic Republic," *The Musical Quarterly,* 85 (2) (2001): 311–341.

Potter, Pamela. "What Is 'Nazi Music'?" *The Musical Quarterly,* 88 (3) (2005): 428–455.

Potter, Tully. *Adolf Busch: The Life of an Honest Musician* (Vol. 1, 1891–1939). London: Toccata Press, 2010.

Prieberg, Fred. *Musik im NS-Staat.* Frankfurt: Fischer Verlag, 1982.

Radano, Ronald & Philip Bohlman, eds. *Music and the Racial Imagination.* Chicago: University of Chicago Press, 2001.

Reuveni, Gideon. *Reading Germany: Literature and Consumer Culture in Germany before 1933.* New York: Berghahn Books, 2006.

Roberge, Marc-André, "Focusing Attention: Special Issues in German-Language Music Periodicals of the First Half of the Twentieth-Century," *Royal Music Association Research Chronicle,* 27 (1994): 73–74.

Rose, Paul Lawrence. *Wagner: Race and Revolution.* New Haven: Yale University Press, 1996.

Roseman, Mark, "National Socialism and the End of Modernity," *The American Historical Review,* 116 (3) (2011): 688–701.

Roseman, Mark. *The Villa, The Lake, The Meeting: Wannsee and the Final Solution.* New York: Penguin Press, 2002.

Roshwald, Aviel & Richard Stites, eds. *European Culture in the Great War: The Arts, Entertainment and Propaganda, 1914–1918.* New York: Cambridge University Press, 1999.

Ross, Alex. *The Rest Is Noise: Listening to the Twentieth Century.* New York: Picador, 2007.

Ross, Corey. *Media and the Making of Modern Germany.* New York: Oxford University Press, 2008.

Ross, Corey & Karl Christian Führer, eds. *Mass Media, Culture and Society in Twentieth-century Germany.* New York: Palgrave, 2006.

Rudinow, Joel, "Race, Ethnicity, Expressive Authenticity: Can White People Sing the Blues?" *The Journal of Aesthetics and Art Criticism,* 52 (1) (1994): 127–137.

Rydell, Anders. *The Book Thieves: The Nazi Looting of Europe's Libraries and the Race to Return a Literary Inheritance.* New York: Viking, 2017.

Ryding, Erik & Rebecca Pechefsky, *Bruno Walter: A World Elsewhere.* New Haven: Yale University Press, 2001.

Sachs, Joel, "Some Aspects of Musical Politics in Pre-Nazi Germany," *Perspectives of New Music,* 9 (1) (1970): 74–95.

Saerchinger, César. *Artur Schnabel: A Biography.* New York: Dood, Mead & Company, 1957.

Said, Edward. *Culture and Imperialism*. New York: Vintage, 1993.

Schachiner, Memo. *Politik und Systematik: Wiener Musikwissenschaft im Wandel der Zeiten—Die Ära Guido Adler (1898–1927)*. Vienna: MC Publishing, 2008.

Schivelbusch, Wolfgang. *The Culture of Defeat: On National Trauma, Mourning and Recovery* New York: Picador, 2004.

Schonberg, Harold. *The Great Pianists*. New York: Simon & Schuster, 1963.

Schorske, Carl. *Fin-de-Siècle Vienna: Politics and Culture*. New York: Vintage, 1981.

Schwartz, David. *Listening Awry: Music and Alterity in German Culture*. Minneapolis: University of Minnesota Press, 2006.

Skelton, Geoffrey. *Wagner at Bayreuth: Experiment and Tradition*. New York: George Braziller, 1965.

Small, Christopher. *Musicking: The Meanings of Performing and Listening*. Middletown: Wesleyan University Press, 1998.

Smith, Helmuth Walser. *The Continuities of German History: Nation, Religion and Race across the Long Nineteenth Century*. Cambridge: Cambridge University Press, 2002.

Solomon, Maynard. *Beethoven*. New York: Schirmer Books, 1998.

Spotts, Frederic. *Bayreuth: A History of the Wagner Festival*. New Haven: Yale University Press, 1994.

Spotts, Frederic. *Hitler and the Power of Aesthetics*. New York: Overlook Press, 2004.

Steinweis, Alan. *Art, Ideology & Economics in Nazi Germany: The Reich Chambers of Music, Theater and the Visual Arts*. Chapel Hill: The University of North Carolina Press, 1993.

Stern, Fritz. *Dreams and Delusions: The Drama of German History*. New Haven: Yale University Press, 1999.

Stern, Fritz. *Five Germanys I Have Known*. New York: Farrar, Straus & Giroux, 2007.

Stern, Fritz. *The Politics of Cultural Despair: A Study in the Rise of the Germanic Ideology*. Berkeley: University of California Press, 1961.

Strobl, Gerwin. *The Swastika and the Stage: German Theatre and Society, 1933–1944*. Cambridge: Cambridge University Press, 2007.

Thelen-Frölich, Andrea Therese. *Die Institution Konzert zwischen 1918 und 1945 am Beispiel der Stadt Düsseldorf*. Kassel: Verlag Merseburger, 2000.

Traverso, Enzo. *The Origins of Nazi Violence*. New York: The New Press, 2003.

Vaget, Hans Rudolf, "Wagnerian Self-fashioning: The Case of Adolf Hitler," *New German Critique*, 101 (2007): 95–114.

Wagner, Wolfgang. *Acts: The Autobiography of Wolfgang Wagner*. Weidenfeld & Nicolson, 1994.

Waligórska, Magdalena, "A Goy Fiddler on the Roof," *Polish Sociological Review*, 4 (2005): 367–382.

Watkins, Glenn. *Proof Through the Night: Music and the Great War*. Berkeley: University of California Press, 2003.

Weber, Eugen. *The Hollow Years: France in the 1930s*. New York: W.W. Norton & Company, 1994.

Weber, Thomas. *Hitler's First War: Adolf Hitler, The Men of the List Regiment, and the First World War*. New York: Oxford University Press, 2010.

Weiner, Marc. *Richard Wagner and the Anti-Semitic Imagination*. Lincoln: University of Nebraska Press, 1995.

Weissweiler, Eva. *Ausgemerzt! Das Lexikon der Juden in der Musik und seine mörderischen Folgen*. Köln: Dittrich-Verlag, 1999.

Weitz, Eric. "Weimar Germany and Its Histories," *Central European History*, 43 (4) (2010): 581–591.

Weitz, Eric. *Weimar Germany: Promise and Tragedy*. Princeton: Princeton University Press, 2007.

Widdig, Bernd. *Culture and Inflation in Weimar Germany*. Berkeley: University of California Press, 2001.

Wildt, Michael. *Hitler's Volksgemeinschaft and the Dynamics of Racial Exclusion* (New York: Berghahn, 2012.

Willett, John. *Art and Politics in the Weimar Period: The New Sobriety, 1917–1933*. New York: DaCapo Press, 1978.

Williams, John Alexander, ed. *Weimar Culture Revisited*. New York: Palgrave McMillan, 2011.

Winter, Jay. *Sites of Memory, Sites of Mourning: The Great War in European Cultural History*. Cambridge: Cambridge University Press, 1995.

Wipplinger, Jonathan O. *The Jazz Republic: Music, Race, and American Culture in Weimar Germany*. Ann Arbor: University of Michigan Press, 2017.

Worthen, John. *Robert Schumann: Life and Death of a Musician*. New Haven: Yale University Press, 2007.

Wulf, Josef. *Musik im Dritten Reich: Eine Dokumentation*. Gütersloh: Sigbert Mohn Verlag, 1963.

Zimmerman, Andrew. *Anthropology and Antihumanism in Imperial Germany*. Chicago: University of Chicago Press, 2001.

Internet Sources

Adolf Hitler, "Appeal to the German People, January 31, 1933." http://germanhistorydocs.ghi-dc.org/sub_document.cfm?document_id=3940.

Arnold Brecht, "On Cardinal Pacelli and Radio in the Early 1920s." http://germanhistorydocs.ghi-dc.org/sub_document.cfm?document_id=3871

Bernhard vom Brocke, "'Scholarship and Militarism': The Appeal of 93 to the Civilized World." October 4, 1914. http://germanhistorydocs.ghi-dc.org/sub_document.cfm?document_id=938

Bob Simon, "Lang Lang: Piano Prodigy." CBS News. 2005. http://www.cbsnews.com/stories/2005/01/07/60minutes/main665508.shtml?CMP=ILC-SearchStories

Duarte, Diogo P., "Buchenwald Goethe Eiche." *Wikimedia Commons*. Last modified August 10, 2007. https://commons.wikimedia.org/wiki/File:Buchenwald_Goethe_Eiche_2007.JPG.

"Fritz and Else Laqueur." *Yad Vashem: The Central Database of Shoah Victims' Names.* http://yvng.yadvashem.org

George Grosz, "Siegfried Hitler, 1923." *Harvard Art Museums/Busch-Reisinger Museum, Gift of Erich Cohn.* http://www.harvardartmuseums.org/art/310541.

Hans Severus Ziegler, "Entartete Musik." 1938. http://www.dhm.de/datenbank/dhm.php?seite=5&fld_0=RA000311

Hans Severus Ziegler, "Juden gegen Wagner," *Entartete Musik: Eine Abrechnung*, 1938 https://archive.org/details/EntarteteMusik_758.

Harry Hopps, "Destroy This Mad Brute: Enlist," Library of Congress Prints and Photographs Division. http://www.loc.gov/pictures/item/2010652057/.

Joseph Goebbels, "Der Rundfunk als achte Großmacht." *Signale der neuen Zeit*, 1933. http://research.calvin.edu/german-propaganda-archive/goeb56.htm

Louis Raemaekers, "War Cartoons." Library of Congress Prints and Photographs Division. http://www.loc.gov/pictures/search/?q=louis%20raemaekers%20&co=pos.

Moriz Violin, "Letter to Heinrich Schenker, February 2, 1922." Schenker Documents Online. http://www.schenkerdocumentsonline.org/documents/correspondence/OJ-14-45_13.html

o.Ang. "So siedelt der deutsche Arbeiter." *Bundesarchiv.* http://www.bild.bundesarchiv.de/index.php?barch_item=en_agb.

Reinhold Brinkmann, "Harvard's Paine Hall: Musical Canon & the New England Barn." Last modified 2010. https://archive.fo/EEyyH.

Various Authors, "Simplicissimus: Illustrierte Wochenschrift". *Simplicissimus: eine historische Zeitschrift.* http://www.simplicissimus.info/index.php?id=5.

Wilhelm Busch, "Finale Furioso." *Wikimedia Commons.* Last modified January 6, 2007, https://commons.wikimedia.org/wiki/File:Busch_Werke_v1_p_404.jpg.

Index

Abert, Hermann 101
Action League for German Culture 8
Adler, Guido 18, 20, 24, 99, 112
  Internationale Gesellschaft für Musikwissenschaft 98
Adorno, Theodor 21, 100, 123–4, 178, 180
Allgemeine musikalische Zeitung 17, 21, 97, 157, 160–2
American orchestras, German imports 93
Arbeitsgemeinschaft deutscher Musikkritiker 22
Arionenzeitung, Ten Commandments 105
Armin, Georges 154–5, 167 n.31
Arrau, Claudio 60, 148, 150, 157, 168 n.39

Bach, Johann Sebastian 1–2, 5, 26, 41, 43, 57, 66, 77, 96, 99–100, 104, 129, 147, 155, 164–5, 177–9
Baroque music 5, 66, 104
Battistini, Mattia 38, 153
Bayreuther Blatter 22, 125, 131
Beethoven, Ludwig van 1–2, 7, 23, 25–7, 35, 41–3, 58, 60, 66, 72, 74, 77, 79, 89, 93, 97, 104, 111, 129, 133, 147–8, 150, 164, 173, 177–80
Bekker, Paul 18, 20, 23, 49 n.26, 96–7, 100, 115 n.23, 143 n.32, 143 n.39, 149
  Richard Wagner: Das Leben in Werke 129–30
Benjamin, Walter 55, 113
Berg, Alban 6, 19, 179–80
Berl, Heinrich 160, 168.n 53
Berliner Tageblatt 25, 142 n.27
Berlioz, Hector 43, 151
Bieder, Eugen 112
Bismarck, Otto von 1
Blessinger, Karl 31–2, 50 n.49, 109
  Die musikalische Probleme der Gegenwart und ihre Lösung 32
Blume, Friedrich 112, 116 n 44, 119 n.90
Boetticher, Wolfgang 112, 119 n.90
Bohemia 23

Botticelli, Sandro, *The Birth of Venus* 30
Boyé 17
Brahms, Johannes 43, 63, 77, 94–5, 100–10, 155, 164, 177
  Symphony No. 1, C Minor 94
  Zigeunerlieder Op. 103 94
Brecht, Arnold 80, 179
Breithaupt, Rudolf Maria
  Die Natürliche Klaviertechnik 157
  on race and musical performance 157–63
Bruckner, Anton 20, 24, 43, 140, 150
Busch, Adolf 44
Busch, Fritz 134
Busch, Wilhelm, "Finale Furioso" 65
Busoni, Feruccio 149, 169 n.72
Butting, Max 82 n.27
  on *Rundfunksmusik* 62
  on Wagner's *Der Ring der Nibelungen* 63
Buxtehude, Dieterich 66

Carey, Mariah 126
Caruso, Enrico 152, 154–5
Chamberlain, Houston Stewart 91, 121–2, 123, 125, 129, 180
  Foundations of the Nineteenth-Century 134, 162
Chopin, Frédéric 42–3, 156, 161, 165
Cornelius, Peter 43, 110
Czerny, Carl 150
Cziffra, Georges 165

Debussy, Claude 126, 147, 156, 165
de Fontenelle, Bernard le Bovier 17
de Gobineau, Arthur 125, 129
Deutscher Sängerbund (DSB) 72
Deutsches Volksturm 105
Diebold, Bernhard 129, 143 n.33
Die Musik 18, 22–3, 36, 44, 67
Die Tonkunst, "On National *vs.* International Music" 89

D'Indy, Vincent 126
Dix, Otto 7
Dürer, Albrecht 122, 164

Eichenauer, Richard 164, 169 n.75
Eichmann, Adolf 1
Einstein, Alfred 7, 24–5, 49 n.31, 68, 110,
    118 n 80, 119 nn.81–2, 149–50, 150,
    166 n.11, 172
  US exile 111
Eisler, Hanns 19, 25, 62
Entartete Musik/Kunst exhibitions 171
Epoque, Belle 63
Ernest, Gustav 162, 168 n.60
Europe
  Eastern Europe, creation of 92
  folk music (German) 112
  German speakers 20
  musical boundaries 18–20, 99
  Nazi occupation 165

Filar, Marian 165
First World War 2, 9, 11–12, 19–20,
    29–30, 47, 63–4, 67, 71, 91–3, 99,
    101, 110, 126, 129, 131, 149, 151,
    153, 164, 171–2, 180
Fischer, Edwin 60, 151
Fischer, Fritz 180
Flaffith, John 147–8
Flesch, Carl, *The Problem of Sound in
    Violin Playing* 160
Forkel, Johann Nicholas 100
Fraktur 44
Frankfurter Zeitung 23, 49 n.26
Frederick the Great 121
Friedland, Martin 6, 97, 115 n.29
Fritsch, Theodor 160
Furtwängler, Wilhelm 52, 57, 79, 134, 144
    n.62, 153

Garrett, Mary 126
Gebrauchsmusik 68, 161
Gehrke, M. M. 73, 85 n.77
Geissler, F. A. 36, 41, 51 n.56
George, Stefen 137
Gerigk, Herbert 103, 109
Germanien 109, 112
Germans
  attitude towards foreign artists 39
  Bildung 1, 13, 64, 72, 76

concert life 26, 29, 38, 41, 45–6, 57,
    63, 181
Kultur 1–3, 5, 71–2, 99, 172, 175–7
music criticism 4, 9, 11, 17–20, 23–6,
    164, 181
music traditions 6–10, 100
science and music, achievements 25–6
German Workers' Singers' League
    (*Deutscher Arbeiter- Sängerbund*)
    72
Gemany
  conquest of Poland and
      Czechoslovakia 112
  copyright laws 127
  inflationary pressures 11, 27–40, 58
  interwar period 2, 5–7, 9, 11–12, 20,
      22, 29, 36, 38, 41–2, 63, 65, 74, 107,
      122, 148–9, 153–4
  modernist movements 10
  music education in schools 19
  role of radio 55–65, 67–75
Gierke, Otto von 175, 177
Gieseking, Walter 19, 61, 151, 156, 165
Gigler, Herbert 156–7, 168 n.37
Gluck, Christoph Willibald 97, 110, 117
    n.54
Goebbels, Joseph 75–9, 113, 137, 139–40,
    180
Peer Gynt 75
Goering, Hermann 140
Goethe, Johann Wolfgang von 1, 4, 23, 25,
    94, 122, 134
  Faust 3, 67
  Goethe Eiche (Goethe's Oak) 3–4
Göhler, Georg 34, 50 n.53
Gold, Julius 112
Goodman, Benny 79
Great War 1, 91, 95, 172
Grieg, Edvard 94–5
Grosz, George 7

Hadamovsky, Eugen 77, 79, 86 n.95
Hagemann, Carl 127, 142 n.26
Hamburger Nachrichten 23
Handel, George Frederick 26, 43, 57, 77,
    97, 133, 157
Hanslick, Eduard 18, 24, 64, 112, 125
Hausmusik 57, 70, 73, 76, 82 n.12
Havemann, Gustav 8, 160
Haydn, Joseph 20, 43, 77, 97, 157, 160

Heine, Heinrich 94
Heinitz, Wilhelm 58–9, 61, 65
  Strukturprobleme in Primitiver Musik 58
Hernried, Robert 7, 51 n.68, 94–6, 110, 115 n.19
Heuss, Alfred 3, 5, 18, 21, 25, 62–4, 97, 99–100, 131, 152–4, 158, 160
  as editor of *Zeitschrift für Musik* 96
  Musik im Leben der Völker (exhibition) 67
  as Nazi party's philosopher 22
Heydrich, Reinhard 1, 140
Himmler, Heinrich 11, 109, 113, 118 nn.75–6
Hindemith, Paul 22, 140
Hinkel, Hans 3
Hitler, Adolf 1, 5, 12, 78, 80, 114, 121–3, 132, 135–6, 138–9, 165, 171
Hoffmann, E. T. A. 17
Holocaust 1, 40, 56, 140, 165, 172, 180
Huberman, Bronislaw 37–8, 51 n.59
  "Artists and Concert Life as Affected by the War" 38

Ibsen, Henrik 94
Imperial Federation of German Journalists (*Reichsverband der Deutschen Presse*) 18
internationalism
  conservative trend 95–6
  egalitarian forms 91
  musicologist's views on 94–9, 104–5, 111, 113
International Music Society 18

Jenner, Gustav 101

Kampfbund für Deutscher Kultur 22
Kant, Immanuel 17, 23, 80, 134
Kapellmeistern 65, 85 n.81
Kapp, Julius 18
Keller, Hermann 26, 49 n.39
Kestenberg, Leo 106
Klatte, Wilhelm 18
Kleiber, Erich 19
Klemperer, Otto 153
  Kroll Oper 136
Klemperer, Victor 7, 77
Klimt, Gustav 19
Koch, Ludwig 67, 83 n.48

Kokoschka, Oskar 19
Köllwitz, Kathe 7
König, Wolfgang 76, 86 n.89
Korngold, Erich 19
Krauss, Clemens 134
Kreisler, Fritz 19
Krenek, Ernst 21–2, 25
Kretzschmar, Hermann 18, 20, 24, 93, 101
Kulz, Werner 134, 144 n.52
Kunwald, Ernst 93

Lach, Robert 109, 157
Lamprecht, Karl 177
Lang, Fritz 137
Lauhöfer, Fritz 56, 69–70, 73, 81 n.11
Lautsprechermusik 62
The League of Composers Review 23
Lechthaler, Josef 21
Leichtentritt, Hugo 24, 129
Leschetizky, Theodor 150, 159, 169.n 72
Lifeboat (Hitchcock) 1
Liszt, Franz 43, 64, 77, 147, 151, 156, 161
  Hungarian Rhapsodies S.244 165
Lorenz, Alfred
  Das Geheimnis der Form 130
  nationalism and anti-Semitism 130
Louis, Rudolf 149, 166 n.8
Ludwig, Emil 67, 76
  Wagner oder die Entzauberten 126
Lueger, Karl 91
Lunacharsky, Anatoly 126
Luther, Martin 121

Magic Flute, The 131
Mahler, Gustav 19, 43, 106, 108, 160, 164, 178, 180
Mann, Thomas 124, 128, 136, 176–7, 180, 182 n.12
Marsop, Paul 131, 143 n.42
Marteau, Henri 39–41, 51 n.67
Meisel, Edmund 19
Melos 21
Mendelssohn, Arnold 43, 106, 108, 157, 160–1, 164
Meyerbeer, Giacomo 94–5, 106, 108, 124, 141 n.13, 161, 164
Moser, Andreas 101
Moser, Hans Joachim 11, 26, 46, 89, 91–3, 95, 97–9, 97–100, 100–15, 101–14, 129, 131–2

Berliner Akademie für Kirchen- und
  Schulmusik 106
  choice of works 132
  Geschichte der deutschen Musik 102,
    104, 111
  on goal of music teacher 106
  Kleine Deutsche Musikgeschichte 106
  Lexikon der Juden in der Musik, name
    of 109
  Midsummer Night's Dream 108
  music analysis 102–4
  Musik-Lexikon 106, 111
  nationalism 105
  "On the Particularity of German
    Musical Gifts" 104
  Reichstelle für Musikabteilungen
    102
  working methods 114
Mottle, Felix 135
Mozart, Wolfgang Amadeus 7, 20, 25–6,
  38, 43, 57, 72, 77, 79, 97, 102, 110,
  129, 131, 133, 147, 156, 157, 160,
  165
Muck, Karl 93, 135–6, 172–3
Müller, Heinrich 113
musical modernism 3, 6, 21, 97
  public skepticism 21, 56, 63
musicologists 2–5, 7, 9, 11–12, 19–20,
  23–6, 42, 46, 91–2, 95, 98–101,
  103–4, 106–7, 109, 111–13, 126,
  128–9, 148–50, 157, 160, 164,
  172
  national identity 149–54
  race and performance 149–54
  Weimer critics 147–9
Musikblätter des Anbruch 19, 21, 42–3,
  61, 96
Musik im Krieg 165
Mussolini, Benito 10

Nagel, Wilibald 21, 89–92, 104, 126
  "Kosmopolische oder nationale
    Musik?" 89
nationalism
  conservative critics 154–7
  modern music 149–54
  musicologists view on 89–92, 98–9,
    101, 104
  Wagner's Nazi propaganda 121, 123–7

National Socialism 2, 4, 8, 31, 56–7, 75,
  77–8, 80, 110, 121, 129, 134, 136,
  138, 140, 149, 180
  seizure of power 76
Nazism
  anti-modernism 10, 56
  Bayreuth under 138–41
  "coordination" (*gleichschaltung*) 25, 75
  Enabling Law 138
  foreign and cultural policies 109
  radio broadcast 75–81
  seizure of power 1933 25, 45, 55, 102,
    108
  Volksgemeinschaft 19, 34, 38, 63–4, 67,
    69, 77–8, 83 n.33, 90, 103, 132, 162
Neubeck, Ludwig 76, 86 n.92
Neue Musik Zeitung 3, 19, 21, 26–8, 41, 44,
  56, 62, 69, 81, 126
Niemann, Walter 25, 49 n.33
Nietzsche, Friedrich 122, 126, 180
Nolde, Emil 7
November Group 62
Nuremberg Laws 110, 117

Offenbach, Jacques 106, 108

Paganini, Niccolò 64
Partita in A Minor 1
Pfitzner, Hans 3, 5, 18, 21–2, 25, 77, 97,
  130, 135
  nationalism and anti-Semitism 130
Pfohl, Ferdinand 23, 135, 144 n.55
Piccini, Niccolò 99
Pierson, Frank, *Conspiracy* 1
Pilsung, Sigmund 156
Pisk, Paul 21
Pius XII, Pope 80
Pretzsch, Paul 135, 144 n.47
Puccini, Giacomo 131
Putsch, Röhm 140

radio
  during Weimar and the Third Reich
    55–7
  German society, role in 70–5
  live performance, comparison with
    57–70
  Nazism and 75–81
Raemaekers, Louis 173–5

Raffke 30
Ravel, Maurice 156
Reger, Max 43
Regidür, Roderich 38, 51 nn.61-2, 153-4
Reichel, Anton, "The Austro-German Cultural Mission" 20
Reiner, Fritz 26
Réti, Rudolf 21
Reuss, Heinrich XLV (Prince) 127-8
Richter, Hans 135
Riemann, Hugo 95, 101, 111, 115 n.21
  Kleines Handbuch der Musikgeschichte 95
Robert, J.E 39, 51 n.66
Rochlitz, Friedrich 17
Romanticism 5, 17, 42, 95
  piano playing 151
Rosenberg, Alfred 22, 109, 137, 139-40, 180
  Myth of the Twentieth Century, The 140
Rousseau, Jean-Jacques 17
Ruah, H 89-92, 97, 104, 114 n.1
Rubinstein, Anton 162
Rubinstein, Arthur 156
Rühlmann, Franz 132, 144 n.48

Sachs, Curt 112
Schemm, Hans 139
Schenk, Erich 109
Schenker, Heinrich 18, 42, 52 n.80
Schering, Arnold 24, 101
Schindler's List (Spielberg) 1
Schmitt, Otto 26, 49 n.37, 152, 154, 158, 167 n.21
Schnabel, Arthur 19, 44, 53 n.88, 60, 82 nn.21-2, 150, 159, 166.n 14, 169 n.72
Schnitzler, Arthur 19
Schoenberg, Arnold 6, 8, 19, 22, 41, 43, 61, 106, 111, 163, 178, 180
Schreker, Franz 19
Schubert 1, 20, 26, 43, 72, 95, 111, 148, 155, 157
  String Quintet in C Major 1
Schulreform movement 67
Schumann, Robert 17, 21, 23, 25-6, 77, 79, 155
Schütz, Heinrich 66, 99, 110
Scriabin. Alexander 41
Second World War 1, 93, 105, 123, 165

Sender, "Mozart: His Life and Work" 72
Severus Ziegler, Hans 137
Shaw, George Bernard 126, 134
Signale fur die Musikalische Welt 44
Simplicissimus 30-1, 33, 35, 37, 59, 68-9, 127-8
  "Bayreuth" 127
  "Cultural Exchange" 37
  "Eight against One" 33
  "Radio Endangers Poor Souls" 69
  "Tannhäuser on the Radio" 59
  "The Book. The Books" 35
  "The Glass House Public and Picture 8611" 31
  "Two Corners of the World" 68
Smend, Rudolf 177
Society of German Music Critics (*Verband deutscher Musikkritiker*) 18
Sofronitsky, Vladimir 151
Söhnlein, Kurt 135, 144 n.59
  Tristan und Isolde 135
Sonderweg 1-2, 99, 121, 178
Sozialistischen Monatsheften 62
Speer, Albert 140
Spengler, Oswald 91, 177
Spoliansky, Mischa 19
Sporn, Fritz 66, 83 n.41
  on gramophone 66
Springer, Hermann 18
Stech, Willi 78
Stefan, Paul 21, 24, 43, 53 n.84
  Die Feindschaft gegen Wagner 126
Sternfeld, Richard 161, 168 n.59
Stokowski, Leopold 26
Strauss, J. 43
Strauss, Richard 77, 137
Stravinsky, Igor 43, 140, 147, 163
Streseman, Gustav 67
Stuckenschmidt, H. H. 20, 22-4, 24, 48 n.13, 49 n.26, 55, 60, 74, 81 n.2
Sudeten Germans 20

Tauber, Richard 79
Tchaikovsky, Pyotr Ilyich 43
Third Reich 2-3, 9-11, 55-6, 75, 79, 92, 101-3, 109, 113, 122, 125, 136, 140, 149, 161-2, 165, 171
Tietjen, Heinz 136-40
  Der Fliegende Holländer 136

Toch, Ernst 19
Toscanini, Arturo 134, 136, 152–3
Tovey, Donald 91, 114 n.9

universalism 90–1, 154–7

Verband deutscher Musikkritiker 18, 22
Verdi, Giuseppe 97, 129–31, 140, 143 n.35
Versailles Treaty 34, 37, 92
Violin, Moritz 42
Volga Germans 20
Vollerthun, Georg 77
von Hindenburg, Paul 67, 76
von Hofmannstahl, Hugo 19
von Waltershausen, Hermann Wolfgang 42
von Wolzogen, Hans 22, 125
Vossische Zeitung 23

Wagner, Richard 5, 11–12, 23, 25–6, 43, 60, 63, 74, 89, 105, 110, 121–41, 153, 173, 180
    Bayreuth Festival 124–7, 129, 131, 134–6, 138–40, 142 n.24
    Cosima (wife) 125, 129, 134
    Das Judenthum in der Musik (Jewishness in Music) 124
    Das Rheingold 126
    Die Meistersinger von Nürnberg 123, 127, 139
    as editor of *Bayreuther Blätter* 125
    Flying Dutchman, The 126, 139
    Freigedank (pen name) 124
    French devotees 126
    Gesamtkunstwerke (total artworks) 59, 123
    Hitler's love for 121–2
    instrumental writing 123
    nationalism and anti-Semitism 124
    Nazism and 121
    opera Siegfried 125
    Parsifal 127, 136, 139
    political thoughts 124–6
    prose writings 126
    role in German society 105
    Siegfried 123, 126
    Third Reich, compositions 122
    Wahnfried 124–5, 127, 129, 138, 142 n.25
    Western music 123
Wagner, Siegfried 123, 127, 134–5, 138, 140, 142 n.27, 152
Wagner, Winifred 121, 123, 125, 132, 135–8, 142 n.27
    nationalism and anti-Semitism 123
    relationship with Hitler 123, 132, 135
Walter, Bruno 150
war cartoons 174–5
Warschauer, Frank 61, 82 n.25, 154, 167 n.29
Weber, William 43, 157
Webern, Anton 7, 19
Weill, Kurt 6, 62, 140
Weimar Republic
    anti-semitisms 103
    democracy 1–2, 20, 29, 46, 91, 113
    musical modernism 2–3
    music criticism 25
    radio musical programming 71
Weissmann, Adolf 18, 22, 129
Wellek, Albert 129–30, 143 n.31
Wellesz, Egon 19
Wenz, Josef 131, 143 n.41
Westermeyer, Karl 160, 168 n.51
Wolf, Hugo 43, 77, 101, 110, 133
Wolf, Johannes 101

youth engagement 19, 33, 66, 110, 153, 156, 178

*Zeitschrift für Musik*3 21, 29, 32, 38, 43, 76, 96, 110, 124, 129–31, 148, 155
    Combat Newspaper for German Music and Musical Culture 22
    Semi-monthly for Musicians and Friends of Music 22
Ziegler, Hans Severus 137
Zilcher, Hermann 149, 155–6, 158, 166 n.7
Zimmermann, Reinhold 58, 82 n.16
Zweig, Stefan 20
    The World of Yesterday 44–5

www.ingramcontent.com/pod-product-compliance
Lightning Source LLC
Chambersburg PA
CBHW052043300426
44117CB00012B/1949